RUSTIC
EUROPEAN
BREADS

FROM YOUR
BREAD MACHINE

BY LINDA WEST ECKHARDT
and
DIANA COLLINGWOOD BUTTS
Bread in Half the Time
Dessert in Half the Time

BY LINDA WEST ECKHARDT
America Loves Hamburger
America Loves Chicken
Feed Your Family on Ten Dollars a Day
Barbecue Indoors and Out
The Only Texas Cookbook

RUSTIC
EUROPEAN
BREADS

FROM YOUR BREAD MACHINE

† † † † † † † † † † † † † † † † † † † †

LINDA WEST ECKHARDT

and

DIANA COLLINGWOOD BUTTS

DOUBLEDAY

NEW YORK   LONDON   TORONTO   SYDNEY   AUCKLAND

PUBLISHED BY DOUBLEDAY
a division of Bantam Doubleday Dell
Publishing Group, Inc.
1540 Broadway, New York,
New York 10036

DOUBLEDAY
and the portrayal of an anchor with a
dolphin are trademarks of Doubleday, a
division of Bantam Doubleday Dell
Publishing Group, Inc.

Book Design by Terry Karydes
Illustrated by Martie Holmer

Library of Congress
Cataloging-in-Publication Data
Eckhardt, Linda West, 1939–
Rustic European breads from your bread
machine / Linda West Eckhardt and
Diana Collingwood Butts. – 1st ed.
p.   cm.
Includes bibliographical references
and index.
1. Bread. 2. Automatic bread machines.
I. Butts, Diana Collingwood. II. Title.
TX769.E2264   1995
641.8'12–dc20   94-40186   CIP

ISBN 0-385-47777-5

9   10   8

To our best tasters,

JOE, LARRY, LAUREN, AND KEITH

FOREWORD

RUSTIC European breads, earthy, aromatic, and enigmatic, have become our great passion. We love to tear into a loaf of freshly made, flour-dusted *Ciabatta*, that irregular flat bread shaped like a Medieval Italian slipper, and simply inhale the bouquet that arises from its creamy flesh. We love to make great peasant rounds, crosshatched and baked free-form on a stone.

But, we also love to use our bread machines. So the central question became for us: Can the bread machine be used to make a rustic loaf of bread? The answer is a resounding yes.

We came to know these breads while researching our first bread book, *Bread in Half the Time*. While baking for that book, we learned how to emulate the European village baker's oven by placing unglazed clay tiles or a pizza stone in our oven, then spritzing the baking loaves with plain water. This, we learned, yielded a heavenly crisp crust. We also mastered bread finishes, slashing and coating endless loaves so that each one became a work of baker's art.

But where our first book taught us to make bread in half the time, we now are experimenting with making breads in twice the time, letting the flavors mature and develop into the complex European-style breads we've come to love. And we have developed a way to make these rustic breads using our best kitchen friend, the bread machine.

Making bread with a bread machine has become for us a form of entertainment. We love to make a new kind of bread, call in our friends, and have an impromptu party with nothing more than a good bottle of wine, a loaf of hot, fresh bread, and maybe just a simple salad. The aroma in the house says *home* before our guests even walk through the door. And, the sight of that gorgeous artisan loaf says *we care*, before anybody's even had a bite.

Not that our efforts were initially received with unbridled enthusiasm.

When someone said, "But what is this dirt all over the loaf?," we had to tell them it was flour we'd carefully rubbed onto the dough before we baked it to give it that nice rustic appearance.

One day, somebody said, "How come this bread has such big holes!" Because we finally got it right, we answered. Many European breads, particularly Italian breads, are judged by their large, irregular holes.

Then, one of our obsessive-compulsive kids complained: "But this pizza is so misshapen! It isn't round." It's art we said. We meant it to be irregular.

When we tried to teach our neighbor how to do this, she said, "This dough is so sticky I can't stand it." It's supposed to be sticky. That's how you're going to get those nice big holes. Don't add more flour. Mist your hands and work surface with water so the dough doesn't stick to you.

Somebody's husband commented, "This bread is as coarse as horsefeed." Of course it is. It's got eleven seeds and grains in it. It's supposed to be chewy.

We're hooked on making these breads with the bread machine. It's lots of fun. Sometimes, we even surprise ourselves. We look at each other and wonder how such simple ingredients could yield up such a bread. After all, most of these breads are nothing more than flour, water, salt, and yeast in one form or another. Almost the same ingredients, with modified technique, can make breads as varied as plain French bread, country loaves, or even the venerable pizza.

The rustic breads of Europe represent hundreds of years of craft and emanate from a time when each baker made his mark on the world by transforming these four basic ingredients into his own particular creation. They differ from traditional American breads in that they are usually leaner, that means made with less sugar, and often with little or no added fat. Rustic European breads are distinctive in that they are full flavored, have crisp crusts, and are often flour-dusted with creamy centers. Some have great irregular holes, and others are known for their uniform, small even cells. When making these breads, technique is all.

Most of these breads were developed long before commercial yeast was available and many of them are enriched by the addition of homemade starters, sponges, or sourdoughs. We were thrilled to discover that making starters at home is not all that mysterious, and we can teach you how to make them too. The starter is nothing more than a blend of flour and water, perhaps with a jumpstart of commercial yeast, or another natural yeast-bearing organic material such as grapes, apples, or peach leaves, that is left to grow and mature into a bubbly, lively yeasty brew with which to start to make bread. (See Chapter 3, "Yeasts and Homemade Starters" for a full discussion.)

We first fell in love with the look of rustic breads. On our first trip to Ecce Panis bakery on New York's Upper East Side we saw the window crammed with breads so beautiful they made you cry. Flat breads topped with vegetables and cheese. Round breads dusted with flour. And the aroma was so intense it drifted clear out into the street.

Soon, we were ordering heavenly breads from Zingerman's in Ann Arbor. Then we came to adore Oregon's own homegrown version of rustic European bread, called New Sammy's Cowboy bread and made by that world-class baker, Charlene Rollins.

We also had a few experiences with expensive "famous" breads made by high-profile bakers who shall herein go unnamed, but who have more in common with the naked emperor than with any artisanal baker we know. Which just goes to show, you'd better learn what the stuff is supposed to taste like before you start raving about a bread just because it's ten dollars a pop in a boutique bakery.

It was in Houston's Quilted Toque that we had our first experience baking beside a fine artisanal baker, Brian Dupnik, who turns out loaves so glorious that people who come to the restaurant are content with nothing more than a bowl of soup and Brian's bread for lunch. From Brian we learned how to handle *old dough*, how to manipulate finishes, and how to spring from a given recipe into one we could call our own.

Old dough, as it's known to bakers, is exactly what it says. The baker, after mixing and kneading today's dough, pulls off a quarter of the batch and saves it to add into tomorrow's bread. The addition of this old dough enhances the flavor, the texture, and the keeping qualities of the bread. Brian has buckets of old dough lying about all over his hot steamy bakery just waiting for the next day's baking. More about this artisan baker's technique later (see page 124).

We learned from reading Dan Leader's book, *Bread Alone*, to use only spring water because it won't contaminate the flavor of the bread, and to use organic flours, because they rise in an uninhibited way in the presence of yeast and homemade starters.

One of the best things we learned from Charlene Rollins, and Zingerman's, and Dan Leader was a standard by which to measure such bread. What is rustic European bread supposed to taste like? How should it look? What's the aroma supposed to be? One of the quickest ways to learn is to taste good bread for yourself. See the mail order section of this book (page 307) for a full listing of artisan bakers around the country who regularly do mail order.

Harold McGee unraveled the science of baking bread for us. If we hadn't pored over his book, *On Food and Cooking*, we could never have begun to separate the facts from the folklore about the bread baker's art. So much of what is passed on from baker to baker is charming myth. But when you begin using a bread machine, you're better off if you understand the biochemistry that underlies the process for making bread. Come to think of it, honest information helps anyone who bakes, no matter what the tools.

We learned from Joe Ortiz, author of *The Village Baker* and Carol Field's *The Italian Baker*, some authentic European techniques: how to make over our home ovens into fair approximations of genuine European baker's ovens; how to work with the wet, wet doughs that give those glorious big-holed artisanal loaves; how to finish breads to get that gorgeous artisanal look. And that led us to our own great discovery.

The bread machine is an ideal tool for making rustic European breads.

The secret to many of Europe's best rustic breads is a wet dough. Try to knead such a dough by hand and the temptation to add too much flour is almost overwhelming. Leave the whole gooey job to a bread machine and you'll get the desired results without having to plunge your hands into a mound of dough that more resembles hot chewing gum than anything else.

We also like the bread machine for making these breads because the machine is there, on our counter top, a clean, enclosed chamber where we can leave the dough to mature and ripen into complex tastes. We discovered that the bread machine's *dough setting* was our best ally in making rustic European breads.

All bread machine brands and models we know about have this setting wherein the machine mixes, kneads, and takes dough through the first rise. Then, you can pull it out, shape it to suit, give it a final rise, and bake. Most of the recipes we developed for this book call for the dough setting, although there are also a few recipes that can be made and baked right in the machine. (We particularly recommend the Chocolate Bread, page 278.)

But, we confess. We began manipulating the bread machine to do more than perhaps its manufacturers knew it could do. We learned we could double-knead whole wheat bread by simply running the dough cycle twice. This allowed optimal gluten development and liquid absorption so that we got high, handsome loaves made entirely with whole-grain flours.

Perhaps the handiest thing we learned about using a bread machine was that upon completion of the dough cycle, we could simply leave the dough in the bread machine to continue to ripen and rise.

We also discovered we could make homemade starters right in the bread machine. It's just an old wive's tale that says you can't let metal touch sourdoughs and starters. Commercial bakers have been mixing these starters in big stainless-steel Hobart mixers for years. You can borrow the professional baker's technique and make starters for yourself, right in the bread machine.

In this book, we'll teach you to make a hundred or so traditional rustic European breads using the bread machine's dough cycle, then lift the dough from the machine, knead it by hand, shape it according to the type of bread you're making, give it a final rise, and bake it in your homemade baker's oven.

We'll show you how to make starters at home, how to keep them going, how to use old dough, how to shape breads as beautifully as any you see in artisanal bakeries, how to finish the loaves in an artful way, how to bake on a stone, and how to assess the breads you make so that your standards will be as high as a professional baker's. It's such a satisfying experience making bread. Using the bread machine, you have convenience, and you can hone your skills so that soon you'll be turning out finely crafted European-style breads.

You can use this book successfully just by following the recipes, but if you study the first four chapters you will also learn how to create breads of your own. We've designed the book for both kinds of bread baker: for the person who wishes simply to have new and different recipes to use with the bread machine, and for the Passionate Amateur Bread Baker who wishes to master the baker's craft. A home baker, by beginning to understand the scientific principles behind baking bread and using a bread machine, will have fewer surprises and disappointments in the bread-baking adventure. We hope you'll come to love this process as much as we do.

And did we forget to mention the cost? In certain boutique bakeries around the country, rustic European breads really do sell for as much as ten dollars a loaf. When you consider that a pound loaf of bread may have fifty cents worth of flour, a teaspoon of salt, a quarter's worth of yeast, and some water, you begin to see that you not only get an artist's thrill from making these breads yourself, but sometimes as much as a ten-fold savings cost as well.

LINDA WEST ECKHARDT
DIANA COLLINGWOOD BUTTS
Rogue Valley, Oregon
September 1994

ACKNOWLEDGMENTS

We wish to thank all of the people who patiently, diligently, and generously helped us with this book. Your enthusiasm, comments, and recipe requests inspired us to tackle the traditional European and ethnic bread recipes found in *Rustic European Breads from Your Bread Machine.* We hope we've made the recipes as user-friendly as the bread machine itself.

To Judy Kern, our wonderful editor with a keen eye, many thanks for keeping us on time and on track. Your sense of humor was greatly appreciated through the many months of hard work. To all of the other powers at Doubleday, many thanks for taking us on, and believing in us and this book.

Thanks also go to Erica Marcus and Renana Meyers for their input and wisdom.

Our thanks also to Rita Maas, who photographed the beautiful breads on the cover, and Martie Holmer, who illustrated the text.

We also wish to thank Mildred Marmur, our agent, for taking care of business and for her patience and guidance through the rough spots.

This book would not have been possible without the cooperation and donated bread machines of our friends in the bread machine industry. Thank you. Panasonic, Zojirushi, Sanyo, Welbilt, Seiko, and Hitachi have all manufactured state-of-the-art machines that make bread-baking a pleasure once again.

We particularly wish to thank Fleishmann's Yeast for their enthusiastic support and for the cases of Bread Machine Yeast.

To all of our fellow cookbook authors who have blazed the bread trail, Carol Field, Joe Ortiz, Dan Leader, and Brother Peter Reinhart, thanks for putting words like starter, *chef,* and *biga* in the vocabulary of the home baker. Your books are beautiful, informative, and inspirational.

Closer to home, we thank our children and husbands for being patient with Mom and for not asking "What's for dinner?" while staring at the fifteen different loaves of fresh bread piled on the kitchen table.

To all the employees at Sugarbakers, thanks for letting Diana work on bread instead of cookies through two busy Christmas seasons.

To all the employees of Jefferson Public Radio and "Pie in the Sky," thanks for being patient with Linda when she wanted to do ten shows straight on bread and starters.

Last but not least, thanks to all of our friends here in the Rogue Valley for buying books, tasting bread, and testing recipes. You are our biggest fans and we truly appreciate you all.

LINDA WEST ECKHARDT
AND DIANA COLLINGWOOD BUTTS
Rogue Valley, Oregon
May 1995

CONTENTS

INTRODUCTION

NEAR the end of the research period for this book, after we had read everything we could find about European rustic breads, after we'd made countless loaves, used up several hundred pounds of flour and sea salt, gallons of spring water, and jars and jars of yeast, Diana made a trip to Paris. While other people may travel to seek out a nation's treasures, Diana went for bread.

Using Patricia Wells's good book, *The Food Lover's Guide to Paris*, Diana and her husband, Larry, and the kids, Lauren and Keith, nipped in and out of boulangeries from one end of the city to the other. They returned with sacks and sacks of bread. The plane ride home was long and arduous. Larry is an American pilot, and they fly standby, so coming home the weekend of Easter break they mostly stood by, sustained by loaves of Paris's finest.

A couple of days after the jet lag had subsided, we sat at the pine table in Diana's kitchen, smelling and tasting the remains of these loaves of bread still in their rumpled sacks from the Paris Bakery, Poilane. We came to several conclusions. The breads Diana had found were among the finest we'd ever tasted. And even though somewhat dried out from being in and out of airplanes and hotels with their deadly, dessicating air-conditioning systems, those breads still tasted good.

We didn't have to ask why. We knew why. These breads had been made using time-honored European bakers' techniques, with the addition of starters in most cases. They'd been baked in that humid city situated at the confluence of three rivers. They represented hundreds of years of trial and error, of craft that yielded up breads of great distinction.

We also noted that the bread recipes we'd already developed for this book were—in most cases—as good as any you could buy in a fine Paris boulangerie. And we'd learned to bake these breads by studying books and building on knowledge we already had from researching our first bread book.

That was a comfort. It reinforced our belief that if you can read, follow instructions, learn to observe, develop some standards by tasting great breads, and are willing to have a few less-than-smashing results, you can learn to bake exemplary breads. After all, we'd just done it.

You can understand our motivation. Just think about your own traveling.

Imagine you are in Europe. Somewhere in the heart of Paris. It is 5:30 in the afternoon. You are sitting in a sidewalk café having a glass of wine. City workers rush by, baguettes in hand. Many have already taken big bites out of the end of the loaf. You are starved. You know you can't wait for that 8:00 reservation for dinner.

Across the street is a boulangerie. The line has snaked out the door and down the street. But the aroma is powerful. You take your place. At last inside, you are overwhelmed by the baskets of breads. Crosshatched floured round loaves, oatmeal-covered loaves, a huge round piece of rich brown bread they are slicing off and selling by weight. Baguettes, *bâtards, bon soir*. The transactions take place quickly and in a gentle language.

You are standing at the counter. All you can do is point. This, and this, and this, and this. Your arms are full of breads. Warm, aromatic breads you can hardly wait to tear into.

With nothing more than a glass of wine, sacks full of bread, and your best friend to taste with, you know suddenly this is life as it's meant to be.

But can you take a little Paris home? Can you do this back in River City with nothing more than a sack of flour, sea salt, a bottle of water, and a brown jar of yeast? Oh yeah, and a bread machine on the counter? Yes, yes, and yes, as Molly Brown said. You can. We'll teach you how. We'll bring Europe to you. Close your eyes and chew the bread. You're there.

We haven't attempted to write a comprehensive history of bread and its religious significance. Nor do we pretend that this is a complete survey of the rustic breads of Europe. We've given you our personal favorites, the breads we found to be delicious, challenging, and authentic when taste-tested against rustic breads made by experts.

We've worked out the recipes so that anyone with a bread machine and a willingness to go beyond punching a button will be rewarded with excellent bread. The recipes in this book are little changed from ones you might find in any eighteenth-century European bread baker's manual, except we've taken the process into our own twentieth-century crucible, the bread machine. While this may seem like a contradiction in terms, it's a happy contradiction.

You can now become an artisan baker, shaping loaves of bread with your own two hands, dusting the loaves with flour, slashing them, and baking them in the twentieth-century version of a baker's oven rigged up in your very own modern kitchen (see page 84). And following our instructions, you'll be pleased with the results. You won't have to do the initial mixing, kneading, and raising. You'll have the bread machine to do that for you.

We know there are those of you out there who are gnashing your teeth and swearing that the only real bread is one made from grain you've milled yourself, dough you've kneaded by hand, and baked in a wood-fired oven out in your back yard. To you we say go and God bless. The rest of us are grateful to be able to replicate ancient recipes using modern equipment and techniques when they are available to help us out.

Becoming a Master Baker

Unlike lockstep bread recipes that mislead you into thinking that making bread is a purely mechanical process with no allowance for differences in the weather—rain or shine, dry or humid—or the other myriad elements that affect the outcome of bread, (we find this particularly so in other bread machine recipes) ours will teach you the *craft* of making bread so that you can learn to judge bread, and bread dough, and become a master baker yourself. We'll teach you how to open up the lid to the bread machine, reach in, pinch that dough, and know what it is that you're pinching. We'll teach you what good bread dough should feel like. We'll show you how to let the bread itself take the lead. It's kind of a Zen thing. You become sensitive to the bread. It gives back to you.

Baking bread, whether you're grinding your own wheat and baking in a wood-fired oven or using a bread machine, is mightily affected by the climate, the weather, the activity of the yeast. Make a recipe ten times and you may get ten different results. Learn not to lament these variations but to celebrate the differences.

So, we say, roll up your sleeves, read our book, and prepare to impress your family and friends.

LEARNING THE DIFFERENCE BETWEEN A BÂTARD AND A BAGUETTE

Since rustic European breads are made up of four basic ingredients: flour, yeast, water, salt, and sometimes other additives, the main differences are a result of technique. Walk into a fine bakery and you may be amazed at the variety of breads with foreign-sounding names offered for sale. Here's a rundown of the basic European breads you can learn to make using this book. (See page 75 for shaping instructions.)

BAGEL: The simplest ingredients, flour, water, salt, and yeast, formed into a donut shape, raised, first boiled and then baked. A little malted barley syrup in the boiling water adds flavor and shine to the bagels, and turning them once in the oven halfway through the baking process guarantees a crisp golden crust and a chewy bread with fine holes throughout.

BAGUETTE: In French the word means "wand." This is a long, thin loaf with diagonal slashes. Often made from nothing more than flour, yeast, salt, and water. It may contain additional flours—whole wheat or rye. Usually baked free-form on a stone or baking sheet, or in a special U-shaped pan.

BÂTARD: Translates into "bastard" in English, and is a fat, log-shaped bread with tapered ends. It is slashed a couple of times diagonally, like the baguette, is baked in the same way, and is generally made from the same ingredients, sometimes with raisins, nuts, or other flavor additives.

BOULE: French for "ball," that's exactly what it looks like: a fat, round loaf made from the same ingredients as a baguette or *bâtard*, baked on a stone.

BRIOCHE: An egg-enriched bread, be it loaf-sized or an individual roll, that is traditionally baked in a fluted, buttered mold. It is frequently distinguished by a topknot inserted in the top.

CHALLAH: The traditional Sabbath bread of the Jews, this rich egg-laden bread is braided and baked free-form on a baking sheet or stone.

CIABATTA: "Slipper" in Italian. A flatbread whose shape is said to resemble a Medieval Italian shoe. It has a chewy interior with lots of holes and a mouthwatering floury crust.

CIRCLE BREAD: Any country bread or pain meteil recipe can be used to make this traditional German-style bread distinguished by its disk shape; notched edges; and concentric circle–patterned, flour-dusted top

COURONNE: The crown shape may be made with any French, Italian, or country bread dough. Take a small rolling pin or a dowel and press an indented square into the surface of the donut.

ÉPI: A baguette-type loaf that's been cut and shaped to resemble a wheat sheaf.

FICELLE: Literally a string, in this case a mini-baguette. Makes great bites with soup.

FOCACCIA: An Italian flatbread with a dimpled surface, close cousin to a pizza. The focaccia has olive oil in addition to the usual flour, salt, yeast, and water, and may be flavored with herbs and topped with many things—but never as saucy as pizza.

FOUGASSE: The uptown French version of a focaccia. Originating in Provence, it's often scented with herbs and usually slashed through, then spread to form a decorative flatbread, resembling—among other things—a sun, or a tree shape.

GRISSINI: These are Italian breadsticks. They can be as thin as pencils or as thick as your thumb. Finish them with an egg wash if you wish, with seeds, or with turbinado sugar for a sweet bread.

KHACHAPURI: A cheese-filled bun from the Russian state of Georgia. It's their version of fast food and a welcome addition to any holiday buffet. These freeze well and can be popped out at a moment's notice when company shows up.

KUCHEN: A German coffee cake that's not too sweet, but made tender with eggs.

PAIN AU LEVAIN: A French version of starter-made (sourdough) bread. It can be round, like a traditional baguette, or any of a variety of shapes including buns, sawteeth, *épis*, zigzags, twists, or crowns.

PAIN AUX NOIX: Nut bread; it comes in many shapes, but often in a floury triangle with walnuts or hazelnuts embedded in the top.

PAIN DE CAMPAGNE: A dense country loaf made with a combination of bread flour, whole wheat, and rye flour. Sometimes baked free-form round, or in a Cloche (see page 73).

PAIN MÉTEIL: A mixture of wheat and rye flours baked into a free-form round loaf, traditionally marked with the baker's mark, a kind of monogram used to designate who made the bread.

PAIN ORDINAIRE: The classic French yeast-leavened bread, usually baguette-shaped, with a soft interior and a crisp, thin crust. Best eaten the day it's made. The French buy these twice a day, just to guarantee they'll be eating totally fresh bread.

PANE ALL'OLIO: Everyday Italian bread made with bread flour, yeast, salt, sugar, spring water, and olive oil. Cigar-shaped rolls, crisp on the outside, creamy on the inside, are baked on a stone.

PANE ALL'UVE E NOCI: Italian country bread made with raisins and walnuts.

PANE BIGIO: A round, classic rustic Italian loaf made "gray" with the addition of whole wheat flour.

PANE DE MAIS: Polenta (Italian cornmeal) bread from Italy. Usually a round free-form loaf, but we bake it right in the bread machine.

PANETTONE: Italian Christmas bread laden with fruits and nuts, it's traditionally made with brioche dough and baked in a tall cylinder. The tall domed shape reminds Italians of cathedral domes.

PANINI: Italian rolls in various shapes, they may be torpedoes, globes, or fancy shapes created according to the baker's whim.

PETITS PAINS: The hard rolls of France, crusty on the outside, soft and creamy on the inside. These rolls get their characteristic bite and texture from being raised four times.

PISSALADIÈRE: France's version of the pizza, made with egg-rich brioche dough then topped with a variety of items such as glazed onions and fresh tomato sauce spiked with rosemary needles.

PIZZA: America's favorite Italian flatbread, made of nothing more than bread flour, yeast, salt, and water. Topped with everything from tomato sauces, to cheeses, meats, or shrimp.

STIRATO: From the Italian *stirare*, "to stretch," this Italian bread is just that: a stretched baguette. You can stretch the dough out to fit the limits of your oven. Thirty-six-inch *stiratos* aren't out of the question, provided you have the oven space.

STOLLEN: German Christmas bread. A large *bâtard* filled with fruit and nuts.

TORDU: A simple twist in a baguette gives this bread an interesting look, something like our American donut twists.

TORPEDO: A bread shape popular in both Italy and France that looks just like it sounds, a fat cigar shape tapered at both ends like a torpedo.

RUSTIC
EUROPEAN
BREADS
FROM YOUR
BREAD MACHINE

Baking Rustic European Breads with Your Bread Machine:

A Brief Overview

WHY on earth, you say, would I want to make complicated breads in a machine I bought so that I could make bread simply and automatically? Two reasons. First—if you're anything at all like us—once you get to making breads a lot, you're going to want to expand your repertoire. Second, and perhaps more important, the bread machine is just so damn good at making rustic European-style breads at home. Plus, it saves a lot of money once you've recouped the cost of the machine.

Every brand of bread machine has a dough setting that allows the machine to mix, knead, and raise the dough once before ringing a bell to get you to pull it out, shape it, and raise it a final time before baking in the oven. We particularly recommend using this dough setting for making rustic European breads because it allows you to get your hands in the dough to knead and form the bread into the shape you want. These are the pleasures bakers have enjoyed for hundreds of years. Owning a bread machine need not rob you of this voluptuous sensation. And you will be able to make some very sophisticated breads by taking advantage of particular qualities the bread machine has. One bonus we discovered is that it also makes a good vessel for creating starters and for holding old dough. But more on that later (see page 56).

Machine kneading allows you to work with a very wet dough. And that, dear friends, is the secret to many fine European-style rustic breads. If you could see, as we have, fine bakers plunge their hands into wet, stringy dough to knead the stuff, you'd fall to your knees and say thanks for a machine that will do that part for you. Once the bread machine has done its thing, you're there to hand shape the dough into loaves, raise them, and bake them on a pizza stone in the oven.

We also found out, in the testing for this book, that certain classic European breads are perfectly adaptable to being made on the basic bread setting, which means the machine does everything and kicks out a loaf of perfect bread at the end. You'll find those recipes here as well.

It's the Bread, Not the Machine

Since we've learned so much about the use of the bread machine, we wanted to encourage you to focus on the bread and not the machine. No matter what brand you have, you can make the finest breads. We don't agree that a recipe is designed for one brand of machine and cannot be made in any other. We know this from experience because in traveling around the country, demonstrating our methods, we've had the opportunity to bake many different kinds of bread in any number of bread machines, in all sorts of climates from high and dry to low and humid and in all kinds of weather—sunny, rainy, and variations in between. Learn this new craft for baking bread and you can bake anywhere, with any equipment.

Bread Machine Basics

The recipes in this book are made using one of two settings found on any bread machine. The first is the basic bread setting, in which you layer in the ingredients, punch a button, and the machine does everything: mix, knead, raise, punch down, raise a second time, and bake. The second, and the one we use most often, is the dough setting, wherein the machine mixes, kneads, and raises the dough once, then rings a bell, at which point you remove the bread from the machine, punch it down, rest it, shape it, raise it a final time, add any finish you may desire, then bake it in the regular oven (see page 72 for more details).

Any bread recipe you read will offer a suggested ratio of flour to liquid. Old-fashioned recipes used to suggest a range (from three to four cups of flour). Bread machine recipes, however, tend to be very dogmatic, insisting that you use precisely a certain amount of flour. In fact, the actual amount of flour needed depends on factors not always in your control. The weather, the climate, the barometric pressure, all affect flour and, therefore, the breads you make—even those made in a bread machine. For, you see, flour takes up water from the air—is hygroscopic—which means you may have to adjust the flour-water ratio slightly, regardless of whose recipe you are using, whether or not you're using a machine.

Our grandmothers developed a feel for dough through experience. They might not have understood the science behind it, but they knew when the dough they were kneading by hand on a board was too dry or too wet, just by the way it felt. Turn the kneading task over to a bread machine, and you can only develop this feel by opening the lid and pinching the dough as it kneads.

This means you, like Grandmother, will have to learn to exercise your judgment to get the flour-liquid ratio just right. After the machine has been mixing for a few minutes, simply open up that lid and examine the dough. If the ratio is correct, you will soon have a soft, pliable dough that, during the rest cycle, relaxes to the corners of the bread machine pan. A quick pinch should reveal dough that feels like baby fat: soft, satiny, and pliable.

If you need to add more water—say in the winter when your house is centrally heated and your flour is dry as house dust—you'll be able to tell because the dough will either be crumbly, refusing to form a ball at all, or will form a ball as dense and hard as a fist. If the dough is too dry, you'll need to add water or some other liquid, one tablespoon at a time, until it forms a soft ball. If the dough is a hard fist, lift it from the machine, pull it into several pieces, drop the pieces back into the whirring machine, and add water, a tablespoon at a time, until the dough is soft and pliable. Given experience with the bread machine you'll get to the point where you can actually hear the difference in the sound of the motor. If the dough is too hard, or hasn't enough liquid, the motor may "lug" or strain. If the dough is too wet, the motor may "sing" or whine.

Sometimes, say in a humid climate or on a rainy day, when the flour may have taken up a good bit of water from the atmosphere, your dough may be too wet. It may have so much liquid that it looks more like cake batter than dough. In this case, with the machine still running, add flour, one tablespoon at a time, until the dough firms up. If you find loaves caving in on the top, it's most likely that you are adding too much liquid. This can happen if you're baking in Miami, or New Orleans, or Houston, where the weather and climate are hot and muggy. However, we would warn you that it's better to err on the side of a wet dough than a dry one.

If you're baking in Denver or Albuquerque you will need to make fine adjustments to compensate not only for the dry climate but also for the altitude. It's easy to understand. As you get higher and the atmospheric pressure is reduced, the air becomes "thinner." You simply need less yeast to lift the bread. Think of it like this. There's less resistance at a higher altitude. So you may routinely have to add less yeast to your bread machine in these situations to be sure that the bread doesn't blow out the top of the pan.

Once you become experienced with your bread machine, you'll have fewer surprises, and the results will become less mysterious. There are good scientific reasons why bread machines do what they do, although we're the first to admit it sometimes seems like gremlins at work. But, we say, keep on using the machine. Have fun with it. Don't get too bogged down in the science. If you have a few failures, just think of them as great pigeon food. Throw the bread to the birds and go forward.

QUICK TIPS FOR MAXIMIZING THE RESULTS USING YOUR BREAD MACHINE

Don't I just dump the ingredients into the bread machine and go?

Although we all wish this were as simple as putting gasoline into a car and driving off, it takes a bit more attention to get the results you want. Always start with fresh ingredients. If your bread machine has a preheat cycle, feel free to place cold ingredients directly into the pan. If your machine doesn't preheat the ingredients (you can tell when a machine preheats by the series of little clicks you hear and the minutes that pass before it actually begins to mix the dough) make sure they're at room temperature. If the ingredients have been in the refrigerator, use your microwave to warm them, ten to twenty seconds will usually bring liquids and eggs (broken into a dish) up to room temperature. If you toast nuts, or melt butter, or heat other ingredients, cool them to room temperature before adding them to the bread machine. Stick your finger in and make sure the ingredient isn't too hot to the touch before you add it to the machine. Too hot and it will kill the yeast; too cold and the yeast will shrink. Room temperature's best.

So what's the best way to put the ingredients in?

Layer the ingredients, adding the yeast first, then flours, and finally salt, fats, and liquids. Measure accurately. Use dry measures for flour and other dry ingredients, use liquid measures for water and other liquids. Cut butter, margarine, or shortening into bits before adding it to the bread machine pan.

My machine doesn't have a raisin bread cycle. When do I add fruits and nuts?

When baking breads with fruit, nuts, high egg or sugar content, choose the light crust setting for best results. When adding raisins, fruits, or nuts, be sure they're not clumped together. Knead them in by hand after the dough cycle is complete, or add them at the beep your machine gives on the raisin bread cycle, if you have one. Dust sticky fruits with flour before adding to get them to incorporate more evenly.

What do you mean by a warm, draft-free place?

If you've made dough on the dough cycle and wish to raise the final loaf outside the bread machine, choose a warm, draft-free place. Diana uses the closet where her hot water heater resides. Linda has a cabinet in the kitchen that sits over a heat vent. Other choices are the oven with the door propped open (this is a problem if you need to preheat the oven with a stone in it for thirty minutes, unless you have two ovens). People have written us saying they place dough on a heating pad set on the lowest setting with layers of toweling over it if their kitchen is too cold. One woman said she stuck her dough into the hot clothes dryer. This would never work at our houses. Somebody would be sure to toss in a wet pair of sneakers.

What if I want hot bread for breakfast?

Can you program your VCR? If so, you can probably figure out how to use the delay time start feature found on some bread machines. If you plan to use this feature, choose a recipe without raw eggs or milk. It isn't safe to leave these items outside the refrigerator for such a period of time before they're cooked.

My bread sticks in the bread machine pan and won't come out. What should I do?

Remember to remove the pin first, if your machine has one. Then, rap the pan on a cutting board and the bread will usually fall right out. Remember to remove the blade that may have imbedded itself in the bottom of the baked loaf of bread. Don't wash the bread machine pan in the dishwasher either. It comes with a no-stick finish that could be damaged by harsh detergents. Likewise, don't scratch the bread pan's surface by using metal knives to try and loosen the bread from the pan.

The loaves I make never seem to fill up the pan. What am I doing wrong?

In the first place, your object in making bread is not to fill up the bread machine pan. Some breads are naturally more compact than others and would never rise up over the top of the bread machine pan. But if your bread seems too compact, you may have used insufficient liquid, or too many fruits and nuts, or too much "heavy flour" (rye, whole wheat, or other dark flours). Try adding a tablespoon of gluten flour per cup of dark or whole-grain flour to lighten the loaf. You may also have misread the recipe and used the wrong kind of flour. Check the pull date on your yeast. It could have been old. It's also possible that you forgot to preheat and used cold ingredients to begin. Conversely, you could have poured hot liquids right into the pan and damaged the yeast. Or, you could have added too much salt, which inhibited yeast action. If you dumped the salt and yeast into the machine together, your yeast might also be inhibited.

Were there weather extremes? Was it too cold or too dry? Move your bread machine to a warmer location if your kitchen's cold. Did you open the lid too many times? If you do, you'll cool off the bread machine chamber so that your bread may be inadequately raised and/or baked.

The bread I bake in the machine sometimes suffers from sunken tops. What's wrong?

Sunken loaves may result from too much liquid in the dough or an overproofed dough (an overproofed dough has been allowed to rise too long). Using too little salt can weaken the dough so that the top collapses. If your machine sits in a spot that's too drafty, it can confuse the machine's computer so that the rising and baking times don't work the way they're supposed to; the bread will be inadequately baked and the top will cave in.

Sometimes, for no reason at all, I get an atom bomb mushroom cloud top on the bread. Why?

You may have had too much liquid in the dough, or too much yeast, or your kitchen may have been too hot. Was the recipe too large for the machine? Look in the recipe book that came with your bread machine. A one-pound machine will have recipes with roughly two cups of flour. A one-and-a-half-pound machine will use three cups of flour, and a two-pound machine may call for as much as four cups of flour.

Among the catastrophes that can actually happen with a bread machine, we offer the following just for laughs. You'd never do anything this dumb. Like the man who wanted to surprise his wife with bread and dumped the ingredients into the machine not knowing it had a *pan,* which was at that moment resting quietly in the dishwasher.

Or the person who failed to put the blade into the pan and ran the machine through the whole cycle only to discover a three-inch-high brick at the end. If the bread machine pan and/or blade is not well seated on the shaft, the ingredients don't mix at all, and all you'll get is a brick.

Cleaning your bread machine

We confess. Sometimes our bread machines smoke like a Camels billboard because we have so many crumbs in the bottom. Cleaning the bread machine is low on our list of priorities. But for those of you who care, you can use one of those portable vacuums to lift out the crumbs, or just wipe the cavity with a damp cloth. Don't scrub the bread machine pan with abrasives or you'll ruin the finish. Some manufacturers recommend that you never put your bread machine pan in the dishwasher. It's really not necessary to do more than wipe it out after it's cooled and the crumbs and dough have dried on. Use a soft cloth to protect the finish and go forth.

So You want to buy a bread Machine

Although we expect that most people who choose this cookbook will already own a bread machine, it's possible that some of you don't. Or, like the person who started out with a Yugo, you might be wanting to upgrade to a Porsche. Here's what we'd advise about buying your first or second or third bread machine.

Which one should you choose? Walk into a store and you may see five machines that all look like your basic bread box, priced from ninety-nine to four hundred dollars. How can you make an intelligent selection?

It depends on what you want. Although we'd never buy the lowest-priced bread machine, neither would we purchase the top-of-the-line machine that has unnecessary frills. Buy the best machine you can afford with the features you need and you'll soon have a new friend in the kitchen.

A one-pound machine—the small one—is best suited for small families or couples who eat only a moderate amount of bread and want the machine mainly for convenience.

A better buy and much more versatile is a one-and-a-half-pound machine. With a larger bread pan, you have more flexibility and—trust us on this—once you begin making bread at home, the aroma will have you and your family eating more of it than you did when you relied on store-bought bread. Big two-pound models are also available for large families.

We have worked with almost every bread machine and can say that the brands have more in common than they have differences. Certain features that we believe are critical include: a dough cycle, a cool-down cycle, a pan that can be lifted from the machine for filling. Features that, in our experience, are not needed are a yeast dispenser, a rice cooker, a jam maker, a quick bread-making cycle. Most viewing windows are useless. You can't see enough to do you any good. Open the top and peek into the machine to inspect the dough. It's okay.

No machine is going to do everything but pay the rent. You shouldn't expect it to. If you want to cook rice, buy a rice cooker. If you want to make jam, haul out the jam pot. If you want to make a quick bread or cake, believe us, your conventional methods and appliances will do a better job than any bread machine. A bread machine's for baking yeast bread. Use it and enjoy it.

All bread machines have a removable bread pan with a kneading blade on the bottom. A motor turns the blade to mix and knead the bread. A microcomputer controls the heat and cycles in the machine and guides the bread through the successive cycles to produce either a finished loaf of baked bread or a mound of proofed dough ready for shaping.

Some brands produce a vertical rectangle, others a horizontal. You can also buy a machine that makes a tall cylinder. The vertical rectangle is most popular and slices nicely into squares. This shape fits toasters and is easily accepted by finicky children who like their bread to look the way they're used to it.

All machines have a dough cycle, which we've discussed, and a basic bread-baking cycle that ranges from two hours and fifty minutes to upwards of four hours.

We also like the rapid bake cycle found on certain high-end machines. This cycle speeds up the basic bread-baking cycle to somewhere around two and a half hours. Some machines have a raisin bread setting. If your family likes breads with nuts and fruits baked in them, you might want to hunt for a brand with this feature.

The popular delayed bake timer, available on most machines, allows you to put the ingredients in the machine, set it to start at a later time, and have hot bread at just the moment you want it. Great for Bed and Breakfast operators, or others who want hot bread for Sunday brunch.

Some machines have a preheat cycle that warms ingredients before beginning to mix them. If you choose a machine without this feature, you'll get best results if you warm the ingredients before beginning to make bread.

A power saver will save you if you experience a power outage or if the cord accidentally gets pulled, because the machine will hold its place in the cycle up to ten minutes and will restart once the power is restored. If your machine doesn't restart, just remove the dough from the pan, punch it down, shape it, and place it in a greased loaf pan or on a parchment-covered baking sheet, let it rise to nearly doubled in bulk, then bake it in the oven. If the power outage occurs during the bake cycle, the bread will be doughy inside and will need to be thrown out.

You'll use your bread machine more if you leave it in a convenient place. Think about how much room you have in your kitchen. Where will you put the machine? Choose one that will fit the space you have available.

When you get your new bread machine home, maximize your bread-making experience by using spring water (no off taste), organic bread flour (not all-purpose), and Fleischmann's Bread Machine Yeast. Then prepare to learn the new craft of baking bread.

FEATURES OF VARIOUS

Brand Name	CYCLES				
	Preheat	Rapid Bake	Dough	Whole Wheat	French
DAK	yes	no	yes	no	yes
HITACHI	yes	yes	yes	no	no
MAXIM	no	yes	yes	yes	yes
MK Seiko	no	yes	yes	no	yes
PANASONIC NATIONAL	no	yes	yes	yes	no
REGAL	no	no	yes	no	yes
SANYO	no	no	yes	no	no
TOASTMASTER	no	yes	yes	no	no
TRILLIUM	no	yes	yes	yes	yes
WELBILT	yes	no	yes	no	yes
WESTBEND	yes	yes	yes	yes	yes
ZOJIRUSHI	yes	yes	yes	no	yes

NOTES:

All models have delayed bake cycles except MK Seiko Mr. Loaf HB 211, Regal K6774, and Welbilt ABM 600.

Always check a particular model in the store against the above chart for features you want since particular models may vary from the above chart.

BREAD MACHINES

	CYCLES				Other Features	
Raisin/Nut	Jam/Rice	Cake/Quick Bread	Cool Down		Crust Color	Power Saver
yes	no	no	yes		yes	no
yes	no	no	yes		yes	yes
yes	no	no	no		yes	no
no	no	no	yes		no	yes
no	no	no	no		yes	yes
no	no	no	yes		yes	no
no	no	no	yes		no	no
yes	no	no	yes		yes	yes
yes	no	no	yes		yes	no
yes	no	no	yes		yes	no
yes	no	no	yes		yes	no
yes	yes	yes	yes		no	yes

2

INGREDIENTS

Rustic European Breads are usually made up of four universally and readily available basic ingredients: wheat flour, water, yeast, and salt. In America we sometimes add natural dough conditioners such as milk, butter or other fats, eggs, sugar, or honey. Both in Europe and the United States cheese, fruit, nuts, spices, and herbs are sometimes added for flavor and variety.

The fab four

Under French law, true French bread may contain only the basic four ingredients and sometimes either small amounts of rye flour or minute additions of ascorbic acid, which is allowed because of its close relation to natural vitamin C. The artisan bakers of today create many variations on the basic-four theme, distinguished not only by artful shapes, color, and hue, but also by crust density, texture, and varying degrees of sourness or lack thereof.

Italian bakers also cling to the basic-four rule but work with a stickier dough that contains more water. This flour-to-water ratio produces a bread that is flatter than the French version, with a moister texture and a crumb of large, irregularly shaped holes in the cell structure. The crust is chewy yet soft, especially if it has been brushed with olive oil while still hot. Preferences for specific flours, flour-to-water ratio, shaping, and slashing techniques, even under similar conditions, produce breads that are remarkably personal in style.

Wheat flour

Throughout Europe and America, wheat is the primary grain ground for the flour that is used in bread baking. A wheat berry (which is the seed that was on the stalk), is an edible powerhouse of nutrition. Botanically, there are more than thirty thousand varieties of wheat, and the most nutritious of these berries may contain up to 19 percent protein. The remainder of the berry is made up of complex carbohydrates and—when not overly processed—fiber.

The wheat berry contains three major parts: the bran, the endosperm, and the germ.

The bran is the thin, brown, shiny outer shell of the berry. It is made up mostly of indigestible cellulose fiber and contributes to the proper functioning of our digestive tract.

The endosperm, which would provide nourishment for the berry if it were replanted as seed, makes up the bulk of the grain. While the endosperm is mainly starch, it also contains the proteins gliadin and glutenin. When combined with liquids and mixed and kneaded, these proteins create a super-protein called "gluten." This gluten is an elastic substance that allows bread dough to expand and provides the proper tension to trap and hold the carbon dioxide gas that is expelled by the feeding yeast. This entrapment of gas creates the cell structure of the bread and is what causes the dough to rise and stay up after baking.

The wheat germ is the embryo of the berry and is rich in oil, vitamin E, and protein. (Think of the embryo like an egg yolk, and, as in an egg, this is where the fat is stored.) The oil in the germ turns rancid easily and any grains or flours that contain the germ (such as stone-ground whole wheat or organic bread flour with germ), wheat germ, or whole wheat berries, should be refrigerated or frozen to prolong shelf life. Freezing grains or flour for at least seventy-two hours also kills any weevils that may have infiltrated the product. Once rendered harmless, they can then be sifted out.

When berries are ground in their entirety, the result is whole wheat flour. When the bran and wheat germ are removed, the endosperm that remains is ground to make white wheat flour.

Wheat milled for baking in America is classified as either hard red spring wheat or soft red winter wheat. Hard red spring wheat is grown on the high plains—in Montana, the upper Midwest, and the Southwest. This wheat is planted in the spring and harvested in the fall. Within this long growing period the wheat develops stalk strength and a hard red berry. It is very high in protein content—from 12 to 14 percent. Knowing a flour's protein percentage is important because its ability to produce gluten is directly related to its protein content. High- and low-protein flours are typically referred to as "strong" or "weak," respectively, a reflection of how much muscle it takes to develop the gluten. The hard, "strong" spring wheat flour is preferred for yeast-bread baking.

Soft red winter wheat, planted in the winter and harvested in the spring, grows in milder climates in the South, Southeast, and Midwest. Indiana and Illinois harvest the most soft red winter wheat. The flour made from this wheat is high in starch and has a low protein content of between 10 and 11 percent. Flours made from this high starch, low-protein, "weak" wheat flour are best used for baking tender cakes, cookies, and pastries.

Stone Milling of Flours and Grains

Many commercially stone-ground flours are available on today's market (see page 308 for mail order sources). If your local miller stone-grinds the flour, all the better. Stone-grinding of flour and grains is one of the oldest and slowest methods. Two huge, round, matching, cool granite stones with diameters ranging from five to eight feet and weighing anywhere from 500 to 1,000 pounds are stacked so that one rotates slowly, heavily pressing against the other. Whole grains are poured between the two stones, where the berries are crushed and broken into coarse bits. The grains are passed through this process several times until they become flour of the desired texture—some fine, some medium, and some coarse-ground.

Some mills, such as Spring Mill Park in Mitchell, Indiana, still power their stones with a big waterwheel. Other mills may power their stones electrically. Ancient mills were turned by real horse power. The horse—or other animal—was attached to a pole that was attached to a rod. When the animal walked around in a circle, the rod rotated and turned the stones.

This cool grinding method is considered best because it processes the entire berry, preserving every nutritious part of the grain. The germ, oils, vitamins, and tiny pieces of bran are all incorporated into a freshly ground first-rate flour. At some mills, you can still bring your own grains for stone-grinding.

Commercial whole wheat flour is a recombination of parts from milling: white flour, germ, and bran. Commercial mills pass grain through high-speed steel rollers, then drop the resulting flour down a chute, blowing off the heavier bran and germ. To make whole wheat flour, the commercial miller simply adds back a certain percentage of bran and germ to the white flour. This is the whole wheat flour available at the grocery store. It is lighter and less perishable than stone-ground whole wheat, but still should be stored in a cool, dark cabinet and used within three months of purchase.

Electric Home Grinders

If you want to grind wheat yourself, we strongly recommend one of the home mills on the market. You learned to grind coffee beans, right! Well, believe us, grinding wheat is just as easy. Coarse or fine whole wheat or rye flour can be ground fresh right before use. But remember, unbleached white flour can't be homemade because the machine can't remove the bran and germ.

Types of Wheat Flour

ALL-PURPOSE BLEACHED ENRICHED WHITE FLOUR: The most common commercially milled white flour, it is, by law, vitamin enriched to replace nutrients lost in the milling and chemical bleaching processes. Most large flour companies mill their grain with steel rollers or hammers at a very high speed. This high speed produces friction and, thus, heat, which destroys many of the vitamins in the wheat berry. Other machines remove the germ and all pieces of the bran from the flour.

The flour is then bleached with chemicals and sometimes bromated with potassium. Adding potassium bromate to the flour toughens the dough so that it can stand up to the rigors of machine kneading in commercial bakeries. If you're kneading dough in the bread machine or by hand, however, it's difficult to overwork it you're using all-purpose flour that has not been bromated.

All-purpose flour may or may not be treated with citric acid (vitamin C), which creates an acid environment for thriving yeast (see page 26 for more on ascorbic acid) and acts as a natural dough conditioner. The flour is then enriched with the vitamins and minerals that were lost in the milling process.

Because the germ that contains the oil has been removed, the packaged flour now has a long shelf life. A combination of hard and soft wheat, with 8 to 10 percent gluten protein, all-purpose bleached enriched white flour can be used in any recipe calling for white flour. But because it is a "one-size-fits-all" blend, the bread may not rise as high as bread made with bread flour. All-purpose flour works well for quick breads that are mixed by hand and leavened with baking powder or soda, but it isn't ideal for breads that must stand up to machine kneading and the demands of a yeast fermentation.

Harold McGee, in his fine book *On Food and Cooking*, points out that the enrichment and fortification of white flour with added vitamins may, in fact, make it even more nutritious than whole wheat. For while it's true, says McGee, that whole-grain flour contains more protein, minerals, and vitamins than refined flours, particularly the wheat germ and bran, it is also true that some of these nutrients pass through the digestive system unmetabolized. White flours, however, fortified with added nutrients, present the nutrients in digestible form.

ALL-PURPOSE UNBLEACHED ENRICHED WHITE FLOUR: All freshly milled "white" flour is a pale tan color. It's allowed to age for several months, during which time natural oxidation causes the flour to whiten. Bleached white flour is chemically whitened. Unbleached flour has the advantage of a slightly higher protein content than bleached all-purpose, plus it retains the vitamin E that is leached out during chemical whitening. The aging process used for whitening unbleached flour also improves the bonding characteristics of the gluten, giving you stronger, more elastic doughs that will produce breads with higher volume.

BREAD FLOUR: Bread flour, commonly found in ten-pound sacks, has returned to the shelves of the neighborhood grocery store after an absence of almost thirty years. "Bread flour" is the shorthand term for high-protein, high-gluten, enriched, hard-wheat white flour. It will produce a dough that's elastic and strong, making a sturdy web to hold the carbon dioxide gases released by yeasts, thus yielding the most volume to the dough. Commercial bakers like bread flour not only for its gluten properties, but also because they believe it creates better-tasting bread. Breads made with bread flour will be flavorful, light, and well risen. Since bread flour contains between 12 and 14 percent gluten protein compared to 8 to 10 percent for all-purpose flour, it's better for you. It can be substituted for organic bread flour with good results.

ORGANIC BREAD FLOUR: We call for organic flours in most of our recipes. Organic flours do not contain the bleaches, bromates, and other additives that are sometimes found in all-purpose flour (see page 27). Organic certification laws differ from state to state, but usually "organic" means that the wheat has been grown using only natural fertilizers such as manure and has not been sprayed with pesticides. It also means that the wheat has been tested for traces of pesticides or other chemical residues (and it passed!). The yeast in natural starters thrives when the flour is free of bleaches, bromates, and chlorine.

However, the different types of white flours give only slightly different results; use what is available and affordable to you—organic bread flour, unbleached bread flour, or all-purpose flour. (Bread flour is recommended by most bread machine companies since it has a higher gluten protein count and forms a stronger gluten web, which holds up well under machine kneading. However, we don't believe that it shows a significant difference in the crumb.)

Organic bread flour is made from high-gluten-protein (12 to 14 percent) hard red spring wheat. It is a wheat flour with all the bran sifted off and the germ removed. If you don't like the idea of the nutrient-packed germ being removed from the flour, simply stir it back in using a ratio of one tablespoon of raw wheat germ for each cup of flour.

Organic bread flour is not bleached but lightens naturally to a cream color if it is allowed to age in a cool place for several months. Organic bread flour will vary in color from batch to batch. The fresher the flour the darker it will be. We recommend using the freshest flour you can find, regardless of the color, as it will lose some of its nutrients and vitamins with age. Organic bread flour may also be marked as "unbleached organic bread flour" simply because it hasn't been treated with bleaching chemicals.

Along with the organic certification, the gluten-protein content of the flour should be listed on the nutritional analysis label on the side of the bag. The protein analysis is usually for four ounces of flour, and four ounces of flour should contain twelve grams of gluten protein to be ideal for bread-baking (if the nutritional analysis is figured on the basis of two ounces, you must multiply the gluten-protein percentage listed in grams by two to obtain the correct information).

Breads made with organic bread flour will be flavorful, light, and well risen. Organic bread flour will give you a robust and textured loaf when mixed with natural starters or with whole wheat or rye flour.

Our favorite organic bread flour comes from Giusto's Specialty Foods (see page 310 for mail order specifics). They sell many types of flour, organic and unbleached, pastry, bread, whole wheat, and cake.

We also recommend getting to know your local miller if possible, because his flour will be much fresher than that found on the local supermarket shelf. Local mills sometimes have certain days on which they mill, and you can get your flour straight from the grinder if you know their grinding schedule.

WHOLE WHEAT FLOUR: Milled from the entire wheat berry, whole wheat flour is a light-brown color with visible flecks of bran and feels gritty to the touch. The supermarket brand of whole wheat is usually ground fine to medium and works well in our recipes. Nutritionally superior stone-ground whole wheat will be heavier than the commercial variety and may require an additional tablespoon or two of liquid for the dough to reach the desired consistency. No artificial nutritional enrichment is added to whole wheat flours, since the bran and germ are retained. For bread-baking, make sure the flour has been ground from hard red spring wheat. This information should be on the label on the side of the sack. When buying in bulk, you may have to ask the grocer to show you the big sack or call the manufacturer to find out. We buy stone-ground whole wheat bread flour from King Arthur (see page 310).

The added weight of the bran in the gluten strands can inhibit gluten development. However, the bran also helps raise the dough because it traps the carbon dioxide being released by the yeast. Rising times may vary in the same recipe depending on the size and weight of the bran found in different whole wheat flours. To develop the gluten fully in whole wheat breads, and thereby get a loaf that will rise to its fullest potential, you may need to double knead the dough in the machine (see page 71). Stone-ground flours generally contain larger and heavier flecks of bran than commercially made whole wheat flour. These larger bran flecks will also absorb more liquid, so you may need to add more liquid when working with stone-ground whole wheat flour.

You'll get a chewy, country-style bread. When combined with rye flour and a natural starter you get the best of both grains—the tug-at-the-tooth chew of the whole wheat and the tangy sourness of rye.

Whole wheat flour is more perishable than chemically treated white flours. Because of the oil in it, old whole wheat flour can develop a bitter or rancid taste. Buy only what you can use in three to six months and store it in an airtight container in a cool place—the refrigerator or freezer in the summer (see page 31 for more on storing flours). Taste any flour you're uncertain about. The bitter taste of stale flour is unmistakable.

WHOLE WHEAT GRAHAM FLOUR: Coarse whole wheat flour can be found labeled as "coarse graham flour" in some stores or mills. Developed by—guess who— Dr. Sylvester Graham, a Presbyterian minister who, during the early part of the nineteenth century, advocated its ability to cure intemperance. In his book *Treatise on Bread*

and Breadmaking, Graham championed not only whole wheat flour but also loose cloth-
ing, fruits and vegetables in the diet, and sleeping in fresh air. Even though temperance
may not be the goal in the nineties, we must agree the old preacher was on to something
for a healthy life.

WHITE WHOLE WHEAT FLOUR: Available from King Arthur Flour (see
page 310), this 13 percent protein flour is a favorite of ours. Milled from a new variety of
wheat, it contains all the fiber and nutritional benefits of traditional whole wheat flour
but has a sweeter, lighter taste. It doesn't make white bread, but a lovely nutty whole
wheat.

SEMOLINA GRANULES: When the largest particles of the endosperm of durum wheat berries (a variety of hard wheat grown in cold climates) detach during
milling, they're known as semolina. Pale yellow and granular, semolina resembles cornmeal and can be used to sprinkle on your baking stone, work surface, or parchment paper to keep breads from sticking. Semolina granules *cannot* be substituted for semolina
flour in breadbaking.

SEMOLINA FLOUR: Amber colored and slightly grainy, this flour is milled
from semolina granules. Pulverized, these granules make a coarse flour that is high in
gluten protein. Generally used in making pasta, it cooks up firmly and absorbs less water than pasta made with softer flour. When mixed with organic bread flour or whole
wheat flour, semolina also makes fine Mediterranean breads.

DURUM FLOUR INTEGRALE: The whole-grain version of semolina flour,
durum flour is made from the same hard wheat and is milled using the entire wheat
berry. It has the traditional powderlike, brown-flecked texture of fine whole wheat flour
and a pronounced wheaty taste.

GOLDEN DURUM FLOUR: Ground from the endosperm only of durum
wheat, golden durum flour is the same thing as semolina flour except that it is ground
finer. If you can't find it, you can make it yourself with the help of your blender. Simply
blend one part semolina granules with two parts organic bread flour until a silky fine-
grind texture is achieved.

INSTANT-BLENDING FLOUR: Sold in shaker cans, this flour is made by
combining flour with water, then drying and pulverizing it into an instant-blending powder. It promises no lumps when used to thicken gravies, soups, and sauces but is not suitable for bread-baking. Wallpaper paste maybe.

SELF-RISING FLOUR: Grandma loved it since she didn't have to measure out salt or baking powder when making biscuits because it contains those already. Self-rising flour can be a great time-saver when making quick breads or biscuits, but it is not suitable for yeast breads.

CAKE OR PASTRY FLOURS: These are white flours made from high-starch, low-gluten, soft wheat. They're not suitable for yeast-bread-baking. Occasionally they are mixed with bread flour and help to make the soft insides of hard rolls such as French milk rolls and bollilos. Use this flour when a tighter soft texture is desired in the crumb. Muffins, cakes, and pastry doughs will all benefit from being made with these specialized flours.

GLUTEN FLOUR: Gluten flour is a high-protein, high-gluten flour containing very little starch. Its main use is to lighten heavy doughs made with dark flours such as whole wheat or rye, which have virtually no gluten at all. The addition of a tablespoon of gluten flour per cup of heavy flour will create a dough that rises as nicely as a hot-air balloon. Feel free to add it to lighten any whole-grain bread.

NON-WHEAT FLOURS

The cornerstone of all bread-making is wheat flour. However, it is the addition of non-wheat flours that adds the structure and complex flavors that characterize some European breads. The health breads of France and German pumpernickels all contain small amounts of non-wheat flours.

RYE FLOUR: There are two basic "grinds" of rye flour.

Medium-ground rye flour is what you will find boxed and on most supermarket shelves. It is medium to light brown in color (this indicates the amount of bran processed out) and works well in all our recipes.

Coarsely ground rye flour is often labeled as "pumpernickel." This rye flour is darker in color, indicating that a higher percentage of bran has been left in the flour. It has a rough, coarse, gritty texture like meal. This creates that almost black, chewy, Eastern European–style bread.

Rye flours are processed from the whole rye berry and are therefore considered to be whole-grain flours. Although rye is high in protein, it is low in gliadin and glutenin, the proteins necessary to form gluten and give bread its springy texture. Rye doughs are sticky, tacky, sometimes downright sullen. Since rye breads can be quite dense, we often mix rye with wheat flour. Using two parts rye to one part wheat will create a lighter loaf. A tablespoon of gluten flour (see page 25) added to each cup of rye flour will lighten a rye loaf as well.

POTATO FLOUR: Sometimes labeled "potato starch," potato flour is made from cooked potatoes that have been dried, then ground into a flour that will ferment rapidly and, when added to wheat flour, will create a dough that rises quickly.

DOUGH CONDITIONERS

The purpose of a dough conditioner is to strengthen the web created by the dough to hold up the gases formed when the yeast begins to work. Your bread machine can help you accomplish this by double kneading the dough, which is especially useful for making whole-grain breads (see page 71).

The following are natural dough conditioners that can help strengthen dough, resulting in a bread that rises higher and is lighter in texture.

MALT EXTRACT: Malt extract is not legally permitted in France for making plain French bread, but it is used by Italian bakers as a yeast food or dough conditioner. Malt syrup contains enzymes that help break down the starch in the wheat flour into sugar, which can be used to feed the yeast. Malt extract is a grain product in syrup form (Diastatic Malt Powder is the dry form) made of barley that's been sprouted and mashed. It can be found in health food stores and in specialty food shops. It should be used in tiny amounts—no more than a half teaspoon per cup of flour—so that its taste does not overtake the flavor of the wheat in the bread.

ASCORBIC ACID: Vitamin C, also known as ascorbic acid, creates an acid environment in the dough, which yeast loves. French bakers add it to bread to give their dough a property they call "tolerance." In other words, how much rising time can a wet dough tolerate before it falls? A wet dough that rises for four to six hours is likely to fall if it is not baked at the precise moment it is ready. Vitamin C gives it tenacity, allowing the full development of the dough.

Buy the acid in granular form (ascorbic acid is available by mail order from the King Arthur Baking Catalog, see page 310), and add just a few grains to each cup of bread flour or whole-grain flour, or one thirty-second of a teaspoon to every five cups of flour.

POTASSIUM BROMATE: An additive in some bread flours favored by commercial bakers because it helps the dough endure the rigors of machine kneading. Since some studies have found potassium bromate to be carcinogenic, it's been outlawed in California and some other states. Most commercial bread flour we see these days contains ascorbic acid instead of potassium bromate.

GLUTEN FLOUR: See page 25.

DAIRY PRODUCTS: Milk, cream, powdered milk, buttermilk, and powdered buttermilk not only add to the flavor of bread, but also improve the cell structure so that the web of gluten will hold the gases more efficiently.

GRAINS

WHOLE WHEAT BERRIES: Available at health food stores and some farmer's markets, whole wheat berries are often kneaded into bread dough to add extra protein, fiber, and a sπtrong wheaty flavor to the finished loaf as well as real chewiness to the crumb. Wheat berries are usually cooked (see page 30 for Cooking Whole Grains chart) before being added to bread dough. Sometimes soaking them in water overnight will soften the berries enough so that they can be added to the dough. Test by biting into one before adding it to the bread dough, just to make sure. It should crack open easily on the tooth. Diana cooks the berries and serves them as a nutritious breakfast cereal, saving the leftovers for bread.

SPROUTED WHEAT OR RYE BERRIES: These give breads a nutritional boost along with added flavor and crunch. To sprout berries, simply rinse them with water and drain. Place no more than a half cup of berries in a clean mason jar. Turn the jar on its side and shake it so that the berries are in a single layer. Cover the end of the jar with cheesecloth and set it aside in bright light for a day or two. In several days you will have green sprouts to add to breads, sandwiches, or salads. These are especially nice to have on hand in the dead of winter.

CRACKED WHEAT BERRIES: Cracked wheat berries are the whole berry coarsely cracked. Sprinkled into the dough or onto the crust, they give bread a rustic look and add an extra wheaty-nut flavor. Cracked wheat berries are usually small enough that they don't need to be cooked or soaked before being added to bread dough.

BULGUR: When wheat berries have had their bran removed, and are then steamed, cracked, and dried, the result is called "bulgur." Bulgur must be cooked before being added to bread doughs, but since it has already been steamed, it cooks very quickly (see page 30 for Cooking Whole Grains chart). Bulgur can also be cooked and served as a nutritious breakfast cereal.

We find bulgur ground two ways. The fine grind is primarily used in tabouli and other Middle Eastern salads; the medium grind is for baking and breakfast cereals.

WHEAT GERM: The germ of the wheat berry is the sprouting segment and contains the fat. It is removed from all flours except those that are stone-ground. Wheat germ can be purchased either powdered or whole, then added to most bread doughs. Flours that contain the wheat germ have a shelf life of only three to six months. Storing them in the refrigerator or freezer can prolong that life for an additional three months.

CORNMEAL: Use either white or yellow, but choose stone-ground meal that contains the flavorful and nutritious corn germ. As with any meal or flour containing germ, it needs to be stored in the refrigerator so that the natural oil does not go rancid. Stone-ground cornmeal is used not only in baked goods but also to dust baking stones, parchment paper, or baking sheets.

Degerminated cornmeal is the commercial version found in the supermarket. It contains a lot of starch but very few vitamins or minerals. It is this starch, however, that will dry out the bottom of a bread baked on a stone and keep it from sticking. Use the less-expensive, degerminated cornmeal on baking stones and parchment paper when raising and baking breads so they won't stick, but bake with the more costly stone-ground cornmeal for optimum nutritional quality.

POLENTA: Polenta is simply cornmeal that is cut coarser and larger than ordinary cornmeal. The germ has been removed and most polenta has been enriched with vitamins and minerals. Cornmeal and polenta can be used interchangeably in our recipes unless otherwise stated.

RICE: Today's rice varieties—and there are thousands—are descended from wild grasses. Loaded with vitamins B and E, rice not only adds nutritional value to bread, it also helps bread retain moisture. When brown rice (which still contains the bran and the germ) is added to multigrain breads, it lends its crunchy texture, fiber, nutty taste, and added moisture to the finished loaf.

Long-grain white rice is fluffy and light and contains less fiber and vitamins than brown rice. At our house, leftover rice usually finds its way into a loaf of Brother Juniper's Santa Rosa Struan (see page 112).

MILLET: Agro-scientists suggest that millet, the most ancient of grains, was one of the grasses dinosaurs and their friends were munching on millions of years ago. Millet is rich in iron, calcium, riboflavin, and the B vitamins. A cup of cooked millet is only a step below wheat on the protein ladder.

The tiny, round, yellow millet grains found in natural food stores and some farmer's markets should not be confused with the pet store birdseed variety. Millet for human consumption has been stripped of its outer bran layer. Birdseed has not.

BUCKWHEAT: Buckwheat is actually not a grain at all but the seed of a plant related to rhubarb. Buckwheat itself is not generally found on supermarket shelves, but kasha, which is roasted hulled buckwheat kernels, is the most readily available form of this Russian grain.

Commercially ground buckwheat flour comes in two types, light and dark. Both are 100 percent buckwheat, but the dark contains more fiber particles (hence its darker color) and has a more pungent flavor (similar to molasses).

If you cannot find buckwheat flour in the supermarket, you can grind kasha in a food processor or blender to make flour. One cup of kasha processed in the blender or food processor will become flour in about three minutes. Buckwheat is low in gluten and makes for a tender baked product. Small amounts of buckwheat flour combined with wheat flour make delicious bread. For adding buckwheat to any standard bread recipe, our rule of thumb is one part buckwheat flour to two or three parts organic bread flour.

Cooking Whole Grains
(Per 1 cup unsalted, uncooked grain)

GRAIN	WATER	COOKING TIME	YIELD
Bulgur	2 cups	15 minutes	2$\frac{1}{2}$ cups
Cornmeal	3$\frac{1}{2}$ cups	25 minutes	4 cups
Kasha (buckwheat)	2 cups	10 minutes	3$\frac{1}{2}$ cups
Millet	1$\frac{3}{4}$ cups	30 minutes	2$\frac{1}{2}$ cups
Rice (white)	2 cups	20 minutes	3 cups
Rice (brown)	2 cups	60 minutes	3 cups
Wheat berries	2$\frac{1}{4}$ cups	60 minutes	3 cups

To cook whole grains: Use a heavy-bottomed pan and bring the water to a full rolling boil. Stir in the grain and adjust the heat to a simmer. Cover tightly and cook for the appointed time without lifting the lid. The grain will be cooked when the surface is dotted with steam holes and all the moisture is absorbed. You can add $\frac{1}{2}$ teaspoon salt per cup of uncooked grain at the end of the cooking time.

Bread Machine Baking Tips for Breads Made with Whole Grains and Whole-Grain Flours

◆ Salt whole grains (and beans too) *after* cooking. Adding salt to the cooking water or liquid before cooking can make it difficult for some grains to absorb water.

◆ Rinsing whole grains to remove dust and foreign material is optional.

◆ Cook whole grains like pasta, *al dente,* which means slightly chewy.

◆ For a high-domed whole-grain bread in the bread machine, keep the ratio of specialty grains and flours, which usually have little or no gluten protein, small in proportion to organic bread flour or organic whole wheat bread flour. Our rule of thumb is about a half cup of whole grains or low-gluten whole-grain flour to two and a half cups of organic bread flour or organic whole wheat bread flour.

Storage of flours and whole grains

Flours absorb objectionable odors and love to make a home for fluttering kitchen insects, so it is most important that you buy fresh flours and store them properly.

Shop in a store that has a high turnover in bakery products. Flour purchased at a neighborhood convenience store is most likely to be old and strange tasting. If you can locate a grocer who stocks baker's supplies in bulk and seems to cater to home *boulangers,* by all means get your baking supplies there. Look for date codes on boxed flours.

Buying in bulk can save you money, but, savings are nil if you waste flours and grains because of improper storage. Once you have the flour home, repackage it in an airtight, opaque canister or bucket and label it. Store labeled flour in a cool cabinet, closet, or pantry. More than once, we've placed flour in a tin and were sure we'd never forget what it was, only to stare at it in bewilderment six months later.

We like canisters that are easy to lift and have a wide open mouth so that flour can be measured out easily. King Arthur Flours (see page 310) sells good lidded buckets to hold either ten or twenty-five pounds of flour.

Placing a couple of bay leaves in the flour discourages weevils. Apparently bugs hate bay leaves as much as vampires hate garlic. Placing flour that contains weevils or their eggs in the freezer for seventy-two hours will kill the bugs, which can then be picked or sifted out. You can tell if you have bugs if you notice that the flour shifts when moved slightly; it's resettling into spaces made by the bugs' movement. White spider web–looking hairs are another sign of buggy visitors.

Liquids

Bottled spring water is the first and foremost liquid we use. If you live in an area with good, sweet water, go ahead and use it in your bread. But, if your water is heavily chlorinated, or has too many minerals, use bottled spring water.

Beers and ales also make good breads. We especially like the taste of ale with rye and other dark, heavy flours. The added sugars and starch provided by the beer give the yeast a little something extra to feed on and will cause the breads to rise a little higher.

All liquids should be at room temperature when they are added to the other ingredients in the bread pan. If necessary, warm the cold liquids in the microwave at 100 percent power for fifteen to twenty seconds to remove the chill.

Salts

Salt adds flavor and brings out other flavors in bread. It also acts as a yeast retardant and thereby keeps the dough on a slow, steady rise so that the flavors have time to develop. A salt-free bread will be high-rising and light but also very bland tasting.

SEA SALT: Sea salt is made from evaporated seawater and tastes pure and natural, without the metallic taste you get from plain table salt. Sea salt may or may not contain magnesium carbonate, an anticaking agent. We tested our recipes with sea salt and recommend it. Sea salt tastes saltier and purer than any other salt we know of.

TABLE SALT: American mined table salt is FDA required to be washed free of its trace minerals and magnesium. Some companies go farther still and add magnesium carbonate as an anticaking agent so that it will pour freely. Untreated salt can absorb moisture from the air and will clump in humid climates. A few grains of rice added to the salt shaker will help keep salt pouring freely. If you are using this salt in the recipes recommending sea salt, you may need to add just a pinch more than the recipe calls for to compensate for table salt's slightly less salty flavor.

KOSHER SALT: Kosher salt crystals are larger than those of other salts and are frequently sprinkled on the top of flatbreads. Kosher salt is the least salty, and if you're using it in these recipes, you'll need to add more than we've called for. A good rule of thumb is that two teaspoons of kosher salt equals one teaspoon of sea salt or one and a half teaspoons of table salt.

Sugar

Sweeteners of any type—honey, table sugar, malt syrup or powder, brown sugar, or molasses—furnish food for the thriving yeast and add flavor to the dough. Sugar makes a tender bread and contributes to a good grain and texture as well as to a golden brown crust. Adding sugar to the dough makes the yeast more active than it would be if it were simply allowed to feed on the starches and natural sugars found in flour. Enriched breads, those containing fruit and nuts, or heavy whole-grain breads need more yeast action because of the weight of the added ingredients. Added sugar helps these breads by speeding up the fermentation of the yeast.

Do not use confectioners' sugar in bread-baking. The small amount of cornstarch it contains to prevent caking gives bread a peculiar taste.

Eggs

Most rustic breads do not contain eggs, but the tenderness of brioche comes from egg. Eggs contribute flavor, color, nutritional value, and a richness that cannot be achieved by any other ingredient. In this book, all recipes call for grade-A large eggs unless otherwise indicated. A large egg measures about a quarter cup in volume. If you'd like to add eggs to improve the nutritional content of your bread, remember to displace the same volume of other liquid in the recipe.

If you are concerned about cholesterol, you can substitute a like volume of egg white, that is, one quarter cup of egg white to substitute for every egg called for in the recipe. The resulting bread will not have the golden hue or the rich taste that egg yolks contribute, but it will be cholesterol-free.

One simple way to bring an egg to room temperature quickly is to cover unopened eggs with hot tap water and allow them to stand in a bowl for a few moments before cracking them into the other ingredients. In most recipes, however—unless several eggs are called for—it's okay to add one refrigerated egg to the dry ingredients.

If you wish to halve an egg in a recipe you're reducing by half, break it into a cup, whisk for a moment, then measure off half: about 2 tablespoons. Save the other half to glaze the loaf.

Leftover egg whites will keep in a covered jar in the refrigerator for up to five days. For longer storage, you may freeze them in an airtight container for up to three months. Egg yolks require more careful storage, or they'll develop a hide as tough as boot leather. Place them in a small container, cover with a little water, then cover tightly. They'll keep for three or four days in the refrigerator, but yolks don't freeze well. Drain the water off of the egg yolks before using in your favorite recipe.

To separate eggs, work with cold eggs to prevent the yolk from breaking. Using a knife or the edge of a bowl, crack the egg, then either pass the yolk from shell to shell, letting the white fall into a waiting bowl, or—more foolproof but gooshy—drop the egg into the palm of your hand and allow the white to drip through your fingers.

Fats

Even though fat has become a dicey notion in the nineties, a small measure of fat in bread makes a big difference in taste and texture. Fats in all food carry flavor, and that certainly holds true for bread. You'll notice that most rustic European breads contain very little fat and derive most of their flavor from the long, cool rise and/or the use of starters (see page 47).

Fats make breads softer, giving them a delicate crumb and a lovely golden crust. They also help breads to keep. Any recipe that is laden with fat is likely to produce bread that stays moist and mold-free for up to a week, if properly stored. Think about French bread *(pain ordinaire)*. Totally fat-free, it's only good the day it's made.

Always taste fats before adding them to make sure they're not rancid. Nothing can ruin a loaf of bread quicker than old oil.

BUTTER: For French brioche, butter is a must. We prefer unsalted butter because it makes a fresher, sweeter product and also because it gives you more control over the total amount of salt in the recipe. We've specified unsalted butter in all the recipes. If you're using salted butter, you might want to back off just a bit on the salt called for in the recipe.

LARD: Loathsome old lard makes some of the best country breads there are. If you can buy good, fresh lard, by all means try it in a hearty whole-grain bread. The taste and crumb will be marvelous. We buy inexpensive lard that comes from a Latin American market where the turnover is high.

VEGETABLE SHORTENING: Solid vegetable shortening can be used in any recipe (except for brioche or croissants) measure for measure, as a substitute for butter or lard. You'll lose that buttery taste and yellow cast to the crumb, but will achieve the same tenderness.

OLIVE OIL: We've saved the best for last. We admit it, we're crazy about olive oil and believe that choosing an olive oil is a matter of taste, not necessarily of price. A higher price tag does not always mean a better oil.

For our breads, we like to use a heavier-bodied and full-flavored extra-virgin oil from the first cold pressing of the olive. Cold pressing, that is, processing without heat extraction, makes a better-quality oil. However, most extra-virgin olive oils are not cold pressed because the process is labor-intensive and, thus, expensive. If an olive oil that you're considering is cold pressed, it will be so-labeled since that is a compelling selling point. Many people believe that extra-virgin olive oil, the highest grade, is always made by cold pressing the olives, but this may not always be the case. It is the amount of oleic acid in the oil that determines an oil's grade and it's labeling. To be labeled extra-virgin, an oil must contain less than 1 percent oleic acid, but it does not have to be cold pressed.

Olive oils are like wine. They have different flavors according to the type of olives used, the degree of ripeness of the olives when picked, and the region of origin. However, where wine gets better as it ages, olive oil does not. Some extra-virgin olives come vintage dated; most do not. We try not to buy more than two liters at a time, which we hope to use within three months. Store olive oil in a cool, dark place since heat and light destroy the oil's flavor. For long storage, say up to a month or more, store the oil in the refrigerator. It will turn cloudy and solidify, but will quickly liquefy and clarify when returned to room temperature.

NUT OILS: Walnut, hazelnut, and almond oils tend to be quite expensive. But they are wonderful in bread when teamed with their nuts of origin. All nut oils have been roasted to preserve their characteristic flavor, but this heat hastens their demise and therefore shortens their shelf life. Purchase them from a reputable merchant and buy in small quantities.

OLIVES

Brown, black, green, or purple, large or small, olives play an important part in rustic European breads. The salty tang and richness of the olives and their oil add punch whether they're chopped and slathered on crostini or folded into baguettes or hard rolls.

Olives are imported from Greece, Spain, Italy, and France. Two of our favorites are the Kalamata olives from Greece, which, by the way, are now available pitted in a four-ounce jar, and the larger green Sicilian imports. The only olive we shun is the canned, ripe, black olive, whose taste disappears in bread.

Olives that need to be pitted can be cracked open easily with the flat side of the blade of a large chef's knife. Set the knife over the olives and hit the blade of the knife sharply with the heel of your hand. The olives should now be cracked and the pits can be removed. Olives that are covered with brine will keep almost indefinitely in the refrigerator.

Tomatoes

FRESH TOMATOES: A perfect, vine-ripened tomato is the tomato by which all others are measured. However, these are available only three months out of the year. The other nine months we must learn to substitute what's available at the supermarket. When only a fresh tomato will do for topping a pizza or focaccia, we fall back on fresh Italian plum tomatoes, which are available year-round. Leave them out on the counter or on the window sill for several days, if possible. Maybe it's psychological, but this seems to season them and maybe, just maybe, they will lose a little of that pink tomato soup color and turn flame red instead. Plum tomatoes almost always have a nice meaty texture without a lot of juice. This makes them perfect for topping flatbreads.

CANNED TOMATOES: We are blessed in America to have so many different brands and varieties of canned tomatoes. In the dead of winter, our favorite for sauces and salsas is still the plum tomato. Our second choice is the canned salad tomato. We don't buy expensive imports because we see very little difference in sweetness between the imports and the natives.

SUN-DRIED TOMATOES: Sun-dried tomatoes are vine ripened, then dried on large screens out of direct sunlight. They are then either packaged as is (looking like bright red leather wagon wheels) or they are packed in olive oil, sometimes with herbs. We like the tomato-herb combination for topping breads and in tortas.

The dried red wagon wheels are cheaper but must be steeped in boiling water for a minute or so to soften before use. For those of you watching your fat grams, these may be preferable since they contain no fat. They seem a little bland after steeping, so we add additional salt and a touch of olive oil. Sun-dried tomatoes are available minced, whole, or in halves. We stir the minced into vinaigrettes and tortas and spot breads and pizzas with the others.

Candied citron

Available in the United States mainly at Christmastime, candied citron is made from the citron fruit grown in the Mediterranean, which is as big as a plum and has a bumpy, thick rind. It is most often used in fruitcakes and sweet breads such as panettone. Candied citron often goes on sale after Christmas and will keep indefinitely in the freezer.

Nuts

Nuts—walnuts, pine nuts, hazelnuts, to name just a few—add flavor, natural oils, and crunch to many rustic European breads.

Most nuts taste best in bread if they have been lightly toasted. This is very easy to do in the microwave: Place the nuts in a single layer on a microwave-safe plate, cook on High and watch, stirring every minute or so until browned to taste. Remember to toast on the light side in the microwave because the nuts will continue to cook for another minute or so after being removed from the oven.

ENGLISH WALNUTS: The English walnut originated in Persia (its correct name is the Persian nut) and found its way to England less than 375 years ago. The nutmeat is cream colored and has a biting, pungent tang. It adds flavor and, when left in large chunks, a bit of beauty to the interior of breads. It can also be ground fine and used as a flavorful and nutritious substitute for part of the flour in wheat breads and other baked goods. A good rule of thumb is one part nut flour to five parts bread flour.

HAZELNUTS: In our recipes, we speak of hazelnuts and filberts interchangeably, as they are, to all intents and purposes, the same nut.

As with every rose there is a thorn, so it goes for the hazelnut, which is prized for its flavor but cursed for its skin. The hazelnut skin is bitter and must be removed before the nut can be used in most recipes. Lucky for us, this is easily done by toasting the nuts in the oven or microwave and then rubbing the hot nuts in a towel to remove the skin, or by blanching them in boiling water for ten to fifteen minutes and rubbing the cooled nuts in a towel.

Hazelnuts start to lose their flavor and go stale before going rancid, so they should be used soon after purchasing. Freezing is a good way to store them for periods of up to two years.

PINE NUTS: Pine nuts are the seeds extracted from pinecones of a certain variety of pine tree. Most of these nuts are imported from Italy and tend to be expensive. As pine nuts can turn rancid quickly, store them in the freezer. Pine nuts are a key ingredient in pesto and can be tossed in a salad of Italian greens and prosciutto. Sprinkled on focaccia with melted onions, they have no rival.

CHEESE

MOZZARELLA: Mozzarella is best known as a pizza cheese, and the marriage of mozzarella and tomatoes on a crisp crust is indeed a blessed union. We don't think very highly of the vacuum-sealed, plastic-wrapped rounded bricks of mozzarella you'll find in your supermarket's dairy case. We much prefer fresh mozzarella, which is moist, creamy white, and shaped into dimpled, palm-sized rounds. It has a delicate, fresh dairy aroma and flavor. Fresh mozzarella is more expensive than the commercial variety, but it's well worth the price. It is usually sold in bulk or in a small eight-ounce tub. Whey is ladled into the tub to keep the cheese moist. Some companies ladle in a saline solution, which salts the cheese and ruins the taste. Ask your retailer to be sure you are getting the kind packed in whey and not salt. Fresh mozzarella has a shelf life of only seven days, so check the freshness pull date and plan on using it within a day or two of purchase.

PARMIGIANO-REGGIANO (PARMESAN): Parmigiano-Reggiano is not the cheese in the shaker can. Authentic Parmigiano-Reggiano is a partially skimmed cow's milk cheese that is made only in a specially designated area of Italy. Each large wheel of cheese must have, by law, the words "Parmigiano-Reggiano" imprinted into the rind along with the date it was made.

Parmigiano-Reggiano has a dry granule and a brittle crumb. The flavor is robust and sharp. To ensure the freshest flavor, it should be bought in a wedge and grated by hand just before using. It can also be shaved into curls with a swivel-bladed vegetable peeler. Don't try to grate anything but very small pieces in the food processor; large pieces can burn out the motor and dull the blade.

Try topping an olive oil–brushed focaccia with Parmigiano-Reggiano and a sprinkling of fresh herbs, or shave the cheese and toss it into your favorite salad of bitter greens.

PECORINO ROMANO: Pecorino Romano is made from sheep's milk and is a second cousin to Parmigiano-Reggiano. Both taste robust, tangy, and sharp, but Pecorino Romano also tastes salty. It is an excellent cheese to shave or sprinkle over breads, especially breads topped with tomatoes and garlic. Bread-crumb stuffings also get a lift when a little Pecorino Romano and a few minced, fresh herbs, are added.

PROSCIUTTO

Prosciutto is a very fine, dry-cured Italian ham that can be found in the deli departments of most large groceries or in specialty food stores. Prosciutto is very versatile and adds texture, color, and flavor to salads, flatbreads, and rolls. Thinly sliced prosciutto will do what we call "frizzle" when it comes in contact with high heat from the broiler or in the oven. Sprinkle frizzled prosciutto on top of a fresh slab of focaccia topped with fresh mozzarella and a slice of plum tomato for an Italian version of a B.L.T.

HERBS

Fresh herbs always enliven a bread with flavor and aroma. We grow our own and suggest that you do the same. If this is not possible, many large supermarkets now sell bundles of fresh herbs in the produce section. Make sure they look fresh and have no black spots. Pinch off a leaf and taste to be sure the herbs you buy are worth their price tag.

BASIL: Fresh basil is one of our favorite herbs for pizza and flatbread toppings. It is easy to grow, and in the spring it can be found at the local nursery in a six-pack of small plants. It can also be grown from seed. The six-pack will give you six nice bushy plants, each growing to be about two feet tall. Linda's daughter, Katherine, has kept one plant growing in a pot in New York City for three years simply by watering it a little each day and always pinching off the cluster of leaves that forms at the top right before flowering. If the plant can't make flowers, it will not reach the end of its life cycle. Basil is sensitive to cold and will die with the first frost. Plan on bringing it inside before that time as you won't get a second chance. Freezing will turn the delicate leaves black. We take one day in September and simply do nothing but make pesto for the freezer. The oil in the pesto keeps the basil bright green. Don't buy dried basil; just substitute another fresh herb.

OREGANO: Oregano is a hardy herb and grows easily in an indoor pot or in the ground. We like the dwarf or creeper varieties, which, if planted in a protected spot, will grow and stay green in mild climates even in the winter. Use oregano in tomato sauces and to dust the tops of flatbreads and pizzas. Dried oregano is a fine substitute for fresh. One half teaspoon dried is equal to two teaspoons fresh.

ITALIAN FLAT-LEAF PARSLEY: Diana grows Italian flat-leaf parsley year-round in her outdoor herb garden here in Oregon. Planted close to her heat pump, it is kept from freezing by the circulating air from the pump. Don't knock yourself out, though; flat-leaf parsley is one fresh herb your supermarket will almost certainly carry. Curly parsley can be substituted for flat-leaf, but never use dried parsley.

ROSEMARY: Fresh rosemary is preferable to dried in our recipes, but if you must use the dried, remember that one half teaspoon is equal to two teaspoons fresh. When adding fresh or dried rosemary to breads, be sure you crush the needles to release their flavor and fragrance. If you are baking for children or the elderly, be sure to mince the rosemary, as the needles can be sharp and uncomfortable in the mouth.

3

Yeasts and

homemade starters

Yeasts

No one knows whether yeasts were first discovered by bakers or brewers. Yeast spores, in the presence of grains, at specific temperatures and over time, cause fermentation that sets in motion a chain of events yielding both a fine loaf of bread and a great bottle of beer.

Either way, it's a cinch that one day grains that had been set aside—whether in the form of meal for porridge, or ground to make an ancient "mead" or beer—began to bubble and ferment, because of the natural yeast spores that cling to grains—spores being microorganisms in a dormant state. No doubt early cooks noticed that fermented batches of porridge and drink took on a different texture and an altered flavor. They liked it. Yeast baking and brewing had begun. If we were asked to bet, we'd say the two arts probably developed simultaneously over time. After all, man cannot live by beer alone.

There are about 160 species of yeasts. Single celled fungi, they not only raise bread and brew beer, some species also spoil fruit or cause infections. But the yeasts that raise bread, *Saccharomyces cerevisiae*, so named because they consume sugar, are well designed to do their job. They merely metabolize starch and sugar, producing carbon dioxide and alcohol, which raises the dough and then evaporates during the baking process. What these particular strains of yeast *don't* do is release other noxious odors or flavors.

The yeast action takes place within a certain scientific framework. First of all, the yeast spores must be alive. (That's why yeast packages are pull-dated. Old yeast dies.) Second, the temperature of the mixture must be within a certain range. Too cold and the yeast will not activate; too hot, and you will kill the yeast. The ideal range is between 70° F. and 98° F. From the scientific standpoint, yeast action is optimum at 95° F.

But this is not to say that science and the baker's art are in complete agreement. The ultimate flavor of the bread is affected by the temperature at which the yeast action (fermentation) takes place. The cooler the dough, the slower the fermentation, the more complex flavor development is achieved. (See page 44 for further discussion of fermentation.)

Commercial Yeast

You can buy yeast in several forms. The most recently developed, and to our mind the most successful yeast to use in a bread machine is called, plainly, "bread machine yeast." Fleischmann's makes it, and it's a new strain designed to work best in lean doughs and in bread machines. Made to be added with the flour, without proofing, this yeast is ideal.

What, you say, is a lean dough? That's one with little or no added fat, sugar, milk, or eggs. Since that pretty well describes rustic European breads, we feel this yeast was made for us.

Right behind that, and sharing certain key features, is 50 percent faster active dry yeast. This yeast was designed to speed up the mixing and rising properties of the bread and is a strain that can also be mixed right in with the dry ingredients instead of being "proofed." Actually, the time saved has more to do with the fact that it isn't necessary to "proof" this type of yeast than with the time it takes to rise. Some bread bakers fear losing flavor and control by using 50 percent faster yeast, but it is our experience that even a slow fermentation can be successfully begun by using this yeast in combination with a homemade starter. It is also recommended for use by many bread machine manufacturers.

Active dry granular yeast was developed during World War II to help the army keep its soldiers in bread. It will work in any of these recipes, but it must first be dissolved in warm water in the presence of a little flour and/or sugar. That's what's known as "proofing," and you'll see the yeast begin to bubble up within four or five minutes provided it is *proved* to be, indeed, active and alive. Then you mix the lively, bubbly, flour-yeast slurry into the dough. If you use this kind of yeast in our recipes, remember to subtract the amount of water you used to proof the yeast from the total you add later on.

Cake yeast preceded the dry yeasts and is sold in the refrigerator case of some grocery stores. One square of cake yeast may be used interchangeably with a two-and-a-half-teaspoon packet of bread machine dry, active dry, or 50 percent faster active dry yeast. Cake yeast must be dissolved in warm water with a little flour and sugar, "proofed" as it were, and will also work in any of these recipes.

Every strain of commercial yeast, every brand of yeast, has a slightly different flavor. Make a lot of bread using different brands and types of yeast and you'll eventually choose your favorite. With subtle variations, yeasts can be interchanged, measure for measure, in any bread recipe. Remember that two and a half teaspoons of dry yeast equals one square of cake yeast.

As each strain converts carbohydrates in the grain to alcohol and CO_2, it yields a distinct taste. If you use a large *volume* of any type of yeast, you'll get a really beery, yeasty flavored bread. If you use a smaller amount and allow the natural fermentation to take place, causing the bread to rise more slowly, you'll get a different, and some say better, taste, because the content of the gases released will be slightly altered. In the presence of less yeast, the fermentation process is more complete, fewer residual yeast by-products remain in the dough, and the complex flavors we love the best come through.

Europeans originally had to give their dough a long rising period because of their particular kind of "weak" (low-gluten) flour. In the United States, we have higher protein, high-gluten flours to begin with, the envy of many European bakers, but we have had to make allowances in these recipes to achieve authentic European results.

We also stress that yeast will work best in the presence of pure water without a lot of minerals and salts to retard its action and chemically alter its taste. Unless you have pure water from the tap, without chlorine added or a lot of natural minerals, we urge you to use bottled spring water in these recipes. It will give you superior bread, because it will help your yeast to work at its most efficient best.

Two other critical points we must restate about yeast: Salt retards the action of yeast. If you take the salt out of any one of these recipes, you may see the bread blow up inordinately. That's because the yeast went crazy without the salt to govern it.

Breads with a lot of sugar require more yeast, because the little yeasty beasties just go crazy and get drunk on the sugary dough. So when you notice us calling for more yeast in sweet breads, it's to feed those voracious little beasties who do love their sugar so.

It's easy to remember the yeast action equation. Yeast in a dry, inert state, is brought back to life by being mixed with warm spring water (about 95° F.), flour, perhaps some sugar or malt powder, and usually a little salt to make a dough. The yeast begins to eat and grow, giving off CO_2 and alcohol, and will continue to eat until all the nutriments are gone. The kneading action not only creates a web to hold the CO_2 gas, but moves the molecules around so that those hungry little yeasties can find more food to eat.

When using commercial yeast, keep these points in mind.

◆ Buy yeast and use it within its pull-dated time. It's a living fungus and dies when it's old.

◆ Store yeast in the refrigerator or freezer to preserve it.

◆ Buy only as much as you expect to use within a three-month period.

◆ Start yeast with *warm* liquids (about 95° F.) to activate the spores. Cold liquids retard yeast activity; excessive heat kills yeast.

◆ When layering ingredients in the bread machine pan, separate the yeast from the liquids by adding the yeast first, covering it with flour, then adding salt, fats, and liquids.

◆ To save money, buy yeast in bulk, either in brown jars, or in foil packs from stores that keep yeasts under refrigeration so that you can be assured it is lively.

◆ Occasional bakers should buy pull-dated yeast in three-strip foil packs. Each packet contains two and a half teaspoons of yeast.

How can you tell if the yeast you're planning to use is active? Bakers call this "proofing" the yeast and it works with any of the three basic types of yeast: active dry, 50 percent faster active dry, or cake. Using a two-cup glass measure, dissolve a teaspoon of sugar in a half cup of warm water (110°–115° F.). Sprinkle a packet of yeast (two and a half teaspoons) slowly over the top and stir. Set a timer for ten minutes. Within three or four minutes, the yeast will have absorbed enough liquid to activate and should start rising to the surface. At the end of ten minutes, the yeast should look bubbly and will have multiplied to the one-cup mark. It will have developed a rounded crown. That is active yeast. If the yeast is dead, it will have few or no bubbles and will not have increased in volume. Remember to reduce the liquid in the recipe by the half cup of water you used to proof the yeast.

CHEMICAL LEAVENING: BAKING POWDER AND SODA

Not to be confused with yeast breads, quick breads rise because of a chemical action caused by baking powder and/or soda. While yeast creates carbon dioxide gas that blows up yeast dough in much the same way you blow a balloon after chewing bubble gum, quick breads create carbon dioxide gas when a basic compound, such as baking soda, comes in contact with an acid, such as buttermilk or yogurt, and makes a mini-bomb in the batter that holds long enough for the oven heat to "set" the reaction and keep the cake or quick bread up. Baking powder is made by mixing both acid and basic compounds into a single inert powder that is activated in the presence of water or other liquids.

So-called double-acting baking powder offers two sets of chemical reactions: the first when the batter is mixed and the second when it's placed in the hot oven. In this way the quick bread or cake is doubly assured of finding its way to your table high, light, and desirable.

This book contains no recipes for quick breads calling for baking powder or baking soda.

Homemade starters

Bakers made yeast bread for aeons before commercial yeasts were available for sale. They were able to make their own homemade natural starters because yeast is ubiquitous in organic materials. Yeast spores are found in flour; in dairy products; on plant matter including grapes, apples, or peach leaves; in dried cumin powder, and in many other sources that bakers have discovered in their efforts to make starters at home.

Why bother making an old-fashioned starter when yeast is for sale at the store! Bread made from a homemade starter tastes different from that made with commercial yeast. The texture is chewier. The crust may be crunchier. The keeping qualities are greatly enhanced.

This explains the basic difference between *pain ordinaire* and *pain au levain*. The French know that *pain ordinaire*, plain French bread, a simple mixture of flour, water, salt, and commercial yeast, is good for only a day. *Pain au levain*, made from a homemade starter plus flour, water, and salt, is more substantial, will keep longer, and will have a more complicated, interesting taste.

We knew we wanted to make breads with starters after Diana returned from her Paris trip with a rumpled sack full of breads she'd bought in Parisian boulangeries. These breads were three or four days old. Although a bit dried out, the breads weren't stale. The flavor was delicious. This, we said to each other, is what we're after right here in our own kitchens.

How Starters Were Developed

Bakers, using trial and error, have experimented with various organic compounds to activate starters. Beginning with a mixture of flour and water, they've added organic grapes, apples, or peach leaves; cumin powder; yogurt; milk; or any number of other organic materials to begin the growth process that brings the mixture to life. Once the mixture bubbles vigorously, the grapes, or peach leaves, say, are fished out and discarded while their yeast spores stay behind to leaven the dough.

And, as we have learned from discussion of commercially prepared yeasts, yeast spores are activated in the presence of warm liquids, with flour and perhaps a little sugar to eat. This means it is possible to make your own homemade starter with nothing more than flour and water. The flour itself provides not only the nutriment for the yeast, but the yeast spores themselves, which are clinging to the organic flour.

Strictly speaking, the starter you make at home won't be plain old *Saccharomyces cerevisiae*, the strain of yeast found in commercial packages; it will contain airborne molds as well. Without getting too deep into the biochemistry of bread, just know that molds float through the air, yeasts do not. Yeasts cling to organic matter. When you begin creating your own starters, you'll be getting a mixture of these two particular types of living matter, yeast and mold, which will bubble up into a starter that may be—dare we say it— better than anything you can buy.

Make a simple starter with flour and water, adding a pinch of commercial yeast for insurance that it will start, and soon you'll have a bubbling mixture that will make a tasty bread. Feed this starter over a period of days or weeks, stirring it, covering it, and letting it stand, and soon airborne molds from your own kitchen will attach themselves to the starter and its character will begin to change.

You get a secondary fermentation from these airborne molds that will produce lactic acid, which gives a more or less sour taste to bread.

What Makes San Francisco Sourdough Unique?

Airborne molds explain why a bread made in San Francisco will taste different from one made in Provence, even if you follow the same recipe exactly. The air you breathe and that the starter takes its molds from, differs from locale to locale. Different airborne molds float through San Francisco's air than through the air of Provence. Not to mention your home town, which will have its own unique load of airborne molds. This is what makes breads taste different from place to place and we say *vive la différence.*

Making Your Own Homemade Starters

Let's put the science lesson behind us now and begin making our own homemade starters. After all, bakers famous and infamous have been making starters with no more real idea of how the process worked than most of us understand about how a television signal works.

First of all, make starters using organic bread flour and spring water. The additives in chemically treated flour or water inhibit the yeast and mold growth. Makes sense, doesn't it! They treat flour and water to prevent the growth of unwanted bacteria. That will also prevent the growth of the Lactobacillus we're after when making starters at home. Don't ponder this too long or you'll soon get into some "Meaning of Life" questions that are best not tackled by bakers. After all, you're a person of action. Don't think about the meaning of life, just make it.

One word of encouragement we'd like to add. Making starters gets easier with experience. If you're not happy with the results the first time, keep trying. This isn't all science. It's also art, and luck and love. We love the challenge. We think you'll love it too.

Our big discovery is that the bread machine is an ideal incubator for homemade starters. Simply run flour and water, with perhaps a pinch of commercial yeast to kickstart the process, through the dough cycle of your bread machine, then let it sit there to capture airborne molds, and within two or three days, you'll have a starter all your own with which to make fine breads. If you want to use the bread machine for making bread during this time, you may, of course, transfer the starter to a glass jar, cover it, and place it in a warm, draft-free place in your kitchen.

Making starters is always an adventure since no two of them will ever be exactly alike. Some will be mild and docile. Others will be sour and spunky. Each starter is as individual as a child.

Learning How to Read Starters

Perhaps the most important thing for you to learn when beginning to make breads with starters is how to read the starter. What you're embarking on is not a purely mechanical process. You can't just set a clock, go away, come back, and expect the starter to be made. You must learn to judge the starter by the way it looks, the way it tastes, and the way it smells. Some starters are ready to use in twenty-four hours. Other times, the same starter recipe might take as long as four or five days to be ready for use. You can learn to read the signs. It's not so different from directions in a bread recipe that say, "raise until doubled in bulk." You may know from experience that a yeast bread might achieve this rising in as little as twenty minutes, but other times it might take more than an hour.

The same is true for starters and starter-made breads, only more so because you're dealing with a yeast and mold growth that's less controlled, wilder—if you will—and therefore as unpredictable as romance and just as exciting.

When a starter is active, it will have inflated some from the original volume you mixed up. It will be a pleasant tan color, have a liquid appearance in the middle, like hot chewing gum, and, when it's young, a sweet, wheaty smell that becomes increasingly sour as it's allowed to stand and mature. As a starter gets older, it may fall and not have the high volume of a young starter. That's okay. This older, tangier starter will still work well in breads and will produce a loaf that's more like our American sourdoughs.

Sourdough starter will have gaseous bubbles in it. Stir it vigorously and the aroma from the released gases will waft up your nose and make your mouth water because it smells so wheaty and nice.

If you're using a recipe that suggests the starter may be ready to use in five days, re-member that this is only an estimate. Based on the molds in the air where you live, and the kind of wild yeasts available in the flour and, perhaps, in other organic materials you may have added—say peach leaves or organic grapes—the starter might be lively and quick and ready to use in two days. It might also be languid and sluggish and take upwards of ten days.

You must let the rhythms of the starter lead you. Observe it daily. Note how much it has risen in the container. Note the activity of the starter by the number of bubbles you see on the surface and in the middle. See if the texture changes from day to day. It should become more and more sticky and liquid as time passes. The aroma should become more and more sour.

It's normal for a thick crust to develop on the surface of the starter. Stir it back in. The starter will rehydrate. Not to worry.

And best of all, remember, this is not a matter of life or death. If you don't succeed in making starter the first time or the first three times, don't despair. You'll get it. Keep trying.

Following this discussion are recipes for a group of starters we've developed particularly for use with the bread machine. Use them interchangeably in our recipes and you'll begin to see the infinite permutations of bread-making. In the recipe section of the book, you'll see recipes that call for these starters. Use the ones listed here, then jump off and make some of your own.

Storing Starters and Keeping Them Alive

We don't believe that making and keeping a starter is like getting married—it's not a lifetime commitment. Make and use a starter for a few weeks, feeding the starter as you use it to replenish and replace what you use in a recipe. Then, when you get bored with taking care of it, throw all the starter into today's bread, or give it away.

Starters, like commercial yeast, become most active at a temperature of 95° F. Excessive heat kills them while less heat will cause them to become inactive. The refrigerator or freezer is used to store starters until you want to use them.

Mix up a starter using one of the recipes listed below and keep the mixture at room temperature for several days so that the yeast activity will be most lively. But once the starter is well made and "ripe," as defined by the recipe, transfer it to the refrigerator until you're ready to use it.

Place a ripe starter in a large Ziploc bag or a big glass jar at least three or four times larger than the volume of the starter. Mark the container with the contents and the date. Cover and refrigerate. Use it within three or four days, or you'll need to feed the starter. The French call this "refreshment," and it means exactly what you'd think. To feed or refresh the starter means simply to provide new nutriment for the yeasts and molds in the form of additional flour and water.

The Care and Feeding of a Starter

Whenever you remove a starter from the refrigerator, first sniff it. The aroma should be sweet and sour, but never rotten (like spoiled meat). If you get this "off" smell, throw it out. Another way to tell if your starter's gone off is to see if it's accumulated any pink-tinged liquid on top. That indicates unwanted bacterial action and means—throw it away.

Measure off one cup of starter to use in today's recipe, to give to a friend, or to discard. To feed the starter, first stir it vigorously to rearrange the flour molecules, molds, and yeast spores, to add oxygen, and to give off some carbon dioxide. Now add a half cup *each* of organic bread flour and spring water and again stir vigorously to mix thoroughly. Recover the starter and leave it in the warm kitchen overnight, or until the starter shows bubbles on the surface. Then, refrigerate until needed.

You should feed or use some starter weekly. Although some experts swear that starters never die, they just become dormant and can be revived six or eight months after being left in the back of the refrigerator, we do not recommend this. Not because the starter might not be alive, but because it can also pick up off-tastes and unwanted microflora in the refrigerator.

Our practice is to make, feed, and use a starter for a matter of weeks or months, then discard it. After all, we're sport bakers. We do this mainly for fun. When summer comes, we've got other priorities besides the care and feeding of starters.

Using Homemade Starters in Your Bread

Before using starter in a recipe, bring it to room temperature. We usually just set the container on the kitchen counter. But when we're in a hurry, we sometimes place the starter in the microwave set at 10 percent power and heat it for about twenty seconds just to raise the temperature to about 70° F. If you warm it in the microwave, you'll notice the starter getting visibly more active and beginning to grow right before your very eyes. Break the starter into small pieces and add it to the bread machine pan on top of the flour mixture.

We would encourage you to use starter in a recipe *even if the recipe doesn't call for it.* If you're using the dough setting on the bread machine, you can add a cup of starter to any recipe without changing another thing in the recipe. Add the starter. Let the machine begin to work, open the lid, and make any necessary fine adjustments to the flour-water ratio by adding one or the other, a tablespoon at a time, so that you get a soft, satiny dough, then let the dough setting continue. Pull the dough out, save a cup for your next day's baking, shape the rest to suit yourself (see page 75 for shaping suggestions), raise it again, and bake. See! You've just invented a new bread and started a batch of "old dough" in the process. You're on your way to becoming a master baker.

LEARNING EUROPEAN BAKER'S TERMS

When you study European baker's techniques you'll begin to see various foreign terms used to describe the process of making homemade starters. Here's a brief rundown of terms you're likely to run into.

SPONGE: In this method, a small portion of the total dough is made early and allowed to ferment for two to ten hours. This enhances the flavor and strength of the dough without being as much trouble or as time-consuming as making a full-fledged starter that may take days to ripen. You can turn any bread machine recipe into a sponge method recipe by following this technique. Sponges can be made easily in the bread machine itself. Simply mix half the flour with all the water and yeast and run the machine on the dough setting. Let the starter sit for the required time called for in the recipe. Then add the remaining flour, salt, and any other ingredients called for. Run the machine again on the dough setting and you will have a well-developed, flavorful dough with which to make bread.

POOLISH: A French term for "sponge." Similar to the sponge described above, it's made separately, using a recipe, then added to a variety of bread doughs. One easy way to do this is to use the bread machine's dough setting and make the *poolish* right in the machine (see page 00). The dough setting will see to it that the gluten develops the long strands that are ideal for your own homemade starter.

BIGA: The Italian version of a homemade starter. Italian bakers start it with flour, water, and a shot of yeast. Some let it work for twenty-four hours before beginning to bake. Others, who prefer a more sour flavor, leave it for up to seventy-two hours. This is something that you, the mad scientist in your own bakery, should decide for yourself after some experimentation. How sour the flavor will be depends upon the particular microflora in the air, as well as the length of time you allow the *biga* to work.

CHEF: This is the French term for the original flour-water mixture the baker uses to begin his starter. The original fermentation takes from two to ten days and is as individual as the baker and his (or her) room. This fermentation brings about a lactic acid action, and the airborne Lactobacillus causes the bread to have a more or less characteristic "sour" flavor. While an American sourdough starter may be the texture of pancake batter, a *chef* makes a stiff dough.

LEVAIN: The French word for leavening. After a starter or *chef* is begun, it's mixed with additional flour and water to make the *levain*, or leavener for the bread. The *levain* is usually ready to use within eight hours or so, although it can be held overnight or used as soon as two hours after mixing the *chef* with additional flour and water.

OLD DOUGH: Just what it says. Make bread in the bread machine using any recipe—it may or may not begin with a *biga, chef,* or *levain*—but before you shape the bread for the final baking, pull off about one cup of the dough and save it for the next day's baking. That's the "old dough" that will enhance and improve the taste and texture of the next bread. Store the old dough, covered, in the refrigerator or right in the bread machine pan. It's up to you and will depend on how often you bake. If you don't bake every second or third day, you're better off refrigerating it. Always let old dough warm to room temperature before adding it to today's bread as directed in the specific recipe.

RECIPES FOR VARIOUS STARTERS

THE BASIC *CHEF*

French bakers call the foundation of the starter by the term *chef.* It's the beginning of life in the French bakery. It's easy to make in your own kitchen and it differs from American-style sourdough in that the mixture makes a stiff dough, not a thin batter.

½ cup organic bread flour
⅛ teaspoon bread machine yeast
¼ cup room temperature spring water

Make a mound of the flour on a board. Sprinkle the yeast on top and stir it in. Make a well in the mound. Now pour the water into the well. Mix the flour, yeast, and water with your fingers on the bread board until all the water is absorbed and the texture is like a stiff dough. Place the dough in a small jar, cover it with a lid, and set it aside in a warm place for two or three days. Now it will look wrinkled and have a dry crust, but the middle will be bubbly and smell wheaty and sweet. Remove it to the bread board, add 1 cup more organic bread flour and ½ cup more warm spring water and knead it again into a hard ball. Place it back in the jar, cover, and let it stand a couple of days or until it looks like a smooth, tan marble. Break it open and you'll see it's beginning to be runny in the middle and smells more sour.

Finally, transform the *chef* into a *levain* by mixing it with an additional 1 cup of organic bread flour and ½ cup warm spring water in the bread machine, letting it work through the dough cycle. Then let it stand in the machine for 8 hours or so. Now you're ready to bake.

You'll have about 2 cups of the mixture, known to French bakers as the *levain*, or leavening. Pull off a cup and store it in the covered jar in the refrigerator. Use the other 1 cup of the starter for your first *Pain Levain* (see page 94).

Within a week or so, either use the remaining starter, or feed it by adding ½ cup organic bread flour and ½ cup spring water. Knead again into a ball, cover, and let it stand in a warm place overnight, then refrigerate.

BREAD MACHINE *LEVAIN*

This is an easier way to make the French baker's starter or leavening. You can do it directly in your bread machine using the dough cycle.

1 cup organic bread flour
$1/4$ teaspoon bread machine yeast
$1/2$ cup room temperature spring water

Process all ingredients through the dough cycle, then leave the *levain* to "work" for 2 to 5 days, or until it smells and tastes pleasantly sour and is bubbly and light. During this time you may store it in the machine, or transfer it to a jar with a lid, and keep it in a warm, draft-free place. Knead the dough a couple of times during the process, to stir the mixture and admit more airborne microflora. After about a week, if you haven't used the starter, pull off a cup to give away or discard, and feed the rest by kneading in $1/2$ cup organic bread flour and $1/2$ cup spring water. Leave the starter in a warm place overnight, then refrigerate until needed. The aroma will continue to become more sour and the tan, bubbly dough will have a crusty surface and a runny middle. Stir the crust back into the starter any time you're working with it. No need to discard it. It will rehydrate once it's remixed.

BREAD MACHINE *POOLISH*

The bread machine chamber is an ideal home for a French-style sponge. Simply make the *poolish* in the bread machine. Then, 10 hours or so later, add the ingredients to your favorite European bread and make the bread in the machine using the dough setting. Shape, raise, finish, and bake the bread on a stone. It's the best of all possible worlds.

$^3/_4$ cup organic bread flour
$^1/_2$ teaspoon bread machine yeast
$^1/_2$ cup room temperature spring water

Combine the flour, yeast, and water in the bread machine pan and process on the dough setting. Or, if you prefer, beat the mixture by hand, 100 strokes. Cover and set it aside or simply leave it in the bread machine.

Within 2 hours it will rise and bubble, at least doubling in volume. The *poolish* will continue to work and will peak in about 10 hours, when it will "drop," and fall back to its original volume. For fuller flavor development, place the *poolish* in the refrigerator after 4 or 5 hours or overnight. Let it return to room temperature before using. Pour all the *poolish* into any bread recipe made on the dough setting to complicate and improve the taste and texture of the bread.

YOGURT STARTER

Since yeasts also reside in milk products, you can make a fine starter by incubating plain yogurt with milk, then mixing it with organic flour. This will yield a taste similar to that of San Francisco sourdough breads because the lactose in the milk product "sours" in much the same way that airborne molds do in San Francisco.

1 cup 2 percent milk
3 tablespoons plain nonfat yogurt
1 cup organic bread flour

Place the milk in a 2-cup glass measure and heat it in the microwave to 100° F., about 45 seconds at 100 percent power or on the stove top in a small pan until warm. Stir in the yogurt, cover tightly with plastic wrap, and place it in the warmest place in your kitchen, ideally about 80° F. Let the mixture stand until it forms a curd and doesn't readily pour, about 24 hours, then stir in the flour. Whip it with a fork to both combine and aerate the mixture, then re-cover and let it stand until the mixture is full of bubbles and has a good sour smell, from 2 to 5 days. If a clear liquid separates out, stir it back in; if the liquid is pink, throw the starter out and begin again. The pink color means you have captured undesirable airborne bacilli, airborne pathogens that have spoiled your starter.

If you don't use the starter within 3 or 4 days, feed it with ½ cup flour and ¼ cup milk so that the yeast and molds will have a new supply of food to keep them alive. Cover and leave out in the warm kitchen overnight or until the starter is bubbly and light. Once the starter is made and bubbly, store it in the refrigerator.

RYE SOURDOUGH STARTER

Making a rye sourdough is not difficult. You'll need about 3 days to do it, but only a moment's attention each day. After you've made the starter, use some to enhance the flavor of any rye or wheat bread. A rye starter is a welcome addition to a whole-wheat-bread-flour bread as well. Make your own good peasant bread this way.

If you wish, dump all the starter into your recipe for dark bread, process on the dough setting, then pull off a cup of the dough and hold it back for the starter (old dough) you'll need in a few days.

2/3 cup room temperature spring water
1 cup organic medium rye flour
1/8 teaspoon bread machine yeast

Stir the water, flour, and yeast together in a clear glass or plastic container with a tight lid. Cover and put it aside in the warm kitchen for 24 hours. The next day, add another 1/2 cup of flour and 1/3 cup warm spring water. Stir vigorously to mix and aerate the mixture. Cover and set it aside in the warm kitchen for another 24 hours. On the third day, repeat the addition of flour and water. Mix again and let it stand for 8 hours or so. It will double in bulk and be lively and bubbly. Glutenous strands will stick to the spoon you stir with, and the taste will be unmistakably tangy and sour. Now, you may refrigerate it or use it in bread dough.

To use this starter, bring it back to room temperature, then add a cup of it to any rye bread recipe. Feed the starter by adding equal parts (about 1/2 cup each) flour and water every few days. Store it in a clean, covered jar in the refrigerator after the first 3 or 4 days.

ITALIAN WINTER *BIGA*
FOR ROLLS AND WHEAT BREADS

Carol Field first introduced us to Italian-style homemade starters known as *biga* in her wonderful book, *The Italian Baker.* We've converted the process to a bread machine and find it wonderfully versatile. The longer you allow the *biga,* or homemade starter, to stand, the more sour the flavor will become. Use these starters after allowing them to sit in the bread machine overnight, or leave them to ripen and sour for a few days to achieve a different taste.

¹/₄ teaspoon bread machine yeast
³/₄ cup plus 2 tablespoons spring water
1³/₄ cups plus 2 tablespoons organic bread flour

Add the yeast, water, and flour to the bread machine pan and process on the dough setting until the starter has mixed for 5 minutes, then turn off the machine. Let the *biga* sit in the bread machine or in a covered jar overnight, or for a minimum of 10 hours. Remove the starter to a 2-quart glass or plastic storage container. Cover it tightly and store it in the refrigerator for up to 2 weeks. Alternatively, store it in the warm kitchen for a few days, stirring from time to time to further "sour" the taste. Feed this starter as you would any other: Add ¹/₂ cup each organic bread flour and spring water, knead thoroughly, cover, and set aside in the warm kitchen overnight or until it becomes bubbly and active again.

DURUM FLOUR *BIGA*

This *biga* is a bit earthy and seductive. Made with durum flour usually reserved for pasta, it has a rich, robust bread flavor and will give off a sweet, warm smell that lingers in the kitchen during its rest and after baking.

½ teaspoon bread machine yeast
1⅓ cups spring water
2⅓ cups plus 2 tablespoons golden durum flour (not durum integrale)

Place the yeast, water, and flour in the bread machine pan. Process on the dough setting until the *biga* has mixed for about 5 minutes, then turn off the machine. Let the *biga* sit in the bread machine pan from 8 to 24 hours. Then remove it to a glass or plastic container, cover, and refrigerate until ready to use.

Feed this starter as any other: Add ½ cup organic bread flour and ½ cup spring water, stir vigorously, cover, and let it stand on the warm counter overnight or until bubbly and light, then refrigerate.

NATURAL GRAPE STARTER

For making real bread—bread that can't be gulped, bread that's chewy and crusty, that tastes so good you can hardly bring yourself to swallow—begin with organic grapes that will offer their own yeasts to your homemade starter. Buy organic grapes at a natural foods store, or better yet, go grape picking during the season. Wild mustang grapes make a heavenly starter. So do any number of vineyard grapes that a kindly vintner might allow you to pick.

You can also make a starter using organic peach leaves and following the same process. You may have to find a peach orchard before you begin, but this starter, which we learned about in an old Oklahoma Dust Bowl cookbook, makes a fine earthy starter.

1½ cups organic bread flour
2 cups room temperature spring water
½ pound organic green grapes on the stem, unwashed

In a medium-sized glass or plastic bowl, whisk together the bread flour and spring water until it's lump free. Submerge the grapes in the mixture, cover with plastic wrap, and set aside in a warm room from 4 to 7 days. Feed the mixture every day with a few spoons of additional flour and water, keeping the ratio 3 parts flour to 4 parts water.

Within a few hours the mixture will begin to bubble and expand. The starter is ready to use once the aroma is tangy and the taste is sweet and sour all at once, usually on about the third day. If the starter just lies there after a couple of days, heavy and lifeless, throw away most of it and feed it again with ½ cup flour and ⅔ cup water. Let it sit for about 12 hours, and look to see if it's started bubbling again. If it's still dead, throw it out and start over.

Once you have a lively homemade grape starter, strain out and discard the grapes. Then, transfer the starter to a clean glass jar, cover, and refrigerate. To use the refrigerated starter, bring it to room temperature and give it a little feeding of 2 tablespoons flour and 3 tablespoons water. Let it stand in your warm kitchen overnight, then use it in the recipes.

QUICK TIPS FOR SUCCESS WITH HOMEMADE STARTERS

Where do I start?

Use a container at least three times bigger than the volume of the starter ingredients. After all, you want the starter to grow. Keep a lid or plastic wrap handy to cover the starter while it's working.

Why do I have to use organic flour and spring water?

Chemical additives inhibit the growth of starters. Using organic flour and spring water guarantees that you won't be introducing restrictive additions that would stop your yeast from working.

How can I tell if my starter's working?

Learn to recognize a lively starter. It should be a light tan color, bubbly, with a sweet/sour aroma and taste, and when stirred it should remind you of hot bubble gum because it strings up in long supple strands. Whenever you check the starter, mix it thoroughly so that you add plenty of "air" with its attendant load of airborne molds. Check the starter a couple of times a day. It should be bubbly and light within a few hours.

How fast your starter grows depends on how warm the mixture is, how warm the room is, how much yeast you've introduced, how much airborne mold the mixture picks up, and maybe how lucky you are. It could be hours, it could be days. Be patient.

Where's the best place for me to make a starter?

Make a starter right in the bread machine, or in a bowl with a lid. Then, find a warm draft-free place in your house and let it bubble for several days. When Diana isn't using her bread machine, she uses the closet with the hot water heater, which, in her house, holds at a toasty 85° F. Although Linda almost always makes starters right in the bread machine itself, on cold winter days, she sometimes places starters in a covered bowl in a cabinet that sits over a heat vent in the kitchen.

How do I store the starter?

Once you've made the starter, and after several hours or days, when it's bubbly and ready to use or store, place it in a large glass jar, cover, and refrigerate.

How and when do I feed it?

Starters should be fed equal parts flour and water, about a half cup each, every three to five days. You can always give starter a little snack of flour and water just to make it more lively. Give the starter time to digest its food before using or refrigerating it. At least two hours to begin. This is one time you really want gas after a meal.

So how do I use the starter once it's been made and refrigerated?

Warm all starters and liquids to room temperature before adding them to bread dough. Either leave the starter on the counter top for a couple of hours, or, if you're in a hurry, place it in the microwave for ten to twenty seconds at 100 percent power. You'll see it begin to bubble and rise right before your very eyes. Break the starter into small pieces and add it to the top of the flour mixture in the bread machine pan.

How can I tell if my starter's gone bad?

While attracting natural airborne molds into your homemade starter, you may inadvertently have attracted unwanted pathogens that will spoil the mixture. Discard any starter that has a spoiled smell (you know, like rotten meat) or a pinkish tinged liquid on top.

4

MAKING BREAD

CERTAIN physical and chemical changes take place in the presence of time and temperature when you combine flour with liquid, yeast and/or starters, salt, and perhaps other flavor additives to make yeast breads. And, although making bread is both art and science, we hope, in this chapter, to remove some of the mystery so that you will achieve results that don't surprise you. No more lead balloons. No more jaw breakers. No more breads that look like the mushroom clouds of fifties A-bomb documentaries.

MAKING DOUGH: MEASURING, MIXING, AND KNEADING

Measuring the Ingredients

While every bread machine book says to measure your ingredients accurately because being even a tablespoon off can ruin a loaf of bread, these instructions miss the point and will not teach you how to make bread. If you take the same recipe for bread baked in a machine and make it ten times in different weather, or take the machine to Grandma's and make the bread there, you could be in for an ugly surprise. Why? Because flour takes up water from the air. Because rising times are affected by the temperature of the room, the weather, and the climate.

Does this make machine bread-baking impossibly difficult? Not at all. It means that you should open up the lid of the machine from time to time to look at the bread as the process goes along, so that you can fine-tune the dough and get exactly what you want by adjusting the flour-liquid ratio.

Using the dough cycle obviates many of the problems. You have more latitude with this setting. You'll be handling the dough. You'll be raising it a final time outside the machine. You'll be baking it in your regular oven. The craft will become more familiar to you the more loaves of bread you handle.

Using the dough cycle also means you can make a large recipe—using three cups or more of flour—in a one-pound machine as well as in a one-and-one-half or two-pound machine. Why! Because you're not using the machine to bake the bread. It won't rise out of the top of the pan and make a mess.

But we do come back to that original instruction. *Always begin with precise measurements.* Choose dry measures for dry ingredients and liquid measuring cups for liquids. Then, keep additional water and flour close by your bread machine to make fine adjustments during the first fifteen minutes of the knead cycle.

Putting in the Yeast

Measure and *place bread machine yeast* or *50 percent faster active dry yeast* in the bottom of the bread machine pan before adding the flour. This keeps the yeast separated from the liquids so that if your machine has a preheat cycle, the yeast won't begin working before the machine starts mixing the ingredients. If, however, you're using *regular active dry granular yeast,* first dissolve it in a little warm liquid, then add it to the mixture *as it is kneading* to guarantee that all the yeast will be dissolved. Crumble *cake yeast* into a small bowl and mash it with warm liquid to dissolve it, then add it to *kneading dough* in a bread machine. (See page 43 for further discussion of yeasts.)

Layering Ingredients into the Bread Machine Pan

After placing the yeast in the bottom of the pan, stir the flour to aerate it, then scoop your measure into the flour, level it off with a knife, and dump the flour into the bread machine pan. Never pack flour into the measure. You'll get too much. Measure and add the remaining dry ingredients, such as salt or sugar. You'll note that this layering technique separates the salt from the yeast. This optimizes the yeast action because salt retards yeast and it's best not to put them side by side in the pan.

Measure liquids into a liquid measure, holding the container at eye level or setting it on a flat surface to make sure you have a precise measure. If your machine has a preheat cycle, dump the liquids on top of the dry ingredients. (You'll know if your machine has this cycle by the series of little clicks you'll hear for several minutes while the machine warms up the ingredients before the actual mixing begins.) If your machine doesn't have this cycle (it begins mixing immediately when you turn it on), you should preheat liquids to room temperature by placing them in the microwave at 100 percent power for fifteen to thirty seconds. You needn't be too precise about this. All you're trying to do is knock the chill off. Stick your finger into the liquid before placing it in the machine. It should feel slightly cooler than body temperature. Remember the old principle: Cold inhibits yeast action. Too much heat will kill it.

Once you have all the ingredients layered in the pan, start the machine on the appropriate setting.

Temperature of the Room

Be aware that the ambient temperature affects yeast action. If your kitchen is hot, yeast action will be quicker. If your bread machine is placed in a cold room, or close to a cold air duct or an air conditioner, yeast action is slowed down. You may wish, if you have the room, to move your bread machine around to keep it in a space as close to a 70° F. as possible.

Machine Mixing the Dough

Once the machine begins mixing the dough, you'll want to check it after about ten minutes or so to see if the water-flour ratio seems to be about right. If the mixture is crumbly and will not form a ball, the mixture is too dry. Adjust it by adding more liquid, one tablespoon at a time, until the mixture forms a soft ball. If the mixture forms a hard cannon ball, it is also too dry. Lift the dough ball out of the machine, break it into four or five pieces, replace it in the bread pan, add additional liquid, a tablespoon at a time, and let the machine continue to knead it. Feel free to restart the machine if necessary to give the dough enough time to knead. It's almost impossible to overknead bread dough in the machine.

If the dough looks more like cake batter than dough it could be too wet. Add flour, one tablespoon at a time, until the mixture firms up into a soft dough. Be advised, however, that many Italian-style breads are made with very wet doughs. Don't add too much flour or you won't get those nice big holes you're after.

Developing a Well-Fermented Dough in the Bread Machine

Fermentation is the heart of yeast baking. By this process, yeast, and perhaps molds, begin to eat the starch in the flour, giving off gases that cause the bread to rise. This is true whether you're making bread by hand or using a bread machine.

But before the yeasts can get at the starch, the flour molecules must be broken down by kneading. When kneading begins, the proteins in the flour that make gluten begin to unfold and to mix thoroughly with the liquid. Look in your machine a couple of minutes after mixing begins and you'll see it looks like a shaggy mass. If you looked through a microscope you'd see that in the beginning the gluten molecules look like tangled hair. But as the process continues, the mixture straightens out, becomes more fluid, more elastic, and the gluten begins to become distinct long, straight strands in the dough. Look into the machine after fifteen minutes or so, and you should see a soft ball of dough with a satiny sheen to the surface.

At the same time, the starch in the flour becomes available so that the yeast can eat it and give off the gases that are then trapped in the web formed by the gluten.

This explains why you must wait a few minutes before leaving your bread machine to do its work. Give the machine about fifteen minutes to knead, then look inside and see if the dough ball looks soft and elastic. It won't get this way unless the flour-water ratio is correct. And you may have to make the minor alterations we've discussed to get the dough just right. After a few minutes of kneading it should, in most cases, feel like soft, smooth baby fat. Go ahead. Open up the machine, pinch that dough. See if it feels soft and supple.

The cycle will complete by mixing, kneading, and resting the dough in sequence, then the machine has a preset period for the dough to rise the first time. This whole cycle—mixing through rising, is approximately two hours on most bread machines. (Check your machine manual for precise time.) At the end, the dough should have about doubled in bulk.

Dough Cycle and How You Can Manipulate It

If you're using the dough cycle, however, you're not chained to the automatic timer in the machine. Following recipe directions, you can work the dough on the dough cycle, then leave it in the machine to continue to ferment and rise. Or, you can pull the dough out of the machine, place it in a bowl, cover it, and let it continue to rise slowly, perhaps in the refrigerator, or in a cool place in your house. This additional slow fermentation will give homemade starters a chance to develop and produce the complicated taste that characterizes European rustic breads.

Double Kneading Whole-Grain Doughs

You can run whole grain doughs through the dough cycle twice to double-knead them and improve the absorption of liquid by the flour molecules. Because whole-grain flours are less refined, they may need additional time and manipulation to achieve maximum lift in the dough. Double kneading helps and it's easy to do with a bread machine. If you're in a hurry, and don't want to wait the two hours or so it takes the dough cycle to complete, simply turn the bread machine off and restart it at the point when the dough is "resting" after the first kneading period is over. If you don't want to watch it that carefully, just run the dough cycle twice. You can also run the dough cycle once, and the regular bake cycle next, if you wish to bake whole wheat bread right in the machine.

Breads with Starters

If you're adding a homemade starter to the bread, be sure the starter is at room temperature before adding it to the pan. If you forgot to remove it from the refrigerator ahead of time, just place it, in a microwavable dish, in the microwave and heat it for ten to fifteen seconds at 100 percent power, or until the starter is about room temperature, 70° F. *Don't* overheat a starter or you'll kill it.

Place the starter on top of all the other ingredients at the beginning of the dough cycle and let the machine work through the entire cycle, adding additional resting time at the end as directed by the recipe.

Fully fermented dough will have stretched the gluten to the maximum of its elasticity, and if you poke your finger into the dough, the impression will remain.

Removing the Dough from the Machine, Punching It Down, Letting It Rest

Remove the dough to a lightly floured surface, and punch it down. This relieves the tension in the gluten and expels some of the carbon dioxide gas that's formed by the yeast. Squeeze the dough and you'll see it's easy to work now. Form it into a tight ball, cover it with the bread machine pan, and let it rest on the counter. This allows the gluten to relax even further so that you can roll out the dough without it springing back. It also moves the flour molecules around and makes more starch available so that the yeast can again begin to work.

Some European rustic bread recipes call for more than two fermentation periods. Second, or even third rising periods will work faster than the first because of the change in molecular structure that has clearly taken place and the multiplied yeast spores in the dough. Flavor development occurs as the molecules are shifted around so that the yeast and other molds can digest more of the starch and sugars in the dough.

But whether the recipe calls for the traditional two fermentation periods or more, you will give the bread dough one final rise in the shape you choose for baking. Once you put the bread in the hot oven, the yeast will give one final push ("Let me out of here," it says, "it's too damned hot") and the bread will rise as much as one third more, the so-called oven spring.

Forming and Baking European Rustic Loaves

Tools

BAKING PANS AND SHEETS: If you don't have a baking stone, shape free-form loaves and place them on dark metal baking pans lined with parchment paper and coated with cornmeal or spritzed with cooking spray for the final rise and for baking. These pans will yield the best brown crusts because they absorb and retain heat. If you prefer glass baking pans, prepare the pans in the same way and turn the temperature of the oven down twenty-five degrees for best results. Crusts will be a lighter, more golden color.

BAKING STONE: Turn your home oven into a fair facsimile of the ancient unglazed clay baking ovens found in European villages by simply buying baking stones or tiles to line the bottom oven shelf. Place a pizza stone, or unglazed quarry tiles from your local tile supply store (see page 312 for mail order sources) on the middle shelf of the oven. Preheat the oven with the stone in place for at least thirty minutes before shoveling the bread on it to bake. The porous texture of the clay helps distribute the heat in a way that will produce a fine crispy crust on your breads.

BANNETON: Europeans like to raise some breads in woven reed baskets made in round or oval shapes. These give a rustic beehive look to the breads, which are then turned out onto a hot stone for baking. You can buy a *banneton,* which is simply a basket lined with cloth, or you can make one at home by lining a basket yourself with coarse cloth or canvas. Work a generous amount of flour into the surface of the cloth so the bread won't stick. Place the round ball of dough in the well-floured *banneton,* cover, and let it rise until nearly doubled in bulk, then simply turn it upside down directly onto the baking stone in the preheated oven or onto a peel (see below) so that you don't risk burning yourself while flipping the dough into the hot oven. The resulting bread will be rustic looking and luscious, with the *banneton* pattern baked into the surface of the loaf.

LA CLOCHE: An instant bread oven, this is an unglazed clay base and bell that will give you heavenly loaves of country bread. Order La Cloche if you can't find one in your local cookware store (see page 312 for mail order sources). To use La Cloche, raise the dough the final time in the bell with the lid on, then place the whole thing on the bottom shelf of a 450° F. preheated oven to bake. The finish on the bread will be crisp, golden, and delicious. This is easy, and it's foolproof. Remove the Cloche from the oven at the end of the baking period, carefully raise the lid, and voilà. Picture perfect bread: round, golden, aromatic.

PARCHMENT PAPER: Using parchment with a peel and a baking stone gives great results. The shape you so carefully create won't get distorted from being moved around because you can use the paper to hold the shaped dough while it rises, then place the paper on a baking sheet or on the peel you use to shovel the bread dough right onto the hot baking stone in your oven. And no, the paper won't catch on fire in the hot oven.

When the bread's baked, remove it from the oven, peel off and discard the paper. Your bread will have a great brown, crisp bottom, your oven will be clean, and there won't be any mess at all. Such a deal. Buy parchment paper at a good cookware store, from a catalog, or in better supermarkets.

PASTRY SCRAPER: Handy as heck, this tool helps you lift and turn the dough as you form it. It also can be used to clean the work surface of flour after you're done. Use a scraper to divide the dough in pieces for rolls.

PEEL: You've seen this wooden tool at the pizza parlor. It looks like a big wooden paddle with a long handle. It's what the baker uses to shovel pizza and bread into the oven. Get one. You'll love it. They're available, along with parchment and baking stones, from good cookware stores or catalogs. Dust the peel with cornmeal or cover it with parchment and place the bread on it for the final rise. Then, just before baking, give the peel a trial shake to make sure the bread doesn't stick, and shovel it directly onto the hot baking stone. It's mighty close to what the village baker did in the fourteenth century.

ROLLING PIN: While it is not used for every bread, we recommend a heavy rolling pin at least fifteen to eighteen inches long. We also use a variety of dowels the same length, but of varying diameters—from the size of a pencil up to the thickness of your thumb—to form crown loaves and other specialty shapes. The circular end of the dowel can be used to make decorative indentations in the bread.

WATER SPRAYER: We can't say too much about the necessity for a water sprayer. Spray wet dough and the work surface before attempting the final shaping. Spray your hands. Then use the sprayer to mist the oven during the first five to ten minutes of baking to get that crisp crust we love on rustic European breads. Open the oven just a crack and shoot the water into the top portion of it, closing the oven as quickly as possible so as not to cool it unnecessarily. Avoid spraying the oven light or you may break it.

WORK SPACE: For best results, choose a work surface at least twenty-four inches square to knead and shape the dough. The work surface can be made from a variety of materials. Our very favorite is maple. However, we also like Formica. When working with a wet dough, such as for Italian breads, we can spray the Formica surface with plain water before rolling it out and—although it sounds like a contradiction—the wet dough won't stick to the super-sealed Formica surface. We also spray our hands when working with wet dough.

You may also use marble, which provides a cool, dispassionate surface for both kneading and rolling. Other helpful surfaces include pastry cloths well impregnated with flour and Tupperware plastic that's dusted with flour and can be rolled up and put away when you're not using it. Makes for a tidy work space.

Whatever work surface you're using to shape the final bread, take care not to work in any unnecessary flour. Sprinkle flour onto the surface then rub your hands over the surface until only a thin film of flour remains. All you're trying to do is prevent the dough from sticking.

Shaping the Dough

After you've allowed the dough to relax for ten to fifteen minutes, roll it or shape it, according to the recipe and your own whim. Listed below is a series of traditional shapes. Choose one of these, or invent your own.

Since most European rustic breads are baked free-form, it's important to work the dough enough to pull the gluten net tight so that the bread will hold its shape while its baking. Don't be shy about manipulating the dough. After you've let it rest, flatten it with your hands, roll it up into a tight cigar shape or ball, then skid it across the work surface to tighten the gluten web. Now you're ready to shape it into one of the many possible forms. You can increase your bread repertoire exponentially simply by taking a basic *pain au levain, pain ordinaire,* or country bread and shaping it in different ways.

BAGUETTE: With a rolling pin, roll the dough away from you into a long oval about eight by twelve inches. Fold the dough in half lengthwise by bringing the twelve-inch edge farthest away down over the edge closest to you. Seal the edges by pressing the seam with your extended thumbs. Now roll the dough a quarter turn up so that the seal is on top. Again flatten the dough into an oval with the rolling pin. Press a trench along the twelve-inch-

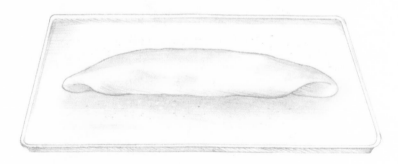

Baguette

long center of the dough, then fold it in half toward you again, and this time, seal the edges by pressing with the heel of your hand. Now roll the dough back and forth, sliding your hands along the length, making a sixteen-inch-long sausage roll. Place the roll seam side down on a cornmeal-dusted peel or parchment, or in a special baguette baking pan to rise a final time before slashing and baking. Make three or four quick, sure diagonal slashes in the bread just before baking.

Bâtard

BÂTARD: Roll the dough away from you into an eight-by-ten-inch oval. Pull the ten-inch side of the dough toward you and flatten it with your hand, then pull the dough over and roll the bread so that it's seam side is down. Now pull the ends of the dough out so that you have a bread so that is fat in the middle and tapered on both ends. Set it aside to rise on a cornmeal-covered peel or parchment paper, or on a cornmeal-dusted baking sheet.

BOULE: Pull off a piece of dough—it can be a quarter of the dough, half, or all the dough. Begin pulling the dough into a ball over your fingers, turning the ball and tucking the dough under until you have a mushroom cap–shaped piece with a flat bottom. Turn and pull the dough until the top is perfectly smooth and globe shaped. Place the bread flat side down on cornmeal-dusted parchment or a peel or baking sheet for the final rise.

Boule

BRIOCHE: Roll the brioche dough into a ball as described for the *boule*, withholding a small amount for the topknot. Roll the small ball, then pinch it into a "teardrop" shape. Punch a hole in the top of the big ball with a skewer and fit the topknot in, pointed side down, before the last rising. Alternately, you can eliminate the topknot, score the top of the ball with a cross, and place a walnut half inside. Brioche dough can also successfully be formed into rolls that are shaped into globes, then raised and baked on parchment, or into mini-loaves shaped and baked on parchment.

CHALLAH: To braid a challah, divide the dough into three equal pieces. Roll the pieces into sixteen-inch-long ropes on a lightly floured surface. Lay the three ropes beside one another on a big piece of parchment, then begin braiding by laying the ropes

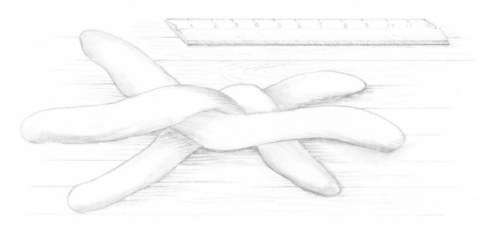

Challah

over one another from the center, like spokes on a wheel. Braid from the center to each end, then tuck the ends under. Place on a prepared baking pan or in a loaf pan for the final rise.

CIABATTA: Roll the dough flat into a quarter-inch-thick oval, then cut it into two rectangular pieces about four by ten inches. Let the pieces rise on parchment or on a cornmeal-covered peel. To finish, splay your fingers widely and mash down the dough. Let the uneven dough rise a final thirty minutes, then bake on a stone.

CIRCLE BREAD: Roll the dough into a ten-inch disk, then transfer it to a cornmeal-covered parchment or peel for the final rise. To get the traditional look, once the dough is puffy and light, lay a round cooling rack with a circular pattern on top of the dough and generously dust the dough with flour. Lift the rack off to reveal the concentric circular pattern. Notch the edges of the dough with a sharp knife or pastry cutter before baking on a stone.

COURONNE: This giant donut is made by rolling the dough into a ten-inch disk, then pressing your elbow into the center to make a hole, thus forming a large donut shape. Lift the donut and gradually enlarge the hole in the center by turning the loop in your

Couronne

hands. Take care to keep the loop intact, and don't tear the dough. Now place the giant donut on parchment paper to rise. Once it has almost doubled in bulk, take a small rolling pin or dowel and indent the top of the bread on four sides forming a square depression in the donut. Flip the donut over and let it rise again. Flip it one final time onto a cornmeal-covered parchment or peel so that the square pattern shows. Quickly finish with an egg wash and bake.

ÉPI: The wheat-sheaf shape is made by first forming a baguette (see above) and placing it on a sheet of parchment. Then, use clean sharp scissors and, beginning at one end, make a diagonal cut three quarters of the way through the loaf. Make the next cut about two inches up the "stalk" from the first cut, but on the opposite side. As you've cut each section, gently fold the dough over and pull it out to form wheat sheaves. Dip the scissors into cold water if you find the dough sticking and make quick, sure cuts so that the sheaf will be cut clean. A baguette should have about ten cuts, five to the side. You can leave the sheaf in a vertical loaf, or you can turn it into a crown by pulling the two ends around and sealing them together before the final rise.

Cutting the Épi

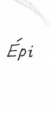

Épi

You can make stars using the same basic process, except you cut the baguette completely into nine pieces, making diagonal cuts with a sharp knife or pastry cutter. Then form the eight-pointed star on a piece of parchment by rolling one piece into a ball for the center and setting the remaining pieces around it. Moisten the points of the star with water and squeeze them into the center ball to make them stick together. If you wish, sprinkle the center of the star with poppy or sesame seeds.

Star

FICELLE: To make this long string, roll the dough out as for a baguette, but keep rolling until the dough is no thicker than a pencil. Raise a final time on parchment.

FOCACCIA: Roll the dough into an irregular fourteen-inch circle a quarter inch thick. Let it rise a final time on cornmeal-coated parchment or a peel until puffy and light, about twenty minutes. Just before baking, dimple the top of the bread with your fingertips and finish it with additional olive oil and the toppings of your choice. If you'd like your focaccia to be thicker, roll it into a twelve-inch circle to begin with.

FOUGASSE: For this French flatbread scented with herbs and usually slashed and cut to form a decorative shape (such as a sun or a tree) roll the dough into a fourteen-inch oval that's about a quarter inch thick, place it on cornmeal-coated parchment, then slash the flatbread into the desired design and raise it a final time.

GRISSINI: Roll the dough for these Italian breadsticks between your hands or on a lightly floured surface. They can be as thin as pencils or as thick as your thumb. Finish them with an egg wash and sprinkle with seeds, kosher salt, or turbinado sugar.

Fougasse

PAIN AUX NOIX: Shape this nut bread into two large triangles or three small ones by rolling the dough into a twelve-inch oval then cutting it into three triangles with a sharp knife or a pastry blade. Dust the bread generously with flour after the first rise, and imbed walnuts or hazelnuts in a row on the top. Raise on cornmeal-dusted parchment.

Pain aux Noix

PIZZA: Roll the dough into an irregular fourteen-inch circle a quarter inch thick. For a classic New York–style pizza, keep rolling until the circle is about an eighth inch thick and sixteen inches in diameter. Transfer it to a cornmeal-coated peel for a few moments while you prepare the final toppings.

SAWTOOTH BREAD: Form a twelve-inch-long cylinder by rolling the dough between the palms of your hands, then flatten the cylinder with a rolling pin and cut the dough into six triangles with a sharp knife or pastry blade. Lay the triangles out on parchment forming an arc and moistening the dough with water to make the points stick together. Raise until nearly doubled in bulk, then finish with an egg wash.

TORDU: Roll the dough into a twelve-by-six-inch rectangle. Using a small rolling pin or a dowel, press an indention two inches wide into the center along the length of the bread. Fold half the loaf sideways along the indentation, until the two sides meet. Twist the dough and stretch it, giving it three twists. Raise on parchment paper.

TORPEDO: Form the dough into an eight-inch disk, then fold the right half over to the middle and press down with the heel of your hand to seal the seam. Now fold over the left half to the middle and repeat. Now fold over the top to the middle, seal, now the bottom to the middle and seal. You'll have a flat, squarish disk that's fatter in the middle. Shape the square into a torpedo by rolling the dough under the palms of your hands to form a log, then pinching the two ends to form points. Turn the torpedo seam side down and raise it on parchment, or keep the seam on top and raise it in a *banneton*, in either case keeping it covered with plastic wrap. Just before baking, slide the dough onto a cornmeal-covered peel. Slash it deeply down the middle, then bake on a stone.

ZIGZAG BREAD: Form as for a baguette (see above), then place on parchment and flour the top heavily with rye flour. Using a sharp knife or razor, cut deep triangles into the surface of the loaf. Cut down almost through the bread, making zigzag teeth. Let the bread rise until almost doubled in bulk.

The Final Rise

The final fermentation period takes place after you've shaped the bread and placed it on parchment paper, on a cornmeal-dusted peel, in a *banneton*, or in a prepared bread pan. Usually, you should cover the bread with plastic or a damp tea towel for this final rise to prevent its drying out. There are, however, some exceptions to this rule. Hard rolls should rise uncovered, for example. Let the recipe be your guide.

If the top of your bread dough dries out, do what Julia Child recommends: Roll it over onto a cornmeal-dusted peel and slash the bottom, which will have retained its moisture, before baking. This guarantees that the oven spring of the yeast will work in a controlled way and that the slashes you have made will be effective. (See Slashing the Loaves below.)

Dry bread dough may crack around the edges or bulge out into a funny-looking loaf during the last crucial oven spring.

Finishing the Loaves

After the bread has been given its final rise, and after you've preheated the oven, you're ready to put the final flourish on the dough to get the finish you want.

There are many ways to get different finishes on loaves of bread or rolls. The reputations of European bakers are often made by the finish they give to their rustic loaves. In the past, when breads were baked in a communal oven, those slashes that make the bread look good and aid the final "oven spring" were actually a way to identify the baker. Develop your own ways with finishes and people will know your breads on sight.

You decide whether you prefer a soft or crispy crust, whether you want the bread crust crunchy or buttery. Glazed or dull. Seeded or floured.

The simplest solution is to do nothing. Your bread will come out of the oven with a crisp, dull finish and a lovely, pale, golden-brown color. Spritz the loaf five or six times with plain water during the first ten minutes of baking and you will have complicated the finish by adding steam. This crust will be thicker, crisper, and a deeper golden-brown.

If you've added whole seeds, nuts, herbs, or other special flavoring ingredients, borrow a trick from the artisanal bakers. Mist the risen dough with plain water or brush it with an egg-white wash, then sprinkle the top heavily with the same seed or nut that's in the bread. Not only does this make the bread look good, it prepares the taster for the flavor and texture to be found inside. If you've used several seeds and nuts, mix them, or place them on the bread in sections, making a design.

FLOUR-DUSTED LOAVES: One of the most popular finishes on rustic artisanal bread is achieved by rubbing flour into the loaf before it bakes. Rub in the flour either before or after the final rise, then slash, and you'll get a wonderful dusted look. If you rub flour into the loaf before its final rise, you can really rub it in, but it will thin out as the bread rises. Wait until the dough has risen and you'll need to use a light touch to avoid deflating the loaf. You may also sprinkle flour onto the loaf through a sieve to get a lightly floured look.

SLASHING THE LOAVES: Slashing the loaf serves a very useful purpose. When the bread is placed in the oven, it will rise one final time by about one third its bulk—the oven spring. If you don't slash your bread before you put it in the oven, it will expand where it wants and may bulge, crack, and tear along the sides. If you're baking the loaf in a bread pan, that's fine. But if you're baking a free-form loaf, it's much better to control the spring by making your own slashes and telling the bread where *you* would like it to go.

To slash loaves of bread, choose an Exacto knife, a French slasher known as a *lame* (available through King Arthur's bread bakers catalog, see page 310) or a razor blade. Hold it at a forty-five-degree angle and make quick, sure, deep slashes in the bread after it's risen and just before baking. Don't try and cheat by using a kitchen knife. Even the sharpest knife won't work—it will just drag through the dough and deflate it. We make these slashes after we've sprinkled the top of the loaf with seeds, or glazed or floured it. That way the slashes stand out in an even more dramatic way.

Practice slashing loaves. Soon you'll become as confident as a surgeon, and you'll begin designing patterns of your own. The tic-tac-toe design so often seen on the top of a free-form round loaf is only the beginning.

TO GLAZE YEAST BREADS: A whole egg whisked with a tablespoon of water gives a shiny, medium-brown glaze. An egg yolk whisked with a tablespoon of milk gives the shiniest mahogany-brown glaze. Plain egg white whisked with a tablespoon of water gives a caramel shine. Brush on the glaze just before baking.

FOR A CRISP CRUST: Mist the oven with plain water several times during the first ten minutes of baking. Don't open the oven wide. Just open it a crack and shoot the water to the top of the oven where it can fall down over the bread. Don't aim right at the oven light either. You could cause it to explode from thermal shock.

FOR A SOFT CRUST: After baking, rub the loaf all over with butter or olive oil while it's still hot. The fat will soften the crust, adding a wonderful rich taste. This is particularly appropriate to sweet or fruit-filled breads.

Baking Bread in Your Own Jerry-Rigged Baker's Oven

Breads in Europe were originally baked in communal wood-fired stone or brick ovens. They created crisp crusts, well-baked interiors, and the traditional breads we've come to know and love. Contemporary commercial bakers ovens are steam injected. This too aids in the crust development. But you can imitate all of this at home by baking with clay and spritzing your oven with plain water (see page 82).

One of the primary differences between European and American breads is that Euro-breads are baked in a very hot oven—sometimes as high as 500° F. And since European rustic breads are known for their fine crusts, it's important to bake them at the high temperatures called for in the recipes. We never trust the thermostat in our own ovens to tell us the truth and always use an independent oven thermometer.

Why wouldn't your oven thermostat be accurate? When manufacturers gave us the advantage of high-temperature self-cleaning ovens, they also built into the stove a device that throws off the thermostat. Don't ask us why they can't solve this engineering problem. Just know that the problem exists and counteract it by using your own independent thermometer to check on the temperature of your oven before you place bread or anything else in it to bake.

A NOTE ABOUT HIGH ALTITUDE BAKING: Gases expand more rapidly in the thin air of high altitudes. This means yeast dough rises quicker. There's less atmospheric pressure to work against the dough. It means the tops of breads may collapse. You can experiment by reducing the yeast by a quarter teaspoon at a time, until you find the right amount for your altitude. You can also experiment with reducing liquids by two or three teaspoons per recipe.

How Do You Know the Bread Is Done?

Baking bread can be divided into three stages. When you first place the bread dough in the preheated oven, it quickly reaches 140° F. During this first part of the baking, the yeast gives its final push, raising the dough one last time (the oven spring) before the yeast is killed by heat. Then the baking enters its second phase, wherein the temperature in the middle of the bread rises to just under the boiling point. The gluten web solidifies so that the bread takes its final shape. The last portion of the baking period occurs when the brown finish that appears as starches and sugars on the surface of the bread caramelize. The interior of the loaf is now above the boiling point and water evaporates out of the loaf.

There are several ways to determine when your bread is done. First of all, check the independent thermometer you put in the oven. Was the oven temperature accurate and has the designated time in the recipe elapsed? Second, does the crust of the bread look brown? Finally, remove the bread from the oven, hold it in a cloth, turn it over, and rap on the bottom to see if it sounds hollow. This means sufficient water has evaporated so that the bread is done. If it only gives off a dull thud, you may need to bake it for a few minutes longer.

Underbaked bread will have a soggy center. Overbaked bread can be as dry as zwieback. If the bread isn't quite done, place it directly on the baking stone for five to ten minutes, then check it again. If you were using a pan, place the bread directly on the oven rack to finish baking a few more minutes.

Cooling the Bread

Resist the urge—don't cut into bread just out of the oven. Proper cooling is the last step in a well-made loaf of bread. Remove the bread from the oven, using the peel if you baked it on a stone, or lifting the baking sheets and/or pans with hot pads. (Always lift bread from the bread machine pan as soon as it's baked as well.) Turn the hot bread immediately out onto a rack to cool. During the cooling period, further changes will take place. You may hear cracking from the bread as the crust takes on its characteristic crazing. But whether or not you hear that, know that the starch inside the loaf is solidifying as the bread cools. Slice hot bread and you'll get a gooey mess. That's because the starches aren't yet solid enough to cut. As bread cools, more moisture evaporates until you have a nice, cool loaf you can slice into perfect pieces.

Choose bread knives with half-moon serrations for best results, and cut with a back-

and-forth sawing motion. Don't mash down on the bread. If you've baked a round free-form loaf, begin by cutting the bread in half, then place the cut side down on the board and cut slices from each half.

Storing of Bread

After you've gone to the trouble to get that nice crisp crust on the bread, don't ruin it by placing the bread in a plastic bag to sweat and soften. Only breads made with eggs and fats store well in plastic. Otherwise, store the bread in a brown paper bag, or loose in a bread box. We do not recommend freezing or refrigerating bread. It takes up unpleasant off-tastes. If you've made bread with a starter, it will have good keeping qualities and may stay relatively fresh for up to a week. Cut into a loaf of bread made with a good starter, keep the cut end down on the cutting board and use the bread as you wish. The crust will get thicker and chewier but the center will remain creamy and fresh. Breads made with commercial yeast only are more fragile. Eat them within a day or two and use the left-overs for croutons, bird feed, or bread crumbs.

Breads enriched with fats and eggs also have greater keeping qualities than breads made with nothing more than flour, yeast, salt, and water. These breads can be success-fully stored in plastic for several days without any untoward effects.

Reheating Bread

We like to place bread in a brown bag, run water over the outside of the bag, and place it in a 400° F. oven for five to ten minutes to reheat. You can also wrap a slice of bread in a paper towel and reheat it in the microwave in ten seconds. We also reheat bread in the toaster oven. But mostly, we just make toast. That extra caramelization on the cut sur-faces of most rustic European breads is just too good to be missed.

Using the Leftovers

The only problem with learning to make bread at home is that there are bound to be left-overs. I mean, you'll probably learn to love making bread so much that the stuff will just stack up in little heels, bits of pizza crust, and quarter loaves that are just too good to throw away. What can you do!

Make bread crumbs by whizzing up old bread in the food processor using the steel blade. Store the crumbs in a Ziploc bag in the freezer.

Cut bread into half-inch cubes, then toss with olive oil and Parmesan cheese if you wish. Lay the cubes out on a baking sheet in a single layer and dry them out in a 200° F. oven, stirring from time to time, until the cubes are golden and crisp, about ten to fifteen minutes. Now you have great croutons for use in salads. Store in a Ziploc bag.

Use the bread in bread puddings.

Feed it to the birds.

Use it to pick up broken glass.

Make a facial out of old bread by dampening the slices with milk and placing them on your face while you lie down for half an hour. Then wash your face and see how much younger you look. It could be the rest. It could be the milk. It could be the bread. Who knows!

Now that you've had this master class in making bread it's time to rip into that sack of flour, plunge your hands into the dough, and bake. You just might find you *can* live by bread alone. Go forth and multiply. We're speaking to the yeast here, you understand. Blessings on you, little ones.

5

Basic Wheat Breads

Pain Ordinaire
No *Pain Ordinaire*
Pain au Levain (with 4 variations)
    with Onions and Bacon
    with Olives and Rosemary
    with Sun-dried Tomatoes and Herbs
    with Toasted Walnuts
Pain à l'Ancienne
Pain de Campagne
Pain de Mie Made Easy in the Machine
Italian Marketplace Bread
Pane all'Olio
Brother Juniper's Santa Rosa Struan
French Bread for the *Banneton*
England's Christmas Bread of 1942
Whole-Meal Bread
Classic Bread Machine Sourdough Bread
Polenta Bread
Como Bread
Brian Dupnik's 11-Seed and Grain Bread
Pane all'Uva
Sweet Butter Loaves from the South of France
Pain aux Noix
Raisin Loaf with a Buttermilk Crumb
Challah
Irish Soda Bread
Greek Bread
Kalamata Bread

PAIN ORDINAIRE
Plain French Bread

Dough Setting
Makes one 14-inch baguette

Light and fluffy with a thin, crisp crust, this is the everyday bread of France that's only at its peak for about 8 hours after baking. Master this recipe and you can have French bread any time you want.

Don't believe for a minute that you can bake real French bread in your bread machine on the French bread setting. Technique is all. Use your bread machine on the dough setting, then form the loaves by hand, bake them on a stone or in a French baguette baking pan. That, friends, is French bread. The ordinary kind.

1¼ cups water
3 cups bread flour
2½ teaspoons bread machine yeast
1 teaspoon salt
1 egg white whisked together with 1 tablespoon water
    for glaze

Combine the ingredients except egg wash in the bread machine pan and process on the dough setting. Remove the dough to a lightly floured work surface and punch it down. Form it into a tight ball and cover it with the bread machine pan. Let the dough rest for 30 to 45 minutes.

BREAD AND ONION SOUP
Makes 6 servings
Don't throw out that stale French Bread.
Make soup. It's easy and it's delicious.

2 tablespoons unsalted butter
2 tablespoons olive oil
2 pounds yellow onions, peeled and
thinly sliced (makes 8 cups)
12 cloves garlic, peeled, crushed,
and minced
Salt and freshly ground black pepper
to taste
1 quart water
1 quart defatted low-fat chicken broth
6 large slices French or country bread
3 large egg yolks

Heat the butter and oil in a soup pot,
then add the onions. Sauté over medium
to low heat, stirring often, for about 30
minutes, or until the onions are dark and
caramelized. When the onions are dark,
add the garlic, salt, pepper, and water.
Mix well, stirring up the good stuff
clinging to the bottom of the pot. Boil for
about 10 minutes on high heat, then add
the broth and continue to simmer over
medium heat for 5 minutes. Adjust the
seasonings with salt and pepper.
While the soup cooks, toast the bread,
then break it into pieces and divide the
pieces among 6 soup bowls. Just before
serving, whisk the egg yolks until thick
and creamy, then whisk in a couple of
tablespoons of hot soup. Pour the egg
mixture into the soup pot. *Do not boil.*
Ladle the soup over the toast
and serve at once.

Divide the dough into two pieces, form each piece into a tight ball, and set aside uncovered for 10 minutes. Flatten each piece into a rectangle about 6 × 3 inches, then form into 2 baguettes (see page 75). Place on parchment or in special baguette pans and cover with plastic or a tea towel while the loaves rise one final time, about 30 minutes. Meanwhile, preheat the oven with a stone in place on the middle rack to 450° F. for at least 30 minutes. Just before baking, brush the loaves lightly with the egg wash, and make 3 or 4 diagonal slashes in the top of each loaf.

Bake the loaves in the preheated oven until golden brown, 25 to 30 minutes. Spritz the oven with plain water 3 or 4 times during the first 10 minutes (see page 82). Turn the bread out and cool on a rack. Eat it the same day it's made.

NO *PAIN ORDINAIRE*

Basic Bread Setting
Makes one 1-pound loaf

Let's face it, sometimes you're tired, you don't want to make a sponge, you don't feel like waiting for a *chef,* a *poolish,* or starter, you want instant satisfaction from your bread machine. Here's our answer. A nice crisp crust with soft, mellow crumb, great for toast or the evening's breadbasket—and it's easily measured into the bread pan in less than 5 minutes.

1 to 1½ teaspoons bread machine yeast
2 cups bread flour
1 tablespoon sugar
³⁄₄ teaspoon salt
1 tablespoon unsalted butter
²⁄₃ cup water
Additional unsalted butter, for a softer crust (optional)

Combine the yeast, flour, sugar, salt, butter, and water in the bread machine pan. Process on the basic bread setting.

Remove the bread from the bread pan to a rack to cool. For a softer crust, immediately rub the top and sides of the loaf lightly with butter or place the warm loaf in a plastic bag. Close the bag and finish cooling.

For one 1½-pound loaf

2 teaspoons bread machine yeast
3 cups bread flour
1½ tablespoons sugar
1 teaspoon salt
1½ tablespoons unsalted butter
1⅛ cups (1 cup plus
2 tablespoons) water

PAIN AU LEVAIN
French Bread From a Starter

Dough Setting
Makes two 14-inch baguettes, one 12-inch round loaf, or
two 12-inch torpedoes

This simple bread is as basic as life and breath. Make it the first
day using any starter (see page 47), then hold back a cup of the
dough and use it the next day in another *Pain au Levain*. Use old
dough 3 or 4 times and you'll see the flavor changes every time.
Soon, you'll have a divine, sour torpedo with largish holes and a
mouth-watering flour-dusted crust. The texture will be chewy, the
crust crisp. You may also form the dough into baguettes or one high
round loaf (see page 75). And because you made the dough with a
starter, it will keep quite well—up to 4 or 5 days.

You'll note we specify organic bread flour and spring water for
this recipe. For best results with this or any starter-made bread always use these unadulterated ingredients.

Holding back a cup of dough, you'll still have plenty the first
day to make two generous torpedoes or baguettes, or one high
round loaf. If you wish to use all the dough the first day, make three
torpedoes or baguettes or one 14-inch, high round loaf.

You can add roasted red and yellow onions, along with leeks,
scallions, and pepper to baguettes, or pecans and raisins to torpedo-
shaped flour-dusted loaves. We love rosemary and olives added to
one big *bâtard* or sun-dried tomatoes and fresh Mediterranean
herbs in a loaf we shape into a flattish round.

But unadulterated *Pain au Levain* is the most basic bread and
the one with which your reputation can be made. It requires that
you run the dough cycle twice, first to make a sponge *(poolish)* with
a starter and additional flour and water, and again with the addi-

tion of the final ingredients. Then, add any extras you wish, shape the loaves, raise them, and bake on a stone, spritzing the oven with water (see page 74). Don't blame us if after you've made this bread 5 or 6 times the people who eat at your table burst into tears. Beauty does that to some of us. We can't help it.

SPONGE:

1¼ cups organic bread flour

½ cup warm spring water

¾ cup any sourdough starter (see page 47), at room
   temperature

DOUGH:

1 teaspoon bread machine yeast

1 cup warm spring water

3 cups organic bread flour

1 teaspoon salt

1 egg white whisked with 2 tablespoons water for glaze

Make the sponge by combining the flour, water, and starter in the bread machine pan. Process on the dough setting.

Now, add the bread ingredients, except egg wash, to the pan. Process again on the dough setting.

Once the second dough cycle is complete, you'll see that you have a wet, soft dough. That's what you want. Remove the dough to a work surface dusted with flour. Cut off 1 cup of dough, place it in a jar, cover, and refrigerate for a *Pain au Levain* that you might make tomorrow or anytime during the next week or so. If you want a heightened sour taste, store the starter in a cool place, but not in the refrigerator.

Divide the remaining dough in two pieces and form it into baguettes, a round loaf, or torpedo shapes (see page xxiii). Place the shaped dough in a *banneton* (see page 73) to rise, or, if you've made torpedoes or baguettes, place on parchment or in a baguette-shaped pan for the final rise. Cover the dough with plastic wrap and let it rise until nearly doubled in bulk, about 1 hour.

Preheat the oven with a stone in place on the middle rack to 450° F. for about 30 minutes. Just before baking, roll the loaves from the *banneton* onto a cornmeal-dusted peel. Slash the loaves diagonally with a razor or sharp knife 3 or 4 times. Slash a round loaf in a crisscross pattern. Glaze the loaves with the egg white wash, then quickly pop them onto the stone in the preheated oven. If you're using a baguette-shaped pan, you can place it directly on the middle rack of the oven instead. Spritz the oven 4 or 5 times with plain water during the first 10 minutes of baking (see page 74). Bake the loaves until done, about 30 minutes for torpedoes or round loaves, 20 minutes for baguettes. The crust will be a lovely caramel color. Turn the bread out and cool on a rack.

To gild the lily,
you may make any of the following additions
to the basic *Pain au Levain*.

PAIN AU LEVAIN
WITH ONIONS AND BACON

After the completion of the second dough cycle, remove the dough to a
lightly floured board. Punch down, then form into a tight ball.
Rest under the bread machine pan for 10 minutes or so, while you cook
3 pieces of bacon until crisp but not dry. Crumble the bacon into the dough
and form the dough into an 8-inch round. Let the dough rise a final time,
covered, on parchment or a cornmeal-covered peel. Cut an X in the middle
of the raised loaf and insert half a large round peeled onion, cut side up.
Now make 4 straight slashes around the edge of the top of the bread,
forming a square. Finish with an egg white wash.
Bake on a stone in a 450° F. oven until the crust is a deep mahogany color
and the bread is done through, about 30 minutes. Cool on a rack.
Leave out the bacon if you wish, and sauté about 3/4 cup onions—red,
yellow, or green onions with tops, and fold into the bread dough instead.

PAIN AU LEVAIN
WITH OLIVES AND ROSEMARY

2 tablespoons chopped fresh rosemary needles
1/2 cup whole pitted Mediterranean black olives

After the second dough cycle is completed, remove the dough to a lightly
floured surface, and knead in the rosemary and olives. Form the dough into
a tight ball, turn the bread machine pan over it, and let the dough rest for
30 minutes. Now, shape into a *bâtard* (see page xx) and let it rise, covered,
on parchment until nearly doubled in bulk, about 30 minutes.
Bake as directed above.

PAIN AU LEVAIN
WITH SUN-DRIED TOMATOES AND HERBS

$^1/_4$ cup oil-packed drained dried tomatoes, chopped after measurement
$^1/_4$ cup chopped fresh sage
$^1/_4$ cup chopped fresh basil

After the second dough cycle is completed, turn the dough out onto a lightly floured surface and knead in the tomatoes and herbs. Form the dough into a tight ball, cover with the bread machine pan, and let the dough rest for 30 minutes. Shape the dough into a *bâtard*, raise, covered, on parchment until nearly doubled in bulk, finish with an egg white wash, and bake as directed above.

PAIN AU LEVAIN
WITH TOASTED WALNUTS

1 cup toasted walnut pieces

After the second dough cycle is completed, turn the dough out onto a lightly floured surface and knead in the toasted walnuts (see page 37). Form the dough into a tight ball, cover with the bread machine pan, and let the dough rest for 30 minutes. Shape the dough into a 10-inch round, raise, covered, on parchment until nearly doubled in bulk, finish with an egg white wash, and bake as directed above.

Pain Paisan

Use the basic dough for *Pain à L'Ancienne* (see page 100) to make other French-style breads. Peasant Bread, or *Pain Paisan,* is basically the same bread but shaped into a thick, elongated oval loaf, then scored into a leaflike pattern by slashing the bread lengthwise down the middle, with angular cuts going off to the sides like tree branches. The loaf is dusted with flour before the cuts are made, then the crust is made golden and easy to chew by being buttered immediately upon removal from the oven (see illustration).

You can also make a Bordeaux-style bread, *Pain Rustique Bordelais,* using the same dough but shaping it into a rectangle. Cut the sides and ends off sharply, holding out about a cup of the trimmed dough for use in another loaf, then let the bread rise a final time, covered, on parchment until nearly doubled in bulk. Flour the loaf after it's raised the final time, then slash it diagonally a time or two across the top. Bake on a stone using liberal amounts of spritzed water in the first 10 minutes of baking to create steam (see page 74). Once baked, the bread will be a lovely brown, with a light texture, a honeycombed crust, and the characteristic pale tan-gray color of Old-fashioned Bread—and you'll have the bonus of a terrific batch of old dough with which to make another loaf later (see page 54).

PAIN À L'ANCIENNE
Old-fashioned Bread

Dough Setting
Makes 2 baguettes

GARLIC SPREAD
Makes 1/2 cup
Use this pungent spread for Old-fashioned or other French breads.

1/2 cup (1 stick) unsalted butter, at room temperature
1 clove garlic, peeled and crushed
1 tablespoon finely chopped fresh parsley
2 tablespoons freshly grated Parmesan cheese

With a fork, whisk together the butter, garlic, parsley, and cheese. Cover and let stand for 1 hour at room temperature.

For a fine lunch, preheat the oven to 375° F. Slice a baguette of Old-fashioned or French bread into 1-inch-thick slices, cutting to the bottom of the loaf but not all the way through. Gently separate the slices and spread both sides of each slice with the garlic spread. Re-form the slices into a loaf and place the loaf on a piece of foil large enough to wrap it completely. Place the wrapped loaf on a baking sheet and bake on the middle rack of the preheated oven for 10 minutes. Unwrap and serve at once.

French bakers added rye flour to plain French bread so that it would keep more than one day. They also liked the complex flavor. This loaf has become one of our favorites as well. Make a bread machine sponge early, then finish the bread hours later for the maximum mystery in the flavor.

This bread is best baked on a stone. Although the baguette is a favorite shape, you may also make a 12-inch round, rolls, a *bâtard* or a *ficelle* (see pages 76 and 80). You may also bake this bread in your bread machine on the French Bread setting if you wish.

It's great with pâtés, fish, and seafood, or as an alternative to rye bread for sandwiches. The leftovers are also good broken up into soups and salads.

3 cups bread flour
1/2 cup rye flour
2 1/2 teaspoons bread machine yeast
1 1/4 cups water
2 teaspoons salt

In the bread machine pan, combine half the flours with all the yeast and half the water. Process on the dough setting. Let this sponge stand in the machine for 6 to 24 hours, then finish the bread.

Add the remaining flours, water, and the salt to the pan. Process on the dough setting (or on the French Bread setting if you wish to bake it in the machine). Remove the dough to a lightly floured surface and knead by hand for a few seconds. Form into a ball, cover with the bread machine pan, and let it rest for about 20 minutes.

Meanwhile, sprinkle a peel generously with cornmeal. With a cooking stone in place on the middle rack, preheat the oven to 450° F. for at least 30 minutes.

For baguettes, cut the dough in two equal pieces and roll into rectangles about 16 × 8 inches. Roll up into 16-inch-long baguettes (see page 75) and place on the peel to rise again, covered, in a warm, draft-free place. When the dough has almost doubled in bulk, make deep, diagonal slashes at a 45° angle in the tops of the loaves with a razor blade or a sharp knife. Mist with plain water and give the peel a trial shake to make sure the bread isn't sticking. (If it is, take a table knife and run it between the peel and the dough to free the bread from the peel.) Open the oven and shovel the bread onto the hot stone. Bake for 10 minutes, misting the oven 4 or 5 times with plain water (see page 74), then reduce the temperature to 375° F. and continue baking for 30 minutes more, or until the bread is evenly browned. The crust will be crisp and golden brown, the slashes will have opened up nicely, and the center of the bread will have irregular holes and be a nice tan color.

Remove the baguettes to a rack to cool. Store in brown paper bags.

BREAD AND CHEESE SOUP
Makes 4 servings
Make this soup using homemade broth
and the taste will sing.

6 cups defatted low-fat chicken broth
Salt and freshly ground
black pepper to taste
4 thick slices
Old-fashioned Bread, toasted
4 ounces Gruyère cheese, shredded

Bring the chicken broth to a boil and
season with salt and pepper.
Meanwhile, toast the bread, then break
it into pieces and divide it among 4 soup
bowls. Divide the shredded cheese
among the bowls, then ladle the hot
broth over all. Serve immediately.

PAIN DE CAMPAGNE
French Farm Bread

Dough Setting
Makes 1 large round loaf

One of the best ways to emulate a baker's brick oven is to bake in a Cloche (see page 73).

You can make an enormous, high-domed loaf of perfectly fragrant bread complete with a thick, crisp mahogany crust and a creamy sour center. This hearty, tangy sour bread is much like those made by the bakers of seventeenth-century France. Only they didn't have a bread machine to do the work. Unlike other claypots, La Cloche does not have to be soaked in water before you bake.

We made this loaf to take to a potluck by making the recipe twice using the dough setting. After the first batch was made, we put it in a Ziploc bag in the refrigerator and made the second. Then, we hand-kneaded the two batches together, formed a big round ball, and let it rise a second time in the Cloche. Finishing the loaf with a generous dusting of flour and cross-hatch marks, we baked it in the Cloche. For smaller gatherings, make the dough *once* on the dough setting and let it rise in the Cloche before baking, following the directions as stated below. The loaf you get will be smaller, but equally crunchy, creamy, and delicious.

If you don't have a Cloche, form the loaf into a round, raise it on parchment, finish as directed, and bake it directly on a stone preheated for 30 minutes in the lower third of the oven. The baking time required will be the same.

For a large loaf, make this recipe twice using the dough setting; for a medium loaf, make the recipe once.

1 teaspoon bread machine yeast

2 tablespoons gluten flour

1 cup whole wheat flour

1/2 cup medium rye flour

2 cups bread flour

1 tablespoon salt

1 cup plain low-fat yogurt, at room temperature

1/2 cup bread machine *poolish* (see page 57)

1 cup water

Process the first batch of dough on the dough setting, then re-move it to a Ziploc bag and refrigerate. Process the second batch on the dough setting, then hand-knead the two batches together and form into one large ball.

Dust the bottom of the Cloche generously with cornmeal and place the dough ball on the Cloche pan. Generously dust the top of the loaf with flour and let it rise, uncovered, for about 20 minutes. Cut a tic-tac-toe pattern in the top with a razor blade, making quick, sure slashes. Cover the Cloche and let the dough rise for 10 to 15 minutes more.

Meanwhile, preheat the oven to 450° F. Place the covered Cloche on the bottom rack of the oven and bake for 1 hour. The loaf will be golden brown and sound hollow when rapped on the bottom. Remove the Cloche from the oven. Re-move the lid and let the bread stand for 10 minutes on the rack in the pan before lifting it to a bare rack to cool com-pletely before cutting.

To cut a large round loaf, make one cut completely down through the bread, then turn the cut side down on the board and cut slices from each half.

BREAKFAST BREAD CUSTARD
Makes 6 servings

1/2 loaf day-old French or country bread
2 eggs
1 cup low-fat milk
1/2 teaspoon freshly ground black pepper
2 large dead-ripe tomatoes, sliced thick
1/2 cup chopped fresh cilantro
2 tablespoons grated Parmesan cheese

Cut the bread into thick slices, then arrange in a 7 × 10-inch ovenproof glass baking pan. Preheat the oven to 350° F. Whisk together the eggs and milk and season with the pepper. Arrange the tomato slices over the bread, then pour the egg-milk mixture over all. Sprinkle with the cilantro and top with the cheese. Bake for 35 minutes, or until the custard sets. Serve in squares, warm.

PAIN DE MIE
MADE EASY IN THE MACHINE

Basic Bread Setting
Makes one 1-pound loaf

Straight from the streets of France, where *pain de mie* is sold in every neighborhood *boulangerie*, comes our version of this famous sandwich and canapé bread. Traditionally made in a *pain de mie* mold or a bread pan with a tight-fitting lid, this bread has a characteristic close, even grain; a thin, crisp crust; and a velvety, soft white crumb. If your machine bakes in a tall, vertical rectangle, slice off the rounded top with an electric knife, and you will have a perfect rectangle of bread ready to use for tea sandwiches or canapés. Let the bread sit for 2 or 3 days and it will make thin, crisp melbas or croutons.

1 to 1$^1/_2$ teaspoons bread machine yeast
2 cups bread or all-purpose flour
$^1/_2$ cup semolina flour
1$^1/_2$ tablespoons sugar
1 teaspoon salt
$^1/_3$ cup instant nonfat dry milk solids
1 tablespoon unsalted butter, at room temperature
$^7/_8$ cup (1 cup minus 2 tablespoons) water

Combine all the ingredients in the bread machine pan. Process on the basic bread setting.

Remove the bread from the pan and cool on a rack. Wrap in a plastic bag or foil to store.

For one 1$^1/_2$-pound loaf

1$^1/_2$ to 2 teaspoons bread machine yeast
3$^1/_4$ cups bread or all-purpose flour
$^3/_4$ cup semolina flour
2 tablespoons plus 1 teaspoon sugar
1$^1/_2$ teaspoons salt
$^2/_3$ cup instant nonfat dry milk solids
2 tablespoons unsalted butter, at room temperature
1$^1/_4$ cups plus 3 tablespoons water

PESTO TORTA WITH TOMATOES

Makes 12 servings

3/4 cup minced sun-dried tomatoes in olive oil, drained
1/2 cup freshly grated Parmesan cheese
1/4 cup freshly grated Romano cheese
1 pound Neufchâtel (light cream cheese)
1/2 cup (1 stick) unsalted butter, softened
1/2 cup sour cream
3/4 cup prepared pesto

Lightly grease a 6-cup mold or bowl, then line the entire surface with plastic wrap. Place the minced sun-dried tomatoes on the bottom of the mold. Place the cheeses, butter, and sour cream in the bowl of a food processor fitted with the steel blade. Process until thoroughly mixed, about 60 seconds. Scrape down the sides of the bowl with a rubber spatula and pulse to mix again. Spoon half the cheese mixture into the mold over the tomatoes. Spread half of the pesto atop the cheese. Then spoon the remaining cheese mixture into the mold and spread it over the top. Spread with the remaining pesto and cover loosely with plastic wrap. Chill for 3 hours or, if you wish, freeze it at this point. It will keep frozen for up to a month. To unmold, remove the plastic wrap from the top, turn the mold upside down on a flat serving tray, carefully pull the mold away, then remove the wrap. Serve with toasted baguette slices or toasted slices of any country bread such as Italian Marketplace Bread (recipe follows).

ITALIAN MARKETPLACE BREAD

ROASTED RED PEPPER AND
BREAD SALAD

Makes 2 servings

Although you can buy roasted red peppers in a jar, if you'll take the time to roast them yourself, you'll like them even better. And this is one good way to use leftover Italian-style white or whole wheat bread.

4 cups French or Italian bread, cut into
1-inch cubes
2 tablespoons olive oil
1 red bell pepper
3 tablespoons drained capers
1 tablespoon fresh thyme leaves,
or 1 teaspoon dried
¼ cup chopped fresh basil leaves plus additional fresh basil leaves for garnish
1 large tomato, cut into wedges
2 green onions with tops, finely chopped
2 small inner ribs celery,
with leaves, chopped
½ cup pitted Kalamata olives

DRESSING

3 tablespoons olive oil
2 teaspoons balsamic vinegar
1 teaspoon Dijon mustard
Salt and freshly ground
black pepper to taste

Preheat the oven to 350° F.
Toss the bread cubes with the olive oil and arrange them in a single layer on a

Our version of this soulful bread is easy and full-flavored. The wheat berries add moisture and a nutritional boost. We like to start the sponge and cook both the wheat berries and the potato the first day. The wheat berries and potato can be held in the refrigerator up to 24 hours until ready to use. However, they will probably lose some moisture during their wait, and you may have to use more potato water to achieve a smooth, elastic, and slightly sticky dough. Check the dough after the first 10 minutes into the dough cycle and add extra potato water if necessary to get the right consistency.

This bread will serve you well as the base for Pesto Torta with Tomatoes (see box on page 105) or any crostini, bruschetta, or crouton that you would like to make with it. It is also excellent toasted for breakfast and served with a thin film of sweet butter and a blanket of honey.

SPONGE:
¾ teaspoon bread machine yeast
1 cup bread flour
½ cup plus 2 tablespoons water

DOUGH:
⅓ cup (about 3 ounces) boiled potato, cooled and slightly
mashed, potato water reserved
½ cup reserved potato water
¼ cup wheat berries, cooked in boiling water for
20 minutes, drained

2¼ cups bread flour

½ cup whole wheat flour

1½ teaspoons salt

Add the sponge ingredients to the bread machine pan and process until the sponge is well combined, about 5 minutes on most machines. Turn off the machine. Let the sponge sit in the machine for at least 12 hours or for as long as 18 hours.

Add the potato, potato water, wheat berries, bread flour, whole wheat flour, and salt to the sponge in the bread machine pan.

If you are using a 1-pound machine, mix and knead the ingredients on the dough setting. Turn off the machine and remove the dough from the bread machine pan to a lightly greased 3-quart plastic or glass bowl and cover with plastic wrap. Raise until tripled in bulk, 3 to 4 hours.

If you are using a 1½-pound machine, process the ingredients on the dough setting, turn off the machine, and let the dough rise in the machine for an additional hour or until tripled in bulk.

Meanwhile, cut a piece of parchment paper to match the dimensions of your baking stone or tiles. Place the parchment paper on a wooden peel or a rimless cookie sheet. Sprinkle cornmeal lightly over the parchment paper. (This bread can also be baked on a heavy baking sheet that has been lightly greased and sprinkled with cornmeal; however, a baking stone or tiles is preferred.)

After the dough has tripled in volume, scoop it out onto a lightly floured surface and knead for 1 minute. Form the dough into a tight ball by pulling the outside edge into the middle and then tucking it inside. Place the dough on the prepared peel or baking sheet. Cover with a tent of heavy-

baking sheet. Place both the bread and the bell pepper (on the oven rack) in the hot oven to roast. Stir the cubes a time or two, and toast until golden brown, about 5 minutes.

Remove to a salad bowl.

Turn the pepper as it blisters and blackens and continue to roast until it's blistered on all sides, about 15 minutes. Then, remove the pepper from the oven to a paper bag for about 10 minutes to sweat. Finally, holding the pepper over a bowl to catch the good juices, peel the skin off using your fingers and a knife. Discard the blackened skin, and the seeds. Cut the pepper into thin strips. Combine with the bread cubes in a bowl.

Add the capers, thyme, ¼ cup basil leaves, the tomato wedges, green onions, celery, and olives. Toss to mix. Whisk together the dressing ingredients in a small jar. Pour over the salad and toss to mix thoroughly.

Divide between 2 salad plates. Garnish with sprigs of fresh basil.

duty aluminum foil that is high enough so that it will not touch the dough as it rises. Raise the bread for 1 hour, or until doubled in bulk. Thirty minutes before the beginning of the estimated baking time, place a baking stone or tiles in the oven and preheat to 400° F.

When the dough has doubled in bulk, spray it with a fine mist of water. Open the oven door and carefully slide the parchment paper off the peel or cookie sheet onto the stone or tiles. (If you are baking the loaf on a baking sheet, merely slip it into the oven.) Spray the oven for 5 seconds with water (see page 74) and close the door. Bake the bread for 15 minutes, then carefully slide the parchment paper out from under the loaf. Bake for an additional 45 to 55 minutes, or until the crust is golden brown and the bread sounds hollow when tapped. Remove the bread to a rack and cool for at least 1 hour before serving.

MUFFULETTA

Makes 6 servings

This New Orleans sandwich originated early in the twentieth century.
Drippy but delicious. Heaven with *Pane all'Olio* (recipe follows).

1 cup chopped
pimiento-stuffed green olives
1 cup chopped Kalamata
or other black olives
$1/2$ cup fruity olive oil
One (4-ounce) jar pimientos, chopped
$1/2$ cup fresh parsley leaves,
cut fine with scissors
One (2-ounce) tin
anchovy fillets, minced
2 tablespoons drained capers
2 cloves garlic, peeled and minced
1 tablespoon minced fresh oregano,
or 1 teaspoon dried
Salt and freshly ground
black pepper to taste
2 rolled loaves *Pane all'Olio* (see page 110)
4 ounces thinly sliced Italian salami
4 ounces thinly sliced provolone
4 ounces thinly sliced mortadella

Combine the olives, oil, pimientos, parsley, anchovies, capers, garlic, and oregano.
Toss to mix, then season to taste with a tiny bit of salt and a lot of black pepper.
Cover and refrigerate overnight so the flavors will marry.
To serve, cut open the breads then pull out the centers leaving a $1/2$-inch-thick shell.
Drain the olive salad and spoon it into the cavities. Top with layers of salami, provolone, and mortadella.
Close the bread, wrap it in plastic wrap, and refrigerate for 30 minutes or so for up to 6 hours to marinate.
Cut the sandwiches into thick slices, spear each one with a bamboo skewer, and serve.
Don't forget to pass the paper napkins.

PANE ALL'OLIO
Italian Olive Oil Bread

Dough Setting
Makes 2 large rolls or 1 medium free-form round loaf

Make a sponge in the bread machine pan first, let it stand for 8 hours to overnight, then make the dough using the dough setting. Shape the dough into 2 cigar-shaped rolls or 1 round free-form loaf, raise and bake it on a stone. Don't be alarmed by the long cooking time. It helps develop the crisp, golden crust and the bread won't burn. Honest.

3 cups bread flour
2½ teaspoons bread machine yeast
1¼ cups warm water
1½ teaspoons salt
1½ teaspoons sugar
2 tablespoons fruity olive oil

In the bread machine pan, combine half the flour, all the yeast, and half the warm water. Process on the dough setting. Let the sponge sit in the bread machine for at least 8 hours or up to 24. Break the dough ball up into 4 pieces, put it back into the machine, and proceed to make the bread.

Add the remaining flour and water, the salt, sugar, and olive oil. Process on the dough setting.

At the end of the dough cycle, remove the dough to a lightly floured surface and knead by hand for a few seconds. Divide the dough into two pieces, cover with the bread machine pan, and let it rest for 5 minutes or so.

Preheat the oven with a stone in place on the middle rack for 30 minutes to 450° F. Sprinkle a peel generously with cornmeal. Now, shape each piece of dough into a cigar-shaped roll about 8 inches long, fat in the middle, and tapered at both ends. Alternately, make one round free-form loaf or a 12-inch cigar-shaped roll. Place the rolls on the peel for the final rising. Cover with plastic wrap and raise in a warm, draft-free place until the rolls are nearly doubled in bulk, about 1 hour.

Just before baking, make a single, deep slash at a 45° angle in the top of each loaf with a razor blade or sharp knife. Spritz the loaves with water. Give the peel a trial shake before you open the oven door, then pop the loaves onto the stone to bake.

Bake for 12 minutes at 450° F., spritzing the oven 5 or 6 times with water (see page 74), then reduce the temperature to 375° F. and continue baking for 40 minutes more. Remove the golden loaves immediately to cool on a rack. Store in brown paper.

BROTHER JUNIPER'S SANTA ROSA STRUAN

Basic Bread Setting
Makes one 1-pound loaf

Tucked away in the heart of Santa Rosa, California, is Brother Juniper's Bakery. The founder of Brother Juniper's Bakery is Brother Peter Reinhart, who graciously agreed to share this recipe with us. According to Brother Reinhart, Struan (pronounced "stroo un") can trace its roots back to Scotland. Brother Juniper's Struan is made from wheat, corn, oats, brown rice, and bran. We've made it a little easier by adapting his recipe to the bread machine, and we use Uncle Ben's Quick Brown Rice, which cooks in 6 minutes in the microwave instead of the 40 to 50 minutes required for traditional brown rice. If you don't have brown rice, don't fret, cooked white rice will work just fine or leftover rice from last night's stir-fry. Just don't eliminate the rice because it's inconvenient to cook. This recipe has no added fat, and it is, therefore, the rice that keeps the bread moist and fresh.

If you can't get to Santa Rosa to visit the bakery, pick up a copy of Brother Juniper's bread book, *Slow Rise as Method and Metaphor*, at your local bookstore. We're sure you'll enjoy every last crumb.

2 teaspoons bread machine yeast
2 cups bread flour
2 tablespoons uncooked polenta
2 tablespoons rolled oats
2 tablespoons brown sugar
2 tablespoons wheat bran

1 teaspoon salt

2 tablespoons cooked brown rice

1 tablespoon honey

¼ cup buttermilk

½ cup plus 1 tablespoon water (the amount of water will
vary according to the moistness of the rice)

Process the ingredients according to your manufacturer's instructions for a basic bread setting. This recipe was developed
using just-cooked rice. If your rice has been sitting in the refrigerator overnight, you may need an extra tablespoon or so
of water. (See page 5 for instructions on monitoring the moisture in bread doughs.) If your machine has a light crust setting, you might want to try it.

Remove the bread from the bread machine pan to a rack
to cool. Wrap to store in aluminum foil or in a clean, brown
paper bag.

For one 1½-pound loaf

2½ teaspoons bread machine yeast
3½ cups bread flour
¼ cup uncooked polenta
¼ cup rolled oats
¼ cup brown sugar
¼ cup wheat bran
2 teaspoons salt
¼ cup cooked brown rice
⅛ cup (2 tablespoons) honey
½ cup buttermilk
1 cup plus 2 tablespoons water (the
amount of water will vary according to
the moistness of the rice)

FRENCH BREAD FOR THE *BANNETON*

Dough Setting
Makes one 1½-pound loaf

The *banneton* is a basket either lined with canvas or one whose weave is coiled to look like a beehive (see page 73 on how to make your own *banneton*). These baskets enable the baker to handle long-risen wet doughs and keep the bread from losing its shape during the second rise.

When making French bread rounds, we recommend quickly inverting the risen bread from the *banneton* onto parchment paper before placing it on a baking stone or tiles. The parchment paper makes it easier for the baker to move the wet dough from the counter to the oven, and the wet dough ensures a chewy crust and bread with irregular holes. This spectacular white bread has a feathery white-floured top and tastes purely of wheat. Serve it in place of the traditional baguette, or it makes a beautiful gift.

SPONGE:
½ teaspoon bread machine yeast
½ cup bread flour
½ teaspoon malt syrup (also called barley malt syrup)
3 tablespoons water
⅓ cup milk

DOUGH:
3 cups bread flour
1 cup water
2 teaspoons salt

For the sponge, combine all the ingredients in the bread machine pan. Process on the dough setting until well mixed, about 5 minutes. The sides of the pan may need to be scraped down with a rubber spatula and the thin batter will have a few small lumps. Turn off the machine and allow the sponge to sit overnight or for at least 8 hours in the bread pan.

Add the dough ingredients to the sponge in the bread pan. Process on the dough setting.

If you are using a 1-pound machine, remove the dough from the bread pan, after it has been mixed and kneaded, to a lightly greased 12-inch bowl, cover with plastic wrap, and let rise in a warm place for 2½ to 3 hours, or until tripled in volume.

If you are using a 1½-pound machine, process the dough on the dough setting. It should triple in bulk and be very bubbly and blistered. Leave the dough in the machine or in a bowl to rest for an additional hour if this has not happened during the previous dough cycle.

While the dough rises, flour an 8-inch *banneton*. Wet your hands, gently deflate the risen dough, and shape it into a round loaf. Place in the *banneton* and cover with plastic wrap or a well-floured towel. Let it rise until it is fully doubled and a finger indention will not immediately disappear, about 1 hour. Thirty minutes before baking, heat the oven with a baking stone in place to 400° F. Right before baking, sprinkle the hot stone lightly with cornmeal. Carefully invert the loaf onto a 14-inch square of parchment paper and place it on the hot stone (the dough can also be baked directly on the stone without the parchment paper) and bake for 1 hour, or until the loaf sounds hollow when tapped on the bottom. Cool on a rack. This bread is best eaten the day it is baked.

PARMA'S BREAD AND CHEESE STUFFING

Makes 6 cups of stuffing

You say you have leftovers when you bake big country-style loaves! Try this easy and light stuffing to spread between the meat and skin of baking chicken breasts, to stuff into fresh zucchini that have been split and hollowed, or as a side dish with scallopini.

3 cups fresh bread chunks, crusts removed, from a firm-textured, country-style loaf
2 cups freshly grated Parmesan or Romano cheese
4 egg yolks
2 large eggs
½ teaspoon freshly grated nutmeg
Salt and freshly ground black pepper to taste

Grind the bread in the food processor until you have fine crumbs. Add the grated cheese, egg yolks, eggs, nutmeg, and salt and pepper to taste. Pulse several times until thoroughly mixed and smooth. Stuff this mixture into chicken breasts or hollowed vegetables. Alternatively, you can bake the stuffing in a buttered baking dish covered with aluminum foil in a 350° F. oven for 30 to 40 minutes. Serve as a side dish with scallopini or other veal dishes.

ENGLAND'S CHRISTMAS BREAD
OF 1942

Dough Setting
Makes one 1-pound loaf

Grandmother Collingwood was a nurse stationed in London during World War II. All of England was trying to make do with shortages and rationing. Fresh milk was scarce, as were sugar and flour. To fight the bleakness of the cold winter and the depression brought on by the war, one nurse at Grandmother's station brought in this bread on Christmas eve, and Grandmother served it back home in the States every Christmas eve until her death in 1990.

The original recipe called for 1/2 teaspoon ground cardamom, but, like the original bakers of this loaf, we were experiencing a shortage of our own; we had no cardamom and so we substituted 1 teaspoon finely minced dried orange peel.

Serve this bread instead of dinner rolls, or use it as the base for your favorite French toast recipe.

1 1/4 teaspoons bread machine yeast
2 1/4 cups bread flour or all-purpose flour
One (6-ounce) can evaporated milk
1/4 cup water
1 tablespoon plus 2 teaspoons sugar
1/2 teaspoon salt
1 tablespoon vegetable oil
1 teaspoon finely minced dried orange peel
1 egg whisked with 1 tablespoon water for glaze

Combine all the ingredients except the egg in the bread machine pan and place in the machine. Process according to the manufacturer's instructions for a dough setting. Meanwhile, lightly grease a large baking sheet and sprinkle it with cornmeal.

Remove the dough from the bread pan to a lightly floured surface and knead lightly to remove any remaining air bubbles.

Form the dough into a ball (divide the dough in half and form 2 balls if making the 2-pound recipe—see sidebar) and place the dough ball(s) on the prepared baking sheet. Flatten the dough ball(s) into a 6-inch circle.

Brush the top of the dough with the egg wash. Use a sharp knife to slash 3 shallow cuts on the top of the dough. Set to rise in a warm place until nearly doubled (40 to 50 minutes). Meanwhile, preheat the oven to 350° F.

Bake on the middle rack of the preheated oven for 40 minutes, or until the bread sounds hollow when tapped on the top. Cool on racks for 20 to 30 minutes and serve warm.

For two 1-pound loaves

2¹/₂ teaspoons bread machine yeast
4¹/₂ cups bread flour or all-purpose flour
One (12-ounce) can evaporated milk
¹/₂ cup water
3 tablespoons sugar
1 teaspoon salt
2 tablespoons vegetable oil
2 teaspoons finely minced
dried orange peel
1 egg whisked with 1 tablespoon water
for glaze

WHOLE-MEAL BREAD

Basic Bread Setting
Makes one 1-pound loaf

A rich, everyday bread you can make right in the bread machine. It's reminiscent of German *brots.* Throw the ingredients in the bread machine and hit the button. Later, it's perfect dinner bread. *Wunderbar.*

If your bread machine calls for 2 cups flour, make the 1-pound loaf. If your machine calls for 3 cups, you'll make the 1½-pound loaf (see sidebar).

2 teaspoons bread machine yeast
²/₃ cup bread flour
¼ cup gluten flour
1 cup whole wheat flour
¼ cup instant nonfat dry milk solids
½ teaspoon salt
¼ cup total of any one or a mixture of the following: rolled oats, sesame or poppy seeds, chopped nuts, raisins, or dates
½ teaspoon ground cinnamon
²/₃ cup warm water
1 tablespoon honey
⅓ cup plain nonfat yogurt

Place all the ingredients in the bread machine pan. Process according to the manufacturer's instructions for the basic bread setting.

Remove the bread to a rack to cool. Store in plastic wrap.

For one 1½-pound loaf

1 tablespoon bread machine yeast
1 cup bread flour
½ cup gluten flour
1½ cups whole wheat flour
½ cup instant nonfat dry milk solids
1 teaspoon salt
⅓ cup total of any or all of the following: sesame or poppy seeds, rolled oats, chopped nuts, raisins, or dates
¾ teaspoon ground cinnamon
1¼ cups warm water
2 tablespoons honey
½ cup plain nonfat yogurt

TOMATO GARLIC BREAD SOUP

Makes 4 servings

6 cloves garlic, peeled
1 tablespoon fruity olive oil plus more for garnish
1 red or yellow bell pepper, packed in vinegar, drained and chopped
1 pound fresh plum (Roma) tomatoes,
or one (1-pound) can tomatoes, chopped, with juice
Salt and freshly ground black pepper to taste
3 cups chicken broth
4 thick slices Whole-Meal or other country-style bread, toasted
Chopped fresh basil, for garnish
$1/2$ cup freshly grated Parmesan cheese

Mince 3 of the garlic cloves and place them in a cold 10-inch skillet.
Add the olive oil and heat. Sauté until the garlic begins to color, then add
the pickled pepper. Simmer a moment, then add the tomatoes and juice.
Season with salt and black pepper. Add the broth and simmer
for about 10 minutes. Correct seasonings if necessary.
While the broth simmers, cut the remaining garlic in half
and use it to rub the toast slices generously. Place a slice of toast
in the bottom of each of 4 soup bowls. Ladle the tomato broth
over the toast. Sprinkle with chopped basil and dust with
freshly grated cheese. Serve hot.
For a more substantial dish, poach 4 eggs in the tomato broth
and place an egg atop each piece of garlic bread in the soup.

CLASSIC BREAD MACHINE SOURDOUGH BREAD

Basic Bread Setting
Makes one 1-pound loaf

Regardless of which starter you choose, you can make a loaf of sourdough bread successfully in a bread machine. We've suggested a booster of bread machine yeast, just for insurance. If your starter is cold from the refrigerator, warm it to room temperature by placing it in the microwave for 10 seconds. For best results, use organic bread flour and spring water at room temperature.

2$^1/_2$ teaspoons bread machine yeast
2$^1/_2$ cups bread flour
1 teaspoon sugar
$^1/_2$ teaspoon salt
$^3/_4$ cup yogurt starter, at room temperature (see page 58)
$^1/_2$ cup plus 2 tablespoons water

Combine the ingredients in the bread machine pan and process on the basic bread setting. Watch the machine for the first 10 minutes. If the dough seems dry, or if the machine lugs, add water, a tablespoon at a time. If the dough is too wet, add flour by the tablespoon until you have a soft dough ball. Remove the bread promptly from the bread machine at the end of the baking cycle and cool it on a rack. Store in a paper bag.

For one 1$^1/_2$-pound loaf

2$^1/_2$ teaspoons bread machine yeast
3$^1/_2$ cups bread flour
2 teaspoons sugar
$^3/_4$ teaspoon salt
1 cup sourdough starter,
at room temperature
(see page 59)
1 cup water

POLENTA BREAD

Basic Bread Setting
Makes one 1-pound loaf

Lard is the fat of choice for this recipe, and before you throw the health book at us for choosing such a recipe, just let us say that lard has been the fat of choice for home bakers for centuries. Only in the last 50 years have we realized the health risks associated with too much saturated animal fat. We suggest moderation in all things, and that goes for lard in baked goods also. The lard in this recipe lends a smoky flavor to the bread and the polenta. A fine tender crumb, with the added crunch of the polenta, makes for a fine "sop" bread for spicy barbecue sauces, French stews, or salad dressings.

2 teaspoons bread machine yeast
2¹/₂ cups bread flour
¹/₃ cup polenta
¹/₂ teaspoon salt
2 tablespoons sugar
2 tablespoons lard or vegetable shortening
²/₃ cup milk
2 tablespoons water
1 large egg

Process the ingredients according to the manufacturer's instructions for a basic bread setting.

Remove the bread from the bread pan to cool on a rack. Wrap in aluminum foil or plastic wrap to store.

For one 1¹/₂-pound loaf

2¹/₂ teaspoons bread machine yeast
3¹/₂ cups bread flour
¹/₂ cup polenta
1 teaspoon salt
3 tablespoons sugar
3 tablespoons lard or vegetable
shortening
1 cup milk
¹/₈ cup water
1 large egg

COMO BREAD

Basic Bread Setting
Makes one 1-pound loaf

Como Bread originated around the lake and city of Como, which is in Lombardy in the north of Italy. It is one of the breads containing *biga*, the Italian yeast sponge. *Biga* doesn't create a sour flavor, but it does contribute an interesting texture and complex flavor. *Biga* needs to be made at least 10 hours before beginning to make the Como Bread, so you will need to plan ahead. This Como Bread can also be made using the dough setting, raised the second time in a *banneton*, and baked for 1 hour on a baking stone that has been preheated for 30 minutes in a 400° F. oven.

Sometimes we let this bread sit for 6 to 8 hours after removing it from the bread pan. This creates a crust more like that of a bread baked on a stone and allows the tender crumb to firm up a bit. Como is an all-purpose wheat bread suitable for the dinner table, sandwiches, or toast. *Ciabatta* (see page 183), another bread from the Como region, is richer than Como Bread because it contains both milk and oil.

1 cup water
1/3 cup Italian Winter *Biga* for Rolls and Wheat Breads (see page 60)
1/2 teaspoon bread machine yeast
2 cups bread flour
1/3 cup whole wheat flour
1 1/4 teaspoons salt

Pour the water and the *biga* into the bread machine pan. Using a rubber spatula, chop and mix the *biga* into the water until most of the long strands of gluten have been severed. Add the yeast, flours, and salt. Process the dough on the basic bread setting.

When the bread has finished baking, remove it from the machine to cool on a rack. For a thicker crust, let the bread sit, uncut, at room temperature for 6 to 8 hours.

For one 1½-pound loaf

1½ cups water
¾ cup Italian Winter *Biga* for Rolls and
Wheat Breads (see page 60)
1½ teaspoons bread machine yeast
3 cups bread flour
½ cup whole wheat flour
2 teaspoons salt

BRIAN DUPNIK'S
11-SEED AND GRAIN BREAD

Dough Setting or Basic Bread Setting
Makes one 1-pound loaf

We met Brian Dupnik while he was baking for Houston's Quilted Toque. He laid his breads out on a barn door they'd transformed into a table in the middle of the restaurant. If you strolled in about midafternoon when the sun was shining in sideways through the clerestory windows and gazed upon the heaps of artisanal loaves, it took your breath away. One of his favorites was this 11-Seed and Grain Bread. Brian began with grains and seeds he mixed by hand in a big plastic bucket before tossing them into the big Hobart mixer.

You can shortcut this process by beginning with a commercial 7-grain whole-grain cereal. We buy ours in bulk at the natural foods store. Look for Arrowhead Mills or other reliable brands. This will give you a mixture that may include wheat and rye flakes, triticale, barley, sunflower seeds, white wheat, and sesame seeds. Then poke through your own larder and add other seeds and grains until you have a total of $1/3$ or $1/2$ cup, depending upon whether you're making this bread in a 1-pound machine or a $1^1/2$ pounder. We prefer to bake this free-form on a stone, brushing the top with an egg wash, sprinkling it with sesame seeds, and slashing it 3 times across the top. That makes the most glamorous of the artisanal-type loaves. But, for ease, just make it start to finish in the bread machine. You'll find it's heaven when toasted.

By the way, don't worry if your additions don't add up to 11. It's not so important that you add 11 different grains and seeds to the loaf as it is that the volume be accurate.

⅓ cup seed/grain mixture (a combination from these
   choices: sesame, poppy, caraway or fennel seeds, barley,
   triticale, wheat berries, steel-cut oats, and/or polenta)
   soaked in ⅓ cup boiling water for about 15 minutes

1¾ teaspoons bread machine yeast

3 tablespoons yellow cornmeal

⅔ cup whole wheat flour

2 tablespoons rye flour

1⅔ cups bread flour

¾ teaspoon salt

1 tablespoon honey

1 tablespoon molasses

¾ cup water

1 egg beaten with 1 teaspoon water for egg wash

Be sure the water has been fully absorbed by the seeds and
grains. While they soak, combine the yeast, cornmeal, flours,
salt, honey, molasses, and water in the bread machine pan.
Process on the dough cycle, adding the soaked seeds after 10
minutes or so. Or, if you wish, process on the basic bread setting and let the machine do the work.

   Once the dough cycle is complete, turn the bread out
onto a lightly floured surface. Punch it down, then form the
dough into a tight ball and turn the bread machine pan on
top of it to rest for 15 to 30 minutes.

   While the dough rests, preheat the oven to 400° F. Spritz
a baking sheet with cooking spray or cover the sheet with
parchment. Form the dough into an 8-inch round loaf. Let it
rise on the baking sheet until nearly doubled in bulk, then
finish with the egg wash. Top with a sprinkling of steel-cut
oats, and bake in the preheated oven until the loaf is golden
brown and done through, about 40 minutes.

For one 1½-pound loaf

½ cup seed/grain mixture
soaked in ½ cup boiling water
for 15 minutes
2 teaspoons bread machine yeast
¼ cup yellow cornmeal
1 cup whole wheat flour
2 cups bread flour
3 tablespoons rye flour
1 teaspoon salt
2 tablespoons honey
1 tablespoon molasses
1 cup water
1 egg beaten with 1 teaspoon water for
egg wash (if using the dough setting)

PANE ALL'UVA
Raisin Bread

Basic Bread Setting
Makes one 1-pound loaf

In this book there are a lot of breads made on the dough setting; however, when you are really pressed for time and are looking for a wonderful bread made totally in the machine, try this Italian favorite bursting with raisins.

Try using the raisin bread setting if your machine has one; if not, let the machine knead in the raisins during the very last 3 minutes of the last kneading cycle. Most machines come with time charts detailing the length of each cycle. If you're still not sure when to add the raisins, wait until the dough has completely finished mixing and kneading, then remove the dough and knead in the raisins by hand. Return the dough to the bread machine pan and let it continue rising. Don't shut off the machine when you remove the dough or the cycle will begin all over.

²/₃ cup plus 2 tablespoons water
¹/₃ cup Italian Winter *Biga* for Rolls and Wheat Breads
   (see page 60)
¹/₂ teaspoon bread machine yeast
1³/₄ cups plus 2 tablespoons bread flour
¹/₃ cup whole wheat flour
1 teaspoon salt
¹/₂ cup moist raisins

Pour the water and the *biga* into the bread machine pan. Using a rubber spatula, chop and mix the *biga* into the water until most of the long strands of gluten have been severed. Add the yeast, flours, and salt. Process the dough on the basic bread setting or the raisin bread setting.

Let the machine knead in the raisins during the last 3 minutes of its last kneading cycle—about 20 to 30 minutes into the cycle.

When the bread has finished baking, remove it to a rack to cool. For a crustier crust, let the bread sit, uncut, at room temperature for 6 to 8 hours.

For one 1¹/₂-pound loaf

1¹/₃ cups water
¹/₂ cup Italian Winter *Biga* for Rolls and
Wheat Breads (see page 60)

³/₄ teaspoon bread machine yeast
2³/₄ cups bread flour
¹/₂ cup whole wheat flour
1¹/₂ teaspoons salt
²/₃ cup moist raisins

SWEET BUTTER LOAVES
FROM THE SOUTH OF FRANCE

Dough Setting
Makes 8 small loaves

These small, torpedo-shaped loaves, split down the middle, make a classy sidekick to the best country stew or European salad. Actually, we like them at breakfast, lunch, and dinner.

2^1/$_2$ teaspoons bread machine yeast
^{1}/$_2$ cup plus 3 tablespoons milk
2^1/$_2$ cups bread flour
^{1}/$_3$ cup light cream
^{1}/$_4$ cup (^{1}/$_2$ stick) unsalted butter, at room temperature
^{1}/$_2$ teaspoon salt

Add the yeast, milk, and 1 cup of the flour (2 cups for the 1^1/$_2$-pound recipe) to the bread machine pan. Process the ingredients on the dough setting until well mixed, about 5 minutes. The sides of the pan may need to be scraped down with a rubber spatula and the thin batter will have a few small lumps. Turn off the machine and allow the sponge to sit for at least 2 hours or overnight if possible.

Add the remaining 1^1/$_2$ cups flour (3 cups flour for the 1^1/$_2$-pound recipe), the cream, butter, and salt. Process on the dough setting (on the 1^1/$_2$-pound machine, process just until the ingredients have been mixed and kneaded, about 20 minutes, and then turn the dough out into a 3-quart, lightly greased large bowl, cover loosely with plastic wrap, and let rise for a total of 3 hours). After the 1-pound machine has finished its dough setting, let the dough rest in the bread machine for an additional hour. Meanwhile, lightly grease a large baking sheet (2 large baking sheets for the 1½-pound machine).

Divide the dough into 8 (16 for the 1½-pound recipe) equal-sized balls. Roll each ball into a cylinder as long as the hand is wide. With the side of your hand, hit the dough lengthwise down the middle, fold it over, and pinch the seam to close. Pinch the ends if necessary to make the traditional torpedo shape (see page 81). The loaves should be about 6 to 7 inches long. Place seam side down on the baking sheet. Cover with a floured cloth and allow the dough to rise until doubled in bulk, about 1 hour. While the dough rises, preheat the oven to 400° F.

With a sharp razor blade or a very thin sharp knife, make a ¼-inch-deep slash down the length of each loaf. Bake on the middle rack of the preheated oven for 30 to 35 minutes, or until nicely browned and firm. Both the top and middle shelves can be used when using 2 baking sheets. Just remember to switch the baking sheets midway through the baking period for even baking and browning.

Remove the loaves from the baking sheet to a rack to cool. Serve immediately.

For 16 small loaves

5 teaspoons bread machine yeast
1⅓ cups milk
5 cups bread flour
⅔ cup light cream
8 tablespoons (1 stick) unsalted butter, at
room temperature
1 teaspoon salt

PAIN AUX NOIX
Nut Bread

Dough Setting
Makes 2 equilateral triangles about 8 inches on the side

A triangular-shaped bread imbedded with hazelnuts and dusted with flour. The rich taste comes from the hazelnuts that are shot through the loaf. Alternatively, you can bake this bread in the bread machine on the basic or raisin bread setting, adding the nuts after the first kneading.

1½ teaspoons bread machine yeast
1¼ cups bread flour
1 cup whole wheat flour
¾ teaspoon sugar
⅓ teaspoon salt
1½ teaspoons butter
⅞ cup water
½ cup chopped hazelnuts
    plus 8 whole hazelnuts for the tops

If you have a 1½-pound machine, make 3 triangles.

2 teaspoons bread machine yeast
2¼ cups bread flour
1 cup whole wheat flour
1 teaspoon sugar
¾ teaspoon salt
1 tablespoon butter
1⅜ cups water
¾ cup chopped hazelnuts
plus 12 whole hazelnuts for the tops

Process all the ingredients except the hazelnuts in the bread machine pan on the dough setting. Once the cycle is complete, remove the dough to a lightly floured surface. Punch it down, knead in the chopped hazelnuts by hand, and form the dough into a tight ball. Rest the dough under the bread machine pan for 15 minutes.

Preheat the oven to 375° F., preferably with a stone on the middle shelf. Divide the dough into two equal pieces. Shape into 2 flat triangles, about 6 inches to the side and ¾ inch thick. Place the dough on a parchment-covered baking sheet or a peel, and set it aside to rise until almost doubled in bulk, about 40 minutes. Embed the tops of each bread with a row of whole hazelnuts down the middle. Lay a ruler over the nuts, then dust with flour. Remove the ruler and bake in the hot oven until the bread is golden brown and done, 25 to 30 minutes.

Pain aux Noix: Lay a ruler over the nuts...

... then dust with flour

RAISIN LOAF WITH A BUTTERMILK CRUMB

Dough Setting
Makes two ¹/₂-pound loaves

Diana's children love this naturally sweet loaf, which, by the way, has no added fat. A healthy and nutritious snack, bursting with big, fat juicy raisins that is good plain—or toasted, buttered, and sprinkled with a little confectioners' sugar.

SPONGE:
¹/₄ teaspoon bread machine yeast
¹/₃ cup plus 2 tablespoons water
¹/₃ cup bread flour
¹/₄ cup plus 2 tablespoons whole wheat flour

DOUGH:
¹/₄ teaspoon bread machine yeast
²/₃ cup water
1¹/₄ cups whole wheat flour
1¹/₂ cups bread flour
³/₄ cup buttermilk, at room temperature
1 tablespoon honey
1¹/₂ teaspoons salt
1¹/₂ cups moist raisins (currants can be substituted for the raisins if you wish)

For the sponge, add the yeast, water, and flours to the bread machine pan. Process the ingredients on the dough setting until well mixed, about 5 minutes. You may need to scrape down the sides and bottom of the pan with a rubber spatula. Turn off the machine and allow the sponge to sit in the bread pan for 10 hours or overnight.

To make the dough, stir and break up the sponge with a rubber spatula. Add the yeast and water and stir for an additional 2 minutes with the spatula. Add the flours, buttermilk, honey, and salt. Process on the dough setting until mixed and kneaded thoroughly, about 20 minutes on most machines. Turn off the machine and, if you are using a 1-pound machine, lightly mist a smooth work surface with water and remove the dough from the bread pan to it. Wet your hands and sprinkle the dough with the raisins. Knead the raisins in thoroughly. Place the dough in a large bowl, cover with plastic wrap, and let it rise in a warm place for about 2 hours.

If you are using a 1¹/₂-pound machine, turn off the machine and add the raisins to the bread pan. Turn the machine back on the dough setting and let it thoroughly knead in the raisins, 5 to 7 minutes. Turn off the machine and let the dough rise in the machine until it is doubled in bulk, about 2 hours.

While the dough rises, line a peel or a rimless cookie sheet with parchment paper. Lightly mist a smooth work surface with water, and with wet hands turn the dough out onto it. Knead the dough several times to remove any air bubbles and divide it in half. With the palm of your hand, flatten each piece into a rectangle about 12 × 6 inches. Starting with the long side, roll the rectangle into a cylinder. With the side of your palm, hit the dough lengthwise down the middle, pinch the seam to close, and roll over. Pinch the ends if necessary to make the traditional *bâtard* shape (see page 76).

Place the *bâtards* on the parchment paper and sift several tablespoons of flour over the tops. Cover with plastic wrap

RISIN' RAISIN ROLLS

Raisin Loaf with a Buttermilk Crumb
can also be made into 12 to 14
round rolls and baked on a stone in a
425° F. oven for 15 to 20 minutes.
For a real breakfast treat,
try rolling hot, just-baked rolls
(or leftover rolls that have been reheated
in a 350° F. oven for 6 minutes) in a
cinnamon-and-sugar mixture.

and let rise in a warm place for 30 minutes. Remove the plastic wrap and, with a sharp razor or a knife, slit the loaves straight down the middle, going no deeper than $\frac{1}{2}$ inch. Cover with plastic wrap and allow to rise again in a warm place for an hour or so, or until the loaves are $1\frac{1}{2}$ times the original size. Meanwhile, preheat the oven with a baking stone in place on the middle shelf to 450° F. for 30 minutes.

Giving a quick jerk of the peel or the baking sheet, slide the breads with the parchment paper onto the baking stone. Quickly spray the oven floor with several squirts of water to create steam (see page 74). Close the door immediately. Repeat the spraying twice more during the first 10 minutes. Bake the bread at 450° F. for a total of 20 minutes, then reduce the heat to 400° F. and bake for an additional 20 minutes. The breads should sound hollow when struck with your knuckle after 40 minutes; if not, continue baking for an additional 5 minutes. Remove the breads to a rack to cool, pulling off any parchment paper that may have stuck to the bottoms of the loaves.

CHICKEN POTAGE

Makes 10 to 12 servings

Add challah (see next page) to "Jewish penicillin" and you get a cure-all that will make you wish you could fake being sick just once and head for the bed to claim your own treatment. The silky smooth puree added to Mama's favorite recipe elevates this homely soup into a sublime treatment.

4 quarts cold water
1 large chicken
1 turkey wing
6 cloves garlic, peeled and mashed
1 large yellow onion, sliced
2 medium carrots, peeled and cut into thick rounds
1 medium turnip, peeled and quartered
2 ribs celery, with leaves, cut in pieces
1/2 cup fresh parsley leaves
1 bay leaf
Salt and freshly ground black pepper to taste
12 ounces fresh or dried egg noodles

Bring the water to a boil in a large soup pot. Add the whole chicken, turkey wing, garlic, onion, carrots, turnip, celery, parsley, and bay leaf. Simmer for about 3 hours, skimming from time to time. About 2 hours into the cooking, taste and adjust the seasoning with salt and black pepper. Discard the bay leaf. Lift all the vegetables from the broth to a food processor fitted with the steel blade. Puree and reserve. Remove the chicken and the turkey wing from the broth. Skim any floating fat from the broth and discard. Skin and debone the chicken, reserving the meat. Discard the skin, bones, and the turkey wing. Return the chicken meat to the soup. Raise the heat to a simmer, add the noodles, and cook *al dente,* about 3 minutes for fresh, up to 8 minutes for dried. Add the vegetable puree to the soup and stir to mix thoroughly. Adjust the seasoning with salt and pepper. Serve warm in big soup bowls.

CHALLAH

Dough Setting
Makes 1 large braided loaf

The traditional Jewish Sabbath bread is trouble-free when made using the bread machine. Make a sponge in the bread machine, let it stand for 8 to 24 hours, then finish the bread on the dough setting. You'll be able to work with a wetter dough, which will guarantee a light, airy, tender, rich bread.

3 cups bread flour
1 teaspoon sugar
1 tablespoon bread machine yeast
1 cup water
1 large egg
1/2 teaspoon salt
2 tablespoons unsalted butter or margarine
1 egg yolk whisked into 2 tablespoons spring water
    for glaze
Sesame seeds or poppy seeds for sprinkling on top

Add half the flour, the sugar, yeast, and water to the bread machine pan. Process on the dough setting. Let this sponge stand for 8 to 24 hours before making the bread.

Add the remaining flour, the egg, salt, and butter to the bread machine pan. Process on the dough setting. When the cycle is complete, remove the dough to a lightly floured surface and knead by hand for a few seconds. Cover the dough with the bread machine pan and let it stand for 10 minutes or so.

Divide the dough into 3 equal pieces and roll each piece into a 16-inch-long strip that's about 1 inch in diameter. Place the first piece on a parchment-covered baking sheet. Lay the other two pieces diagonally over the first, forming a spoke pattern. Form the three pieces into a fat braid (see page 77), beginning in the middle and braiding outward to each end. Tuck the ends under neatly. Cover with plastic wrap and set aside in a warm, draft-free place to rise until almost doubled in bulk.

While the dough rises, preheat the oven to 350° F. Just before baking, brush the top of the loaf with the egg wash. Sprinkle generously with sesame or poppy seeds, and bake on the middle rack of the preheated oven until the challah is a luscious golden color, 40 to 50 minutes. Cool on a rack and store in plastic wrap.

IRISH SODA BREAD

Dough Setting
Makes one 8-inch round, free-form loaf

Classic soda bread calls for nothing more than baking soda to leave the bread. We like the results better when we make this loaf in the bread machine and use a teaspoon or so of yeast to boost the rise. The soda taste is balanced by the sweetness of currants and the bite of caraway seeds. Serve this bread alongside corned beef and Colcannon (see page 139) for a fine St. Patrick's Day celebration.

2 cups bread flour
1 cup whole wheat flour
$\frac{1}{4}$ cup powdered buttermilk
2 tablespoons cornmeal
$1\frac{1}{2}$ teaspoons salt
$\frac{1}{2}$ teaspoon baking soda
1 cup water
1 large egg
2 tablespoons molasses
1 tablespoon honey
2 tablespoons butter
$1\frac{3}{4}$ teaspoons bread machine yeast
$\frac{3}{4}$ cup currants
1 tablespoon caraway seeds

Combine flours, buttermilk, cornmeal, salt, baking soda, water, egg, molasses, honey, butter, and yeast in the bread machine pan and process on the dough setting. Add the currants and caraway seeds just before the final kneading. Remove from the pan, punch down, turn the bread machine pan over the dough, and let it rest for 15 minutes.

Cover a baking sheet with parchment paper. Punch the dough down, and form it into an 8-inch circle, slightly flattened. Place the disk on the parchment paper. Cover with plastic wrap and let it rise until nearly doubled in bulk, about 1 hour.

Preheat the oven to 375° F. Place the rack in the middle of the oven. Cut a large X into the top of the dough with a razor blade. Bake for 15 minutes, then reduce the oven temperature to 350° F. and continue to bake for an additional 15 minutes, or until brown and done through. Serve warm. Store in plastic wrap.

COLCANNON

Makes 8 servings

In Ireland, Colcannon is traditionally served for Halloween. A gold ring, a sixpence, a thimble, and a button are hidden in the dish. The person who finds the ring will be married within the year; the sixpence means wealth; the thimble means spinsterhood; and the button goes to the bachelor.

8 medium russet potatoes, peeled
1 head green cabbage or kale
3/4 cup milk
6 to 8 tablespoons butter
Salt and freshly ground
black pepper to taste

Boil the potatoes in water to cover until tender, about 20 minutes. Quarter the cabbage or kale, wash carefully to remove any sand, then steam it until tender, about 12 minutes.
Once the potatoes are tender, drain them and mash with the milk, butter, and salt and pepper. Stir the steamed cabbage or kale into the potatoes. Now's when you add the gold ring, the coin, the thimble, and the button if you wish. Serve hot and be sure there's a bachelor, a single woman or two, and a few people who could use more money in the party.

GREEK BREAD

Dough Setting
Makes one 10-inch round, free-form loaf

This aromatic loaf, lovely mahogany colored and studded with nuts and seeds, makes a good home for strong cheeses or an accompaniment to Ruby Chicken (see sidebar). Your kitchen will be perfumed, your guests delighted.

2½ teaspoons bread machine yeast
2½ cups bread flour
½ cup instant nonfat dry milk solids
1¼ teaspoons salt
¾ cup water
1 tablespoon mild honey
1 large egg
2 tablespoons unsalted butter or margarine

TOPPING:
⅓ cup freshly grated Parmesan cheese
⅓ cup walnut pieces
2 tablespoons sesame seeds
1 teaspoon aniseseed
¼ teaspoon ground ginger
1 large egg, whisked until frothy

In the bread machine pan, combine the yeast, flour, dry milk, salt, water, honey, egg, and butter. Process on the dough setting.

When the cycle is completed, turn the dough out onto a lightly floured surface and knead a moment or two. Form

RUBY CHICKEN

Makes 6 servings

Easy enough for every day, fancy enough for company. Served with a salad of baby greens, Greek Bread, and a bold red wine, this chicken dish makes a memorable summer dinner.

3 tablespoons unsalted butter
1 tablespoon olive oil
6 skinless chicken breast halves, rib bones left in
3 shallots, minced
½ cup raspberry vinegar
1 tablespoon tomato paste
2 medium tomatoes, finely chopped
½ cup chicken broth
¼ cup cassis liqueur
¾ cup fresh raspberries, for garnish
2 tablespoons chopped fresh chives, for garnish

into a ball and turn the bread pan over the dough to rest for 5 minutes. Now, form the dough into an 8-inch, high, round loaf and place it on a parchment-covered baking sheet. Let the dough rise in a warm, draft-free place until almost doubled in bulk.

Preheat the oven to 350° F. Mix the topping ingredients in a small bowl. Just before baking the bread, spoon the topping onto the loaf. Bake on the middle rack of the preheated oven until the loaf is golden brown and done, about 30 minutes.

Cool on the parchment paper on a rack. Store in plastic wrap. Properly stored, this bread keeps up to a week.

In a 12-inch nonstick skillet, heat 2 tablespoons of the butter and the oil until the butter foams. Add the chicken breasts, meat side down. Cook for 5 minutes, or until golden brown, then turn and cook for 5 more minutes. Add the shallots, turn the heat down, and cook for 10 minutes. Transfer the chicken to a warm platter and reserve.

Pour the vinegar into the pan and bring it to a boil. Boil hard for 2 minutes, then stir in the tomato paste, tomatoes, chicken broth, and cassis liqueur. Simmer, stirring from time to time, until the sauce thickens slightly, about 5 minutes. Swirl in the remaining tablespoon of butter to finish the sauce. Replace the chicken pieces in the pan and turn them in the sauce several times to coat well. Cover and cook for 10 minutes over low heat.

To serve, arrange the chicken pieces on a platter and pour the sauce over them. Sprinkle with the fresh raspberries and chopped chives.

KALAMATA BREAD

Dough Setting
Makes one 12-inch round loaf

Use your bread machine to make a sponge, and you can let it ferment right in the bread machine for up to 2 days. Every day you are able to wait enhances the flavor of the bread. But, as with many flavored breads, this one tastes quite good if you bake it the same day you start. The loaf will be close-grained and aromatic, and with swirls of purplish black Kalamata olives throughout.

SPONGE:
1½ cups water
1 cup bread flour
1 cup rye flour
1 teaspoon bread machine yeast

DOUGH:
1 teaspoon salt
2½ cups bread flour
¼ cup olive oil
1 cup chopped Kalamata olives

Prepare the sponge by combining water with the flours and yeast in the bread machine pan. Process on the dough setting. Allow the sponge to rest in the closed bread machine for up to 2 days before finishing the bread.

To prepare the bread dough, add the salt, bread flour, and oil to the sponge in the pan. Process on the dough setting again. Once the dough setting has finished, turn the soft dough out onto a lightly floured surface and flatten into a rough 12-inch round. Press the olives into the surface. Roll the dough from the edges to the center to form into a round shape, then press down to flatten slightly. Rub flour into the surface of the bread. Let rise, covered, on a sheet of parchment paper until nearly doubled in bulk.

Preheat the oven, with a stone in place in the bottom third, to 375° F. for 30 minutes. Using a razor blade, make quick tic-tac-toe slices in the top of the round bread, or if you prefer a baguette shape, cut diagonal slashes on a long loaf. If you wish, brush on an egg white wash (see page 83). Use a peel to shovel the raised dough onto the hot stone. Bake until browned and done, 30 to 40 minutes.

Cool thoroughly on a rack before cutting.

6

DARK BREADS

Whole Wheat Fruit Crescents
German-Style Whole Wheat Bread
German Onion Bread
Polenta-Millet Bread
Whole Wheat–Walnut Bread
A Rustic Round of Whole Wheat and Walnuts
Pain au Citron
French Countryside Whole-Grain Bread for the *Banneton*
Pain Méteil
Jewish Rye Bread
Danish Rye Sourdough
Sour Rye Bread
Walnut, Mozzarella, and Fennel Crown Bread
Raisin Pumpernickel
Verterkake
Russian Black Bread with Sprouted Rye Berries

WHOLE WHEAT FRUIT CRESCENTS

Dough Setting
Makes a dozen crescent rolls or
1 large crescent-shaped bread

Begin with a mound of German-Style Whole Wheat Bread dough that has been through 2 dough cycles. Use one or more of the fruits listed, taking care that you have a total of 2 cups fresh and/or dried. You can also experiment with other fruits of your choice: dried peaches, cranberries, raisins, or a combination of fruits, or fruits and nuts.

This year for Christmas, we mixed chopped apples, pears, dried cranberries, and pecans for a fruit filling that we scented with a light dusting of cinnamon and nutmeg. We made Christmas Crescents that we then decorated with 3 dried cranberries and a fingernail sliver of red-skinned apple for festive St. Nicholas Breakfast Rolls.

½ cup dried apricots
½ cup dried pitted prunes
½ cup peeled and cored apple
½ cup peeled and cored pear
1 tablespoon fresh lemon juice
1 large loaf recipe German-Style Whole Wheat Bread
    dough (see page 150)
1 egg beaten with 1 teaspoon water for glaze
Granulated sugar to sprinkle on top (optional)

Chop the fruits coarsely and toss with the lemon juice, then cover and set aside while the whole wheat bread dough is being made in the bread machine pan on the dough setting. (Remember to run the dough cycle twice.)

Place a tablespoon of fruit on one half of each oval...

For rolls, punch the dough down, then divide it into 12 equal pieces. Using a rolling pin, roll each piece out into an oval shape with the middle thinner than the edges.

Place a tablespoon of fruit on one half of each oval. Using a pastry brush, moisten the edges of the rolls with water, then fold the oval into a crescent shape and press the edges shut.

Turn the rolls over onto a parchment-paper-covered baking sheet. Brush the rolls with the egg wash. Score the top of each roll with crescent cuts, then finish each bread with a piece of fruit that corresponds with the fruit inside.

Cover the rolls with waxed paper and set them aside to rise until almost doubled in bulk, about 40 minutes.

Preheat the oven to 450° F. Just before baking, sprinkle the tops of the rolls with sugar, if desired.

Bake the rolls in the preheated oven until done, about 20 minutes. Spritz the oven with clear water 2 or 3 times during the first 10 minutes of baking (see page 74). The rolls will be golden brown. Cool on a rack.

To make one large crescent-shaped, fruit-filled bread, roll the prepared dough into an oval shape about 14 × 10 inches. Place the oval on a parchment-paper-covered baking sheet. Cover half of the oval with fruit, leaving a 1-inch margin. Use a pastry brush to brush the edges of the loaf with water, then fold over and pinch the edges shut, forming a large crescent. Brush the bread with the egg wash. Score the top with crescent-shaped cuts, then finish the bread with a piece of fruit that corresponds with the fruit inside. For example, cut a pear half into thin slices, leaving the stem end in place, and fan out the slices atop the bread. Cover the bread with waxed paper and set it aside to rise until almost doubled in bulk, about 40 minutes. Preheat the oven to 450° F. Just before baking, sprinkle the top with sugar then bake on the middle rack of the preheated oven until golden brown, 30 to 35 minutes. Cool on a rack.

... and fold the oval into a crescent shape

GERMAN-STYLE
WHOLE WHEAT BREAD

Dough Setting–followed by the Basic Bread Cycle
or another Dough Setting for a free-form loaf
Makes one 1-pound loaf

Here's a lovely, light whole wheat bread that we like to make using King Arthur's White Whole Wheat flour (see page 310). This flour gives a nutty whole wheat taste without being too heavy. If you can't find it, try to use a "light" whole wheat flour. The darker the flour, the denser the bread will be.

Double kneading this or any other whole wheat bread dough will give this type of flour a better chance to absorb water and give you a lighter loaf.

You can, if you wish, bake this bread in the machine. To do this, you simply turn the machine on the dough setting first, then reset to the basic bread setting and the bread will get that extra kneading it requires to become a high, light loaf. If your bread machine has a whole wheat bread setting–which allows for a longer kneading period–you can eliminate the first dough cycle and just add the ingredients and process on this setting.

This is a perfect dough to use for fruit breads as well (see page 284). Fold in apricots, apples, prunes, or pears for a fine breakfast bread.

1 cup warm water
2^1/$_2$ cups light whole wheat flour
2 tablespoons bread flour
1 tablespoon gluten flour
1^1/$_4$ tablespoons instant nonfat dry milk solids

1 teaspoon salt
1¹/₂ tablespoons unsalted butter
1¹/₄ tablespoons mild honey
2 tablespoons molasses
1¹/₂ teaspoons bread machine yeast

Place all the ingredients in the bread machine pan and process on the dough setting. When the cycle is completed, reset—either to the dough setting again, if you wish to form the loaf into a free-form round, or to the basic bread setting, if you wish to bake it in the bread machine.

If you wish to shape the loaf yourself, remove it from the pan after the second dough cycle is completed, punch it down, and form it into an 8-inch round. Place the round on a peel that's generously sprinkled with cornmeal. Rub flour over the top of the dough. Cover with waxed paper and set the dough aside to rise until almost doubled in bulk, about 1 hour.

Preheat the oven with a stone in place to 450° F. for 30 minutes. Once the dough has risen to almost double in bulk, score the top of the loaf with a razor blade in moon crescents, making quick, sure, curved cuts, until you have about 5 arcs across the top of the bread. Give the loaf a trial shake on the peel, then quickly slide it onto the hot stone and bake until done, 30 to 35 minutes. Spritz the oven with cool water 2 or 3 times during the first 10 minutes of baking (see page 74). When done, the crust should be a deep brown and the loaf should sound hollow when tapped. Cool on a rack.

Whole wheat bread keeps well because the bran in the flour holds moisture.

For one 1¹/₂-pound loaf

1²/₃ cups warm water
3³/₄ cups light whole wheat flour
3 tablespoons bread flour
1¹/₂ tablespoons gluten flour
2 tablespoons instant nonfat dry milk solids
1¹/₂ teaspoons salt
2 tablespoons unsalted butter
2 tablespoons mild honey
1 tablespoon molasses
2¹/₈ teaspoons bread machine yeast

GERMAN ONION BREAD

Dough Setting
Makes 6 large horseshoe-shaped rolls

Using the bread machine dough setting, you can create a sponge that complicates the taste of the wheat bread. Flavor these rolls with sautéed onions, form them into horseshoes, and you'll have a classic German rustic bread that begs for sausage and beer.

ONION SEASONING:
3 cups thinly sliced yellow onions
1 teaspoon sugar
3/4 teaspoon salt
2 tablespoons vegetable oil
1 tablespoon butter

SPONGE:
2 1/2 teaspoons bread machine yeast
1 cup whole wheat flour
2 tablespoons brown sugar
1/4 cup 2 percent milk
1 cup water
2 tablespoons butter

DOUGH:
1 1/2 teaspoons salt
2 cups bread flour

To make the seasoning, sauté the onions, sugar, and salt in the oil and butter over medium heat, stirring occasionally until golden brown. Set the onions aside to cool.

To make the sponge, combine the sponge ingredients in the bread machine pan. Process on the dough setting.

To make the dough, add the salt and remaining flour and ³/₄ of the cooled onion mixture to the sponge in the bread pan. Set it on the dough setting and process.

To form the rolls, generously flour the work surface, then turn the dough out onto it and knead by hand a moment. Divide the dough into 6 equal pieces. Roll each piece into an 8-inch bullet shape, then curve into a horseshoe. Place on a parchment-lined baking tray. Spray water over the tops of the loaves, then distribute the remaining sautéed onions equally over the tops and set aside to rise until nearly doubled in bulk, 30 to 40 minutes.

Preheat the oven to 400° F. Bake the rolls until golden brown and done, about 15 minutes. Cool on a rack.

POLENTA-MILLET BREAD

Dough Setting
Makes one 1¼-pound loaf

Some breads happen to be high in fiber *and* rich in taste and this is one of them. Serve it with hearty fish soups, stews such as cassoulet, or as a base for bruschetta. If you don't have polenta, cornmeal can be substituted. We give directions for the dough setting, although this bread can be made *and* baked in a 1-pound machine. (Alas, the flavor will not be the same.) In either event, serve this loaf warm.

2½ teaspoons bread machine yeast
¾ cup plus 2 tablespoons water
3 tablespoons honey
1½ cups bread flour
½ cup whole wheat flour
⅓ cup millet
⅓ cup polenta
2 tablespoons vegetable oil
1 teaspoon salt

Add all the ingredients to the bread machine pan. Process on the dough setting. Meanwhile, lightly grease a baking sheet or place a piece of parchment paper on a peel.

Remove the dough to a lightly floured surface and knead for a few seconds to remove any remaining air bubbles. Shape into a ball and flatten slightly with the palm of your hand. Place on the prepared baking sheet or peel. Cover the dough loosely with plastic wrap or a damp tea towel and set aside to rise in a warm draft-free area until doubled in bulk, about 1 hour. Meanwhile, preheat the oven to 375° F., inserting a baking stone or tiles if you are not using a baking sheet.

When the dough has doubled in bulk, score the top with a sharp knife or razor blade held at a 45° angle to the bread. Bake for 30 minutes, or until medium brown, on the middle rack of the preheated oven on the baking stone or tiles. Transfer from the baking sheet or stone to cool on a rack. Store wrapped in a plastic bag.

Millet is rich in phosphorus, niacin, calcium, and riboflavin. We buy our millet in a health food store where we can be sure that it is not the variety sold in pet stores to feed birds. The birdseed variety has not been hulled and will not be digestible to anything other than the birds!

WHOLE WHEAT–WALNUT BREAD

Dough Setting
Makes 1 large round loaf

Chunks of roasted walnut mixed with white and whole wheat flours, a *poolish*, water, salt, and yeast; such simple ingredients. Such stunning results. A round free-form loaf, deep mahogany in color, with slashes around the edges and a rich chewy taste—it's heaven with butter and one of our favorites. We use organic flours and pure spring water for best results.

POOLISH:
1/3 cup plus 1 tablespoon water
1/4 teaspoon bread machine yeast
1/2 cup bread flour
1/4 cup organic whole wheat flour

DOUGH:
2 cups walnut pieces
1 1/8 cups water
1/2 teaspoon bread machine yeast
1 3/4 cups bread flour
1 cup whole wheat flour
1/2 cup medium rye flour or meal
1 teaspoon salt
Cornmeal for dusting the top

Make the *poolish* in the bread machine on the dough setting by combining the water with the yeast and flours. Let the poolish sit in the machine from 2 to 10 hours before completing the bread.

While the *poolish* is standing, toast the walnuts in the oven or a toaster oven. Arrange the walnut pieces on a baking sheet and bake in a 350° F. oven until lightly toasted, 10 to 15 minutes. Stir a time or two and taste to see when they begin to taste toasted. Don't burn them. Transfer the nuts to a cool plate and refrigerate until baking time.

When you're ready to make the bread, add the nuts, water, yeast, flours, and salt to the bread machine pan with the *poolish* and process on the dough setting again.

Once the cycle is completed, turn the dough out onto a lightly floured surface. Punch down the dough and form into a tight ball. Cover with the bread machine pan and let it rest for 30 minutes. Flatten the dough with the heel of your hand into an 8 × 10-inch rectangle. Form into a round loaf, or a torpedo (see page 81).

Place the loaf on a peel generously sprinkled with cornmeal. Cover the loaf with plastic wrap or a clean towel and set it aside to rise in a warm, draft-free place until nearly doubled in bulk. Preheat the oven with a baking stone in place on the middle rack to 400° F. for 30 minutes. Just before baking, slash 4 straight lines around the edges of the loaf, forming a box design. Give the peel a trial shake before opening the oven.

Bake on the stone in the preheated oven until the crust is a deep mahogany color and the bread is done through, about 40 minutes. Spritz the oven 6 or 7 times with plain water during the first 10 minutes of baking (see page 74). Cool on a rack. Store in a paper bag.

A RUSTIC ROUND OF WHOLE WHEAT AND WALNUTS

Dough Setting
Makes one 1¹/₂-pound loaf

ROASTED HEADS OF GARLIC
WITH MORELS AND
WHITE MUSHROOMS

Makes 4 to 6 servings

We love to serve this in the spring when
the rich Oregon tilth gives birth to
morels. To stretch the morels, we add
white mushrooms, which act like a
sponge to absorb the surrounding
flavors. The roasted garlic complements
the mild, nutty flavor and creamy
texture of the mushrooms.

1 large head garlic
³/₄ pound morels
³/₄ pound white mushrooms, quartered
or halved if large
¹/₃ cup cold-pressed first-pressing extra-
virgin olive oil
2 sprigs fresh thyme, or a pinch dried
Salt and freshly ground
black pepper to taste

Preheat the oven to 400° F.
Pull apart the garlic cloves and place
them, unpeeled, in a small glass baking
dish. Bake in the preheated oven for
20 minutes. Remove the garlic from the
oven and let it cool to the touch.
When cool, grasp each garlic clove at
one end and squeeze. The clove should
pop out of its skin.

This wheel of rustic country bread, slightly porous, is ready to support any spicy topping that comes along. It's also a great grilling
bread for Crostini or Bruschetta (see page 212). Once again, this is
a rather wet dough, so get ready to form it by the sink with a small
stream of running water in which to wet your hands so the dough
won't stick.

¹/₂ teaspoon bread machine yeast
1³/₄ cups plus 2 tablespoons whole wheat flour
1³/₄ cups plus 2 tablespoons bread flour
¹/₃ cup Italian Winter *Biga* for Rolls and Wheat Breads (see
page 60)
2 teaspoons salt
1³/₄ cups water
¹/₂ cup black walnuts or toasted English walnuts if black are
not available, or more to taste

Add the yeast, flours, *biga*, salt, and water to the bread machine pan. Process on the dough setting just until mixed and
kneaded, about 20 minutes. Remove the dough from the
bread pan to a large, lightly greased bowl. Cover tightly with
plastic wrap and set to rise for 4 hours, or until tripled in
bulk. The dough can be left alone to rise in the refrigerator
overnight or for as long as 24 hours if need be. If you leave
it in the refrigerator for the long, cool rise, bring it back to
room temperature before shaping.

Lightly flour a work surface close to your sink. With wet hands, scoop the tripled dough out of the bowl onto the work surface and flatten it into a 12-inch disk. Sprinkle the surface with the walnuts and press them into the dough with flat palms. Pull the sides of the dough into the middle and form a tight, smooth ball.

Place a 12 × 14-inch square of parchment paper on a peel or rimless cookie sheet. Coat the paper lightly with bread flour. Place the dough ball on the parchment paper and tent it with heavy-duty aluminum foil or cover with a large bowl, making sure the dough has plenty of room to rise and will not touch the foil or bowl and stick. Let the dough rise for 1 hour, or until doubled in bulk.

Thirty minutes before baking, preheat the oven with a baking stone in place to 450° F. When the loaf has doubled, carefully slide the parchment paper with the dough on it onto the hot stone. After about 15 minutes you will be able to pull the paper out from under the loaf, thus insuring a crisp bottom. If a crisp bottom is not important, the paper can be left between the stone and the bread for the entire baking period. Bake until nicely browned and crusty, 30 to 35 minutes. Cool the bread completely on a rack and store it in a brown paper bag for up to 4 days.

In a 9 × 13-inch glass baking dish, combine the garlic cloves, mushrooms, oil, thyme, and salt and pepper. Set the dish in the preheated oven and bake, stirring occasionally, 45 minutes, or until the mushrooms are lightly browned and tender. Remove and cool to just warm. While the mushrooms bake, slice and lightly toast thick slices of Rustic Round Whole Wheat and Walnut Bread. Slather the toasted bread with the just-warm mushroom mixture and serve.

PAIN AU CITRON
Lemon Bread

Dough Setting
Makes two 6 × 4-inch oval loaves

The addition of lemon zest to a rye and wheat bread yields a citrus-scented bread you'll love with seafood and pâtés. Shape the breads like big lemons and form follows function. The crust will be golden brown, and the crumb dense and aromatic. The bread keeps at least 3 days wrapped in nothing but a paper bag.

1½ cups medium rye flour
1¼ cups bread flour
2 teaspoons gluten flour
Grated zest of 1 lemon
1 teaspoon salt
2½ teaspoons bread machine yeast
1 cup plus 3 tablespoons water

Place all the ingredients in the bread machine pan and process on the dough setting, then remove to a lightly floured surface and punch down. Knead a moment or two, then divide the dough into two pieces.

Shape each piece into a football (or lemon) shape—a short, thick oval with pointed ends (see page 161). Place on parchment paper sprinkled with cornmeal and set on a baking sheet. Cover with plastic wrap and let the dough rise in a warm, draft-free place until almost doubled in bulk, no more than 1 hour. Make 3 quick, sure slashes in the top of each risen loaf.

While the dough is rising, preheat the oven to 450° F. Bake until golden brown and done through, about 30 minutes. Remove to a rack and cool thoroughly before slicing.

FRENCH COUNTRYSIDE WHOLE-GRAIN BREAD FOR THE *BANNETON*

Dough Setting
Makes 1 round loaf

A nice thick shell of crust protects and helps retain the moisture of the soft inner crumb of this wholesome whole-grain bread. The mix of grains lends an earthiness that's impossible to achieve in a bread made entirely from white flour.

The slightly tacky, loose dough is best proofed the second time in a *banneton* (see page 73 on how to make a *banneton*), but it is acceptable to proof and bake the loaf on a lightly greased baking sheet. The baking sheet bread will not be quite as high or retain its roundness quite as well as the bread proofed in the *banneton* and baked on a stone.

SPONGE:
1 ¼ teaspoons bread machine yeast
³⁄₄ cup water
½ cup bread flour
¼ cup rye flour
¼ cup whole wheat flour

DOUGH:
½ teaspoon bread machine yeast
½ cup plus 1 tablespoon water
1½ cups bread flour
½ cup whole wheat flour
2 teaspoons salt

For the sponge, add the yeast, water, and flours to the bread machine pan. Process the ingredients on the dough setting until well mixed, about 5 minutes. You may need to scrape down the sides and bottom of the pan with a rubber spatula, and the batter will have a few small lumps. Turn off the machine and allow the sponge to sit overnight or for at least 8 hours in the bread pan.

To make the dough, add the remaining yeast, water, flours, and salt to the sponge in the bread pan. Process on the dough setting.

Meanwhile, flour an 8-inch *banneton* (or lightly grease a large baking sheet). Wet your hands, gently deflate the dough, and shape it into a round loaf. Place it in the *banneton* or on the prepared baking sheet. Cover the dough with plastic wrap or a well-floured towel and let it rise in a warm, draft-free place until doubled in bulk, from 1 to 1 ½ hours. While the dough rises, preheat the oven with a baking stone in place if you are using one, to 450° F. for 30 minutes.

If you are baking on a stone, quickly invert the loaf onto the stone and slash the top in a tic-tac-toe pattern with a sharp razor or a knife. If you are baking on a baking sheet, slash the top of the loaf into a tic-tac-toe pattern and place the baking sheet on the middle rack of the oven. Immediately turn the oven temperature down to 400° F. Bake the loaf for 60 to 70 minutes, or until the crust is dark brown and the bottom of the loaf sounds hollow when tapped with a knuckle.

One of our favorite discoveries during the writing of this book was a new product developed by the Ziploc freezer and storage-bag people. Ziploc has developed a new freezer and storage bag that measures 13 × 15 inches and holds everything except the kitchen sink. We place our bread dough in the *banneton* and then slip it, *banneton* and all, into one of these bags to rise. We then use the same bag to store the *banneton* in the pantry. This large bag will hold up to a 10-inch *banneton* and keeps the dough from drying out during a long rising. It also helps the dough retain heat in a cold kitchen. Dust and curious little fingers are also kept at bay, and the environment gets a break since we aren't continually using plastic wrap and adding it to the landfill. The Ziploc people say this bag will hold 2 gallons, or a 13 × 9-inch pan for the freezer.

PAIN MÉTEIL
Monogrammed
Wheat and Rye Bread

Dough Setting
Makes one 1¹/₄-pound loaf

In America we monogram sheets, towels, and men's shirts; in France they monogram their bread. Sound silly? In days past, communal ovens were used to bake loaves of bread formed at home by French housewives, and the loaves had to be marked by each family to distinguish their bread from their neighbors'. A stencil was made of the family initials or mark, a coat of arms you might say, and laid upon the round of bread. Flour was then dusted over the top and the stencil removed.

Today some French bakeries mark some of their breads with the bakery's initials, a little free advertising for the bakery once the bread is sold to a restaurant and then passed on to the diner. A wheat and rye blend of bread called *Pain Méteil* is still commonly made with an "M" stenciled in flour on top. *Méteil* is French for "maslin," a British word meaning a mixture of wheat and rye as grain or flour.

SPONGE:
1¹/₄ teaspoons bread machine yeast
¹/₂ cup rye flour
¹/₄ cup bread flour
²/₃ cup warm water

DOUGH:
½ cup warm water
2 cups bread flour
½ cup rye flour
1¼ teaspoons salt

Bread flour for stenciling

To make the sponge, add the yeast, flours, and water to the bread machine pan. Process the ingredients on the dough setting until well mixed, about 5 minutes. You may have to scrape down the sides and bottom of the pan with a rubber spatula. Turn off the machine and allow the sponge to sit overnight or for at least 12 hours.

To make the dough, add the water, flours, and salt to the pan with the sponge. Process on the dough setting.

When the cycle has finished, turn the dough out on a smooth surface that has been lightly sprayed with water, and with wet hands knead it to remove any remaining air bubbles. Form into a tight, round loaf. Place the loaf on a parchment-lined baking sheet, cover, and let rise for about 1½ hours. The loaf is ready to be baked when a finger-poke indentation does not bounce back.

While the dough rises, preheat the oven to 425° F. and make your stencil out of a piece of parchment paper, construction paper, or typing paper. Make sure the initial or design is at least ½-inch wide.

With a sharp toothpick, puncture the top of the dough to the depth of about 1 inch at least 9 or 10 times. This will allow steam to escape and will prevent the crust from splitting and marring your design. Place the stencil on the bread and

For a personalized gift,
try making bread monogrammed with
your initials and place it in a beautiful
basket with other homemade delicacies,
such as a jar of
Betty Collingwood's Famous Marinara
Red Wine Sauce
or a Pesto Torta with Tomatoes
(see page 172 or page 105).

sift several tablespoons of flour over the initial or design. Remove the stencil. Bake on the middle shelf of the preheated oven for 40 minutes, or until well browned and the loaf sounds hollow on the bottom when thumped with your knuckle. Remove to a rack to cool. Serve as an appetizer with thick slices of room temperature Fontina cheese or slice thin for sandwiches.

Place the stencil over the bread and sift flour over the design

JEWISH RYE BREAD

Basic Bread Setting
Makes one 1-pound loaf

One of the best ways to eat rye bread is to spread a fresh slice thickly with butter and then top it with rounds of sliced red, white, or purple radish. Also, this bread is quite good for sandwiches and other spreadables such as pâtés or foie gras.

2 to 2¹/₂ teaspoons bread machine yeast
¹/₂ cup rye flour
1¹/₂ cups bread flour
³/₄ teaspoon salt
1 tablespoon caraway seeds
2 teaspoons vegetable oil
2 teaspoons molasses
³/₄ cup water

Add all the ingredients to the bread machine pan. Process on the basic bread setting.

Remove the bread from the bread pan to cool on a rack. Store wrapped in aluminum foil or in a paper bag.

For one 1¹/₂-pound loaf

2¹/₂ to 3 teaspoons bread machine yeast
³/₄ cup rye flour
2 cups bread flour
1 teaspoon salt
4 teaspoons caraway seeds
1 tablespoon vegetable oil
1 tablespoon molasses
1 cup water

DANISH RYE SOURDOUGH

Dough Setting
Makes 1 loaf

You have to start thinking about this bread 4 or 5 days before you're ready to bake to give the sourdough time to ripen. Making the bread is easy, it's just a long, leisurely production. We try to use organic flours and spring water in this recipe for best results with the starter.

Bob Katz, a scientist at the University of Nebraska gave us the recipe. He makes a version of this bread every week, holding back a cup of dough to start his next baking. He got the recipe from Kjeld Olsen, in Copenhagen. We've adapted Bob's recipe to the bread machine and think Bob may want a machine of his very own after he tastes the results.

Open the bread machine lid from time to time and scrape the bread machine pan with a rubber spatula, because rye dough is quite sticky. Flour the work surface well before you turn that sticky dough out onto it for the final shaping too.

1 cup rye sourdough starter (see page 59)
2 cups medium rye flour
2 cups bread flour
2 teaspoons bread machine yeast
1 teaspoon salt
1¹/₈ cups water
¹/₂ cup rye berries, softened

Place all the ingredients except the rye berries in the bread machine pan and process on the dough setting twice, adding more bread flour by the tablespoon at the beginning of the second dough cycle if the dough is too wet.

While the first dough cycle is working, boil the rye berries until soft, about 30 minutes in water to cover, then let them stand in the water, cooling, until the first dough cycle is complete. Drain the berries and add them to the dough for the second dough cycle.

Then, generously spritz an $8^{1}/_{2} \times 4^{1}/_{2} \times 2^{1}/_{2}$-inch loaf pan with cooking spray. Preheat the oven to 250° F.

Scrape the soft dough out onto a well-floured work surface. Pull off one cup of the dough to hold back for another day's "old dough." Place that dough in a jar, cover with a lid, and refrigerate. Form the remaining dough into a loaf shape. Place the dough in the prepared pan, cover, and set aside to rise until the dough is at least level with the top of the pan, perhaps just peeking over. This may take as long as 2 hours.

Bake the loaf for 1 hour at 250° F., then raise the oven temperature to 350° and bake for another hour. The loaf will sound hollow when rapped on the bottom. Turn the bread out of the pan and cool on a rack. Store in a paper bag. Cut into very thin slices.

SOUR RYE BREAD

Dough Setting
Makes 1 large oval loaf

An old-fashioned Jewish rye chock-full of caraway seeds, this oval loaf has a shiny top, uneven holes in the crumb, and a chewy, sour, heavenly taste. It begs for smoked turkey or corned beef.

1 tablespoon bread machine yeast
2 cups bread flour
1 cup medium rye flour
2 tablespoons yellow cornmeal
1½ tablespoons sugar
1 teaspoon salt
1 cup water
¼ cup milk
1 tablespoon vegetable oil
1½ teaspoons caraway seeds
1 egg white beaten with 1 teaspoon warm spring water
  for glaze
Cornmeal for sprinkling on top

Place the yeast, flours, cornmeal, sugar, salt, water, milk, and oil in the bread machine pan. Process on the dough setting. Once the dough cycle is completed, remove the dough to a lightly floured surface. Punch it down and knead in the caraway seeds by hand. Form the dough into a tight ball, cover it with the bread machine pan, and let it rest for 15 minutes or so.

While the dough rests, preheat the oven to 350° F. and sprinkle a baking sheet covered with parchment with cornmeal. Form the dough into an 8-inch oval loaf (see page 75), then place it on the parchment-covered baking sheet. Cover with plastic wrap and set to rise until nearly doubled in bulk, about 45 minutes. Coat with the egg white glaze and sprinkle the top with additional cornmeal. Slash the top in diagonal slashes. Bake in the preheated oven 45 to 50 minutes, or until the loaf is mahogany brown and sounds hollow when tapped. Remove to a rack to cool.

ONE WORLD SANDWICH

Spread thick slices of old-fashioned rye bread with a layer of soft cream cheese, then dot with red salmon caviar, nasturtium blossoms, and snipped chives.
Serve it cold, with an icy shot of vodka.

WALNUT, MOZZARELLA, AND FENNEL CROWN BREAD

Dough Setting
Makes one 2-pound filled bread

A crown-shaped beauty of a bread, each pull-apart piece contains a cheesy, sweet, musky piece of mozzarella—or omit the mozzarella and make an unfilled crown. Serve this bread with the best fried Italian sausages available. The fennel seed in this bread not only complements sausages but also begs for a robust, red wine marinara to dip it in. Why not try bread, sausage, and sauce served on a white plate and garnished with fresh basil or oregano?

1½ teaspoons bread machine yeast
1½ cups bread flour
1½ cups whole wheat flour
1 teaspoon salt
2 teaspoons honey
⅓ cup milk
1 tablespoon unsalted butter, at room temperature
2 teaspoons fennel seed
¼ teaspoon grated nutmeg
⅔ cup plus 3 tablespoons water
⅔ cup chopped English walnuts, new crop if available
3 ounces mozzarella, cut into 7 equal chunks
Milk for glaze

Add the yeast, flours, salt, honey, milk, butter, 1 teaspoon of the fennel seed, the nutmeg, and water to the bread machine pan. Process the ingredients according to your manufacturer's

---

BETTY COLLINGWOOD'S FAMOUS
MARINARA RED WINE SAUCE

Makes 4 cups

This sauce has been a secret in the Collingwood family for more than 30 years, and now Grandma says it's time to share it. Our favorite feature of this sauce is that it can be made with either vine-ripened summer tomatoes or good-quality canned tomatoes when nothing else is available. Never, never make it with pale supermarket tomatoes. Serve it with your favorite bread for dipping as an antipasto, or over spaghetti with Italian sausages.

4 tablespoons cold-pressed first-pressing extra-virgin olive oil
½ cup finely chopped onion
3 cloves garlic, peeled and minced
3½ pounds fresh vine-ripened tomatoes, blanched for 1 minute in boiling water and peeled; or one (28-ounce) can peeled tomatoes in juice plus one (14½-ounce) can peeled tomatoes in juice
3 tablespoons chopped fresh basil (there is no substitute for the basil, some supermarkets are carrying it year-round now)
2 sprigs fresh oregano, or 1 teaspoon dried
2 cups water
1 cup good-quality dry red wine
¼ cup tomato paste
1 teaspoon salt
½ teaspoon freshly ground black pepper
1 tablespoon sugar

instructions for a dough setting. Meanwhile, lightly grease a 6- or 8-inch round baking pan with sides at least 3 inches high (we used a springform pan).

Turn the dough out onto a lightly floured surface and knead it for 1 minute. Flatten the dough into a 10-inch round and sprinkle with the walnuts. Press and knead the walnuts into the dough until well combined. Divide the dough into 7 equal-sized pieces. If you are *not* using the mozzarella filling, roll each piece into a ball. If you *are* using the mozzarella filling, flatten each piece into a disk. Place one mozzarella chunk on each disk and form a smooth tight ball around the cheese.

Place 6 of the balls of dough in a circle in the prepared pan and place the seventh in the middle. Cover with a tent of heavy-duty aluminum foil or a large mixing bowl, making sure the dough will not touch the top and stick. Let the dough rise in a warm place for 40 minutes, or just until it reaches the top of the pan. While the dough rises, preheat the oven to 425° F.

Brush the top of the dough lightly with milk and sprinkle with the remaining teaspoon of fennel seeds. Bake on the middle rack of the preheated oven for 40 to 45 minutes, or until the crust is nicely browned and crisp.

Let the bread cool in the pan for 5 minutes and then turn it out onto a rack to finish cooling. Serve with sausages and marinara sauce or your favorite antipasti.

Heat the olive oil in a deep, heavy-bottomed nonaluminum Dutch oven. Add the onion and garlic and sauté just until limp and starting to brown. Add all the other ingredients and break up the tomatoes with a potato masher or heavy spoon.
Simmer over very low heat for 3 to 5 hours, until the mixture thickens to a sauce consistency. Stir occasionally and smash the tomatoes until the chunks are the size you prefer. *Hint:* Don't go overboard on the onion, it will ruin the flavor of this sauce.
Also, the sugar in your tomatoes will vary depending on the time of year they were picked. A little more sugar may be necessary if they were picked too green.

RAISIN PUMPERNICKEL

Dough Setting
Makes 1 round loaf or 2 baguettes

This is our idea of real bread: nearly black, with the subtle flavors of cocoa, coffee, molasses, and rye. Shape it into a baguette for sandwiches if you wish. It's also terrific toasted and makes a fine base for strong cheese. Make a decision about the flavoring—choose either the caraway seeds or the raisins. The caraway seeds will give the bread a nice bite, while the raisins provide a sweet counterpoint to the tang you get from the combination of coffee, cocoa, and molasses.

1 tablespoon bread machine yeast
1½ cups whole wheat flour
½ cup medium rye flour
½ cup bread flour
1 tablespoon caraway seeds (optional)
1 teaspoon salt
1 tablespoon Dutch process cocoa
½ cup strong cold French roast coffee
¼ cup milk
1 tablespoon blackstrap molasses
½ cup raisins (optional)

Place the yeast, flours, seeds (if using them), salt, cocoa, coffee, milk, and molasses in the bread machine pan. Process on the dough setting. If you are using the raisins, soak them in ½ cup hot water while the dough is working.

Once the dough cycle is complete, turn the dough out onto a lightly floured board. Drain the raisins and knead them by hand into the dough. Then turn the bread machine pan over the dough and let the dough rest for 15 minutes. Shape into a tight 8-inch ball or two 12-inch baguettes (see page 75) and place the bread on a peel you've generously dusted with cornmeal. Cover the dough with plastic wrap and set aside to rise until it's increased in size by about a third. This should take about 1 hour.

Preheat the oven with a baking stone in place on the middle rack to 375° F. for 30 minutes. Dust the top of the bread with rye flour and cut slashes in the top of the loaf. Give the peel a trial shake, then shovel the bread onto the preheated stone. Bake until done, 40 to 45 minutes, or until golden brown and done through. Spritz the oven with clear water 3 or 4 times during the first 5 minutes of baking (see page 74). Cool on a rack. Wrap in plastic to store.

SCANDINAVIAN CRUNCH

Makes 2 sandwiches

1/3 cup low-fat, large-curd cottage cheese
1/2 teaspoon ground cumin
2 tablespoons chopped green onions
with tops
1 1/2 tablespoons chopped fresh parsley
2 tablespoons finely chopped
green bell pepper
4 slices pumpernickel bread
2 ounces Jarlsberg cheese, sliced thin
2 ounces ham, sliced thin
Freshly ground black pepper to taste

Combine the cottage cheese, cumin, green onions, parsley, and green pepper, then spread onto the bread. Lay on slices of Jarlsberg and top with ham. Give a grating of black pepper and run under the broiler to heat until bubbly. Serve hot.

VERTERKAKE

Dough Setting
Makes one large round loaf

A spicy, hot, high, round loaf of almost-black bread with just a hint of bitterness from the addition of dark beer, yet studded with sweet currants. *Verterkake* makes a fine vehicle for cheese or for serving with butter and jam. Try it with lox and cream cheese. It's better than a bagel.

The bread originated in Norway and traditionally has been made only by diehard bread bakers because the dough is sticky and sulky. Make it in the bread machine and you won't even notice. You'll get a dense flavorful loaf to be sliced thin for serving. The bread keeps well and can be made 3 or 4 days before the event at which you are serving it.

2 cups bread flour
2 cups medium rye flour
$^{1}/_{4}$ cup sugar
$1^{1}/_{2}$ teaspoons salt
$^{1}/_{2}$ teaspoon freshly ground black pepper
$^{1}/_{2}$ teaspoon ground cloves
$2^{1}/_{2}$ teaspoons bread machine yeast
$^{1}/_{3}$ cup dark corn syrup
$^{2}/_{3}$ cup warm dark beer
$^{2}/_{3}$ cup warm milk
$^{1}/_{4}$ cup currants

Place all the ingredients except the currants in the bread machine pan and process on the dough setting. At the end of the cycle, turn the dough out onto a lightly floured board and knead the currants in by hand. Then form the bread into an 8-inch round. Place the bread on a piece of parchment paper, cover it with plastic wrap, and set it aside to rise until almost doubled in bulk, about 1 hour.

Preheat the oven to 375° F. Brush the loaf with hot water and prick it lightly with a skewer. Bake in the preheated oven for about 45 minutes, until the crust is shiny and mahogany colored. The baked loaf will sound hollow when rapped on the bottom.

For a frosted look, you can mix 1 tablespoon cornstarch with water and mop it on the bread right before removing it from the oven. The pure white starch will stand out in bold relief from the spicy black bread.

Cool the bread on a rack and slice thin. Store in plastic wrap.

A handy kitchen tool to use for baking is a miniature mop. Wet it, squeeze it out, and you can use it to mop on glazes, egg washes, and other wet finishes. Rinse it, leave it out to air-dry, and the mop is ready for use the next time you need to dab something onto bread.

RUSSIAN BLACK BREAD WITH SPROUTED RYE BERRIES

Dough Setting
Makes 1 large round loaf

Adding sprouts to bread not only lightens the texture, but it ups the ante on nutrition as well. You can, however, make this bread without the sprouts if you want it right away. Make minor adjustments in the water, adding a little more as needed, a tablespoon at a time, during the dough cycle.

1 tablespoon bread machine yeast
1 cup medium rye flour
2$^1/_2$ cups bread flour
1 cup sprouted rye berries (see page 27)
2$^1/_2$ tablespoons cocoa
$^1/_4$ cup strong coffee
1 cup water
1$^1/_2$ teaspoons caraway seeds
1 tablespoon aniseseed
1 tablespoon honey
1$^1/_2$ teaspoons salt
2 tablespoons butter
1 egg white, beaten until frothy, for glaze

Place all the ingredients except the egg white in the bread machine pan and process on the dough setting. When the cycle is complete, remove the dough and punch it down. Knead a moment by hand, then form into a round, free-form loaf. Coat a peel with cornmeal, then place the loaf on the peel, cover with plastic wrap, and set the dough to rise until almost doubled in bulk, about 1½ hours.

Thirty minutes before baking time, preheat the oven, with a stone placed in the lower third, to 400° F. Just before baking, slash a tic-tac-toe pattern on the top of the bread and brush the frothy egg white on top. Bake in the preheated oven for about 45 minutes, or until the bread is shiny and cooked through. Cool on a rack.

RUSSIAN PEASANT

Makes 2 sandwiches

2 tablespoons reduced-fat sour cream
2 teaspoons horseradish, or to taste
4 slices Russian Black Bread
2 ounces ham, sliced thin
2 ounces Jarlsberg cheese, sliced thin
1 small cucumber, peeled and sliced thin

Mix the sour cream and horseradish and spread on 2 slices of bread. Top with slices of ham and cheese. Arrange the cucumber on top. Cover with the remaining 2 slices of bread.

7

Specialty Flatbreads:

Pizza, Focaccia, Fougasse, Flatbrod

Ciabatta
Focaccia (with 7 Variations)
    Grilled Onion Focaccia
    Sage Focaccia
    Bacon Focaccia
    Potato and Goat Cheese Focaccia
    Anchovy Focaccia
    Smoked Mozzarella and Sun-Dried Tomato Focaccia
    Garlic Focaccia
Rosemary-Raisin Focaccia with Pine Nuts
Melted Onion Flatbread with Tomato and Parmesan Cheese
The Mangone Family Pizza
Pissaladière
Olive *Fougasse*
German Limburger Flatbrod with Potatoes
Pain du Soleil
Georgian Khachapuri
Durum Focaccia or Pizza Crust
Italian Mushroom and Prosciutto Pizza
Peperoncini Cheese Loaf
Crostini and Bruschetta:
    Crostini with Artichokes and Melted Mozzarella
    Crostini with Sun-Dried Tomato Torta
    Crostini with Tomatoes, Balsamic Vinegar, Cheese, and Anchovies
    Sage Hen Crostini
    Basic Bruschetta
    Bruschetta with Frizzled Prosciutto
    Bruschetta with Two-Olive Pesto and Fresh Mozzarella
    Grilled Onion Bruschetta with Romesco Sauce

CIABATTA
Slipper Bread

Dough Setting
Makes 2 loaves

Ciabatta is an irregular, flat, flour-dusted Italian-style loaf that looks like an old slipper. The dough is quite wet and perfectly suited to the bread machine. The final bread will have big holes and a supreme taste.

Ciabatta is traditionally started with a *biga*. Begin by making a bread machine *biga* the first day, then, on day two, make the bread dough using the dough setting of your bread machine. Pull off 1 cup of dough at the end of the dough cycle to save for the next batch of bread. On the third day, begin with 1 cup of "old dough" you've warmed to room temperature plus the ingredients of the recipe. At the end of that day, pull off a cup of dough and save it. You don't have to use the dough the very next day either. Store it in the refrigerator in a Ziploc bag for up to 3 days before either refreshing it with 1/2 cup of organic white bread flour and 1/2 cup of warm water, or using it in a new bread.

An easy way to warm the old dough is to put it in the microwave for 10 to 15 seconds. It should be about room temperature. Tear off small pieces and add them to the bread machine as it is processing the new ingredients you've just added.

We did a taste test, here making successive "generations" of *ciabatta* for 15 days in a row. The bread's taste improved in subtle ways for the first 10 days, then seemed to hold until, at the end of the last day, we were tired of this kind of bread and baked the whole volume of dough in the day's *ciabatta*.

If you have a sourdough starter in the refrigerator, you can begin with a cup of starter and the ingredients below. Otherwise, just make the *biga* the first day, then hold back a cup of dough, and make the bread again and again.

2 teaspoons bread machine yeast
1¼ cups water
2 teaspoons instant nonfat dry milk solids
3 cups bread flour
1 teaspoon salt
1 cup Italian Winter *Biga* for Rolls and Wheat Breads
   (see page 60)

Combine all the ingredients in the bread machine pan and process on the dough setting. The dough will be more like batter than dough, but that's what it's supposed to be like. Now's when you say thanks for your bread machine.

Once the dough cycle has finished, liberally sprinkle a work surface with flour and turn out the sticky dough onto it. Sprinkle the dough with liberal amounts of flour. Flatten it and cut it into two rectangles, about 4 × 10 inches each. Cover the bread with a cloth or plastic wrap and let it rise for about 30 minutes. Pull and stretch the dough into two 6 × 12-inch rectangles, then spread your fingers and mash them into the dough to flatten the bread and give it it's characteristic uneven shape. Now, flip the breads over onto a peel you've generously coated with cornmeal, rub the surfaces with flour, cover, and let the loaves rise for an additional 30 minutes.

While the dough is rising, preheat the oven with a stone in place to 425° F. Once the breads have risen, give the peel a trial shake to be sure they will slide freely, then open the oven and shovel the loaves onto the hot stone. Spray the inside of the oven with clear water 3 or 4 times during the first 10 minutes of baking (see page 74). Bake the loaves until golden brown, 25 to 30 minutes. Cool on a rack.

ITALIAN BEET SALAD

Makes 4 servings
For a fine lunch, try *Ciabatta* with a beet salad that uses both the roots and the greens.

1 bunch fresh beets, about 1½ pounds
2 quarts water
1 large red onion, sliced thin
⅓ cup olive oil
¼ cup red wine vinegar
1 tablespoon balsamic vinegar
Salt and freshly ground
black pepper to taste

Cut the stems and leaves from the beets. Reserve the beets. In a large stewpot, bring the water to a rolling boil. Boil the beets in the water until tender, about 25 minutes. Lift the beets from the water and drain. Cut into slices ¼ inch thick and place in a large bowl. Add the sliced red onions, all but 2 tablespoons of the oil, the vinegars, salt, and pepper. Set aside.

Thoroughly wash the reserved beet leaves, then boil for about 5 minutes. Drain thoroughly. Toss the beet leaves with the remaining oil and arrange on a serving platter. Top with the beets and onions. Serve warm.

FOCACCIA

Dough Setting
Makes one 14-inch round flatbread

The toppings for focaccia are as varied as they are for pizza.
Here are some of our favorites. In all cases, the baking time may be changed by whatever you put on the top and how long it takes to cook.

GRILLED ONION FOCACCIA

Sauté 1 cup mixed red and yellow onion slices in a little olive oil until limp, then place them on top of the raised and dimpled focaccia just before baking. Bake for about 20 minutes.

SAGE FOCACCIA

Top the bread with a dozen fresh sage leaves, or 2 teaspoons dried leaves, just before baking. Bake for 17 to 20 minutes.

BACON FOCACCIA

Cook 6 slices of bacon in the microwave until crisp—about 5 minutes at 100 percent power. Then drain and crumble the bacon over the dough just before baking. Bake for about 20 minutes.

POTATO AND GOAT CHEESE FOCACCIA

Cook 4 red potatoes in boiling water until tender, then cut into thin slices and arrange atop the dough. Crumble 4 ounces fresh goat cheese over the dough. Sprinkle with red pepper flakes and rosemary needles. Season to taste with salt and freshly ground black pepper. Brush with olive oil and bake for 20 to 25 minutes.

So what's the difference between focaccia and pizza, you say? Focaccia has olive oil in the dough, it's dimpled, and it's rarely covered with gooey stuff the way a pizza is. Make it in the bread machine and it's easy as the proverbial pie. Finish the top with nothing more than olive oil in the craters you make with your fingers and a sprinkling of kosher salt, or get as fancy as you want. Just keep the gooey sauces for pizza. Think of this as the nineties answer to what's for dinner.

2$^1/_2$ teaspoons bread machine yeast
3 cups bread flour
2 teaspoons salt
$^7/_8$ cup water
$^1/_4$ cup fruity olive oil plus 3 tablespoons for the top
Coarse sea salt or kosher salt for sprinkling on the top

Add the yeast, flour, 2 teaspoons salt, water, and $^1/_4$ cup oil to the bread machine pan. Process on the dough setting. Once the dough cycle is completed, remove the dough to a lightly floured surface, punch it down, form it into a tight ball, and let it rest on the counter under the bread machine pan for 15 minutes.

Preheat the oven with a baking stone on the middle rack to 500° F. for at least 30 minutes.

Roll and stretch the dough on a lightly floured surface into an irregular 14-inch circle. It should be about $^1/_4$ inch thick. Or, if you wish, roll it into a 12 × $^3/_8$-inch circle. This will yield a thicker, chewier bread.

Sprinkle a peel generously with cornmeal and place the dough on it. Set it aside to rise until puffy, about 10 minutes. Rub the surface with the remaining 3 tablespoons olive oil and sprinkle it generously with sea or kosher salt. Poke the surface of the focaccia with your fingertips to dimple the bread. Give the peel a trial shake before opening the oven, then shovel the bread onto the hot stone. Bake until golden brown and cooked through, about 15 minutes. Cool on a rack.

ANCHOVY FOCACCIA

Arrange drained anchovies from a 2-ounce tin atop the raised dough. Drizzle the anchovy oil on top, then dimple the dough and add capers. Bake for about 20 minutes.

SMOKED MOZZARELLA AND SUN-DRIED TOMATO FOCACCIA

Arrange sun-dried tomatoes or tomato bits over the dough, top with smoked mozzarella slices, drizzle with olive oil, sprinkle with basil, then bake for 20 to 25 minutes.

GARLIC FOCACCIA

Peel a head of garlic and divide into cloves. Imbed the cloves into the top of the raised dough, dimple, then drizzle with olive oil. Salt and pepper generously, then bake for about 20 minutes.

ROSEMARY-RAISIN FOCACCIA WITH PINE NUTS

Dough Setting
Makes two 8-inch round flatbreads

This flatbread may be eaten as a snack alongside a glass of wine, or served as part of a buffet. It's sweeter than most such breads and goes nicely with fruit and cheese as well.

2 teaspoons bread machine yeast
2 cups bread flour
$^1/_2$ cup whole wheat flour
$1^1/_2$ teaspoons sugar
1 teaspoon salt
$^7/_8$ cup water
4 tablespoons chopped fresh rosemary needles
2 tablespoons fruity olive oil plus additional for coating
    the dough
$^1/_4$ cup golden raisins (sultanas)
$^1/_3$ cup toasted pine nuts (see sidebar, page 189)

Combine the yeast, flours, sugar, salt, and water in the bread machine pan. Process on the dough setting.

While the dough is being processed, add 2 tablespoons of the rosemary needles to the 2 tablespoons of oil and heat in the microwave at 100 percent power until the oil bubbles, about 1 minute. (Alternately, heat in a small pan on top of the stove.) Add the raisins, heat for 20 seconds more, then set aside. Once the dough cycle is completed, remove the dough to a lightly floured surface. Knead in the oil, raisins, and rosemary by hand, then form the dough into a tight ball. Cover with the bread machine pan and let the dough rest for 15 minutes or so. Preheat the oven with a baking stone in place to 400° F. for at least 30 minutes.

Divide the dough into two equal pieces and roll each one into an 8-inch circle. Place on parchment on a peel. Let the dough rise until puffy in a warm, draft-free place, about 15 minutes. Coat with the additional oil, sprinkle with the toasted pine nuts and the remaining rosemary. Dimple the tops with your fingertips, then shovel the breads onto the hot stone. Spritz the inside of the oven 6 or 7 times with plain water during the first 5 minutes of baking (see page 74). Bake until golden, 20 to 25 minutes. Cool on a rack.

To vary this sweet focaccia, leave out the rosemary and substitute other dried fruits—such as Michigan dried cherries or currants—for the raisins and sprinkle with turbinado sugar.
Makes a great breakfast.
To toast pine nuts: Place the nuts on a flat baking sheet in a 350° F. oven and bake for 3 to 5 minutes, or place them in a dry skillet and shake them over medium-high heat until they begin to color up. Immediately pour them into a cool bowl. They'll burn easily.

MELTED ONION FLATBREAD WITH TOMATO AND PARMESAN CHEESE

Dough Setting
Makes one 12 × 12-inch flatbread

We think this simple bread with the long name is one of the best for antipasto. The filling is dry, not runny like pizza or calzone, thus making it perfect for dinner parties with an Italian theme or just a quick afternoon snack. If fresh Parmesan cheese is not available in your area, substitute any hard aged Italian cheese.

DOUGH:
2 teaspoons bread machine yeast
3 cups bread flour
Pinch salt
1 cup plus 2 tablespoons water
2 tablespoons cold-pressed first-pressing extra-virgin olive oil

FILLING:
2 tablespoons cold-pressed first-pressing extra-virgin olive oil
1 small onion, minced
1 clove garlic, peeled and crushed
1 teaspoon sugar
12 sun-dried tomato halves preserved in olive oil with
    dried herbs, drained
12 fresh basil leaves
2 ounces Parmesan or other aged hard
    Italian cheese, shaved
Milk for glaze
Kosher salt to taste

To make the dough, add all the dough ingredients to the bread machine pan. Process on the dough setting.

While the dough is processing, lightly grease a large baking sheet. Heat the olive oil for the filling in a medium skillet. Add the onion, garlic, and sugar. Sauté for 5 minutes, or until the onion is softened. Cool to room temperature.

Turn the dough out onto a lightly floured surface and knead for 1 minute. Cut it into two equal pieces. Roll one piece into a 12-inch square. Place this square of dough on the prepared baking sheet. Spread the cooled onion mixture over the dough leaving a ½-inch border around the edge. Arrange the sun-dried tomato halves over the onion in 3 rows of 4 tomato halves each. Place 1 basil leaf on top of each tomato half. Sprinkle the tomatoes with the shaved cheese. Roll out the remaining dough into another 12-inch square. Place this square on top of the filling. Press the edges of the dough to seal and then flute.

With a sharp knife, score the surface of the dough with 3 or 4 slash marks. Glaze the top with a light brushing of milk. Sprinkle with kosher salt.

Let the dough rise for 25 minutes. Meanwhile, preheat the oven to 450° F. Right before baking, go back and flute again to seal any opened dough. Bake on the middle rack of the preheated oven for 25 minutes, or until nicely browned. Cut into 12 squares and serve warm, with olives and cheeses as part of the antipasti, or alone.

PIZZETTES

The dough used for Melted Onion Flatbread with Tomato and Parmesan Cheese works equally well for pizzettes. For pizzettes, cut the dough into 12 equal pieces. Roll each piece into a small oval about ¼ inch thick on a lightly floured surface. Transfer to a lightly greased baking sheet. Top with your favorite pizza toppings—goat cheese or mozzarella, pesto, anchovies, tapenade, marinated eggplant, onion, minced sausage, or shrimp—and bake in a preheated 450° F. oven for 8 to 10 minutes. Sprinkle with your favorite complementary fresh herbs, such as chopped basil, oregano, or thyme. Serve hot.

Anchovy paste, pesto, and sun-dried tomato paste in imported tubes are handy to have for last-minute pizzette toppings and make for a fast antipasto.

THE MANGONE FAMILY PIZZA

Dough Setting
Makes one 15-inch pizza

This pizza is a study in contrasts. The creamy smoothness of the mozzarella plays straight man for the smoky Fontina and salty chèvre and prosciutto. We like to serve this in the back yard with a jug of homemade Italian wine. Serve Italian hard cookies for dessert as a grand finale. *Salute!*

DOUGH:

2½ teaspoons bread machine yeast

3 cups bread flour

¼ cup plus 2 tablespoons semolina flour

1 cup plus 2 tablespoons water

1 tablespoon sugar

2 teaspoons salt

2 tablespoons plus 1 teaspoon cold-pressed first-pressing extra-virgin olive oil

TOPPING:

2 tablespoons cold-pressed first-pressing extra-virgin olive oil

½ pound fresh mozzarella, sliced thin

½ pound Fontina or Edam cheese, sliced thin

5 ripe plum tomatoes, sliced thin

4 large cloves garlic, peeled and minced

2 tablespoons chopped fresh basil, or 1 tablespoon dried sweet basil

4 ounces thinly sliced prosciutto, chopped coarse

1 small sweet red onion, sliced thin

1 red or green bell pepper, seeded and diced

6 ounces feta cheese, crumbled, or fresh chèvre goat cheese

For the dough, add all the dough ingredients to the bread machine pan. Process on the dough setting. Meanwhile, preheat the pizza stone or tiles to 500° F. for 30 minutes. Prepare your topping ingredients and line them up in the order listed. (To avoid having cornmeal all over the floor, hold your pizza peel over the sink and generously sprinkle cornmeal–approximately 3 tablespoons–on it to prevent the pizza from sticking.)

When the machine has completed the dough cycle, remove the dough from the bread pan to a lightly floured surface. Knead the dough several times, then roll and stretch it into a 15-inch circle. Place the dough on the prepared peel.

Brush the dough with the 2 tablespoons olive oil, then layer it with the mozzarella and Fontina or Edam cheeses–to form a kind of non-skid surface for the rest of the ingredients. Finish layering the pizza with the tomatoes, garlic, basil, prosciutto, onion, pepper, and feta or chèvre cheese. Give the pie a jerk on the peel to loosen it before opening the oven door, then slide it onto the preheated stone or tiles. Bake for 10 to 15 minutes, or until golden brown on the bottom and bubbly on top.

You may use a pizza screen or pan to bake this pie, but it will not have the crusty brown bottom characteristic of baking on a stone or tiles. Baking the pizza on a screen or pan will take 20 to 25 minutes, or until the toppings are bubbly and lightly browned.

PISSALADIÈRE

Dough Setting
Makes two 12-inch pizzas

Count on the French to try and improve on the pizza. Cooking fresh Roma tomatoes into a sauce, sweating onions in butter until deliciously limp and golden, then layering the whole melange onto a rich egg dough makes a memorable pizza. Lucky you have your bread machine to make the dough. Otherwise this would be just too much work.

1 recipe Bread Machine Brioche (see page 268)
    prepared on the dough setting
2 tablespoons olive oil
6 Roma tomatoes, chopped coarse
2 cloves garlic, peeled and sliced thin
2 tablespoons tomato paste
½ teaspoon sugar
Salt and freshly ground black pepper to taste
1 large yellow onion, chopped coarse
12½ tablespoons (1½ sticks plus ½ tablespoon)
        unsalted butter
1 cup freshly grated Parmesan cheese
½ teaspoon rosemary needles, bruised
One (2-ounce) tin anchovy fillets, drained
1 dozen large ripe black Italian or Greek olives, pits
    removed, cut into large pieces

While the brioche is working in your bread machine, make the sauce and toppings.
    For the sauce, heat the olive oil in an 8-inch skillet

over medium-low heat, then add the tomatoes and garlic and simmer, stirring occasionally, until the tomatoes have formed a paste, about 10 minutes. Now stir in the tomato paste, sugar, and salt and pepper. Cook for 5 more minutes, then set aside.

In a saucepan, combine the chopped onions and butter. Over low heat, sweat the onions, covered, until they're reduced and golden in color, about 15 minutes, stirring from time to time. Set them aside.

When the dough cycle is complete, remove the dough to a lightly floured surface and form it into a tight ball. Place the bread machine pan over the dough and let the dough rest for about 15 minutes. Preheat the oven to 375° F.

Divide the dough into two pieces and roll each one on the lightly floured surface into a 9-inch circle about ³/₈ inch thick. Place the rolled dough onto baking sheets covered with parchment paper.

Sprinkle the dough with Parmesan cheese, then with rosemary needles. Now spread the tomato sauce over that and the cooked onions on top. Arrange the anchovy fillets on top of the onions and bake in the preheated oven until golden and cooked through, 25 to 30 minutes.

A glass of Valpolicella,
Zinfandel, Oregon Pinot Noir
or another dark red wine,
makes this an event to remember.

OLIVE *FOUGASSE*

Dough Setting
Makes two 8 × 10-inch flatbreads

Count on the French to fancy up a plain flatbread. This olive-rich bread is rolled into a rectangle then slashed with a knife to form traditional patterns. The sunburst is popular, or a tree branch, a moon, or a sunflower. You won't need butter with this olive oil–drenched bread. It's a perfect accompaniment to salade Niçoise.

1 tablespoon bread machine yeast
2½ cups bread flour
2 teaspoons sugar
¼ teaspoon salt
½ cup warm milk
½ cup water
¼ cup fruity olive oil, plus extra for coating the dough
⅓ cup chopped Niçoise or green olives

The slashed fougasse

Combine the yeast, flour, sugar, salt, milk, water, and ¼ cup olive oil in the bread machine pan and process on the dough setting. At the end of the cycle, turn out the dough onto a lightly floured board and knead in the olives. Turn the bread pan over the dough and let it rest for 15 minutes.

Divide the dough into two equal pieces and roll each piece into an 8 × 10-inch rectangle. Place each rectangle on a parchment paper–covered baking sheet. Make two rows of 6 to 8 evenly spaced diagonal slashes, cutting all the way through the dough. Open these slits by pulling them well apart with your hands. Coat the flatbreads with olive oil and set aside to rise until the dough is puffed, about 20 minutes.

Preheat the oven to 375° F. After the breads are puffy, bake in the hot oven for 15 to 20 minutes, or until golden brown. Cool on a rack. These are best eaten the day they're made, but they can be stored in plastic wrap.

PAIN AU FROMAGE

Skip the olives in the Olive Fougasse recipe and substitute ¾ cup diced Gruyère cheese. Then divide and roll the dough into 2 rectangles about 4 × 6 × ¼ inch thick.
Make 3 horizontal slashes all the way through the dough.
Place the rolled and cut dough on parchment paper to rise a final time until puffy, about 20 minutes.
Bake on a stone in a preheated 450° F. oven. Spritz the oven with water 4 or 5 times during the first 5 minutes of baking (see page 74), then continue to bake until the *fougasse* is golden and done, about 15 minutes
Eat this bread the day it's made, with a salad of baby greens and a good glass of robust red wine.

GERMAN LIMBURGER
FLATBROD WITH POTATOES

Dough Setting
Makes one 14-inch flatbread

The surprising thing about Limburger is that it has a sweet taste that marries well with flatbreads. Make this pizza-style bread for your Uncle Charlie and don't be surprised if he gets a fond faraway look on his face. Limburger does that to some people. Honest.

DOUGH:
2 teaspoons bread machine yeast
2 cups bread flour
1 teaspoon salt
2 tablespoons olive oil
$^{7}/_{8}$ cup water

TOPPING:
1 cup thinly sliced raw new potatoes
$^{1}/_{2}$ cup thinly sliced sweet onion (Walla Walla type)
4 cloves garlic, sliced thin
6 stalks thin asparagus, sliced in half lengthwise
2 tablespoons olive oil
1 tablespoon fresh thyme, or 1 teaspoon dried
Salt and red and black pepper to taste
3 ounces Limburger cheese spread ($^{1}/_{2}$ jar)

To make the dough, place the dough ingredients in the bread machine pan. Process on the dough setting. Remove the dough from the pan, punch it down, and form it into a tight ball. Cover the dough with the pan and let the dough rest for 10 minutes. Then, on a lightly floured board, roll the dough into a 14-inch circle.

Place the dough on a pizza pan generously sprinkled with cornmeal and set it aside to rise while you prepare the topping and preheat the oven to 425° F.

To assemble the flatbread, toss the sliced potatoes, onion, garlic, and asparagus in the olive oil. Season to taste with salt and red and black pepper. Generously spread the vegetables over the top of the pizza. Top with spoonfuls of Limburger spread. Bake in the preheated oven for 20 minutes, or until brown. Serve hot or at room temperature.

If you have any Limburger left over, you can make the classic Wisconsin Bachelor Sandwich: Limburger, a thick slice of onion, and dark bread.

PAIN DU SOLEIL

Dough Setting
Makes one 1¹/₂-pound 14-inch round flatbread
with 16 sunrays

The bread is a flat round cut into rays like a big smiling sun. Each person just pinches off a sunray and munches. And the color is a kind of rosy pumpkin hue, thanks to the dried tomatoes. The flavor, suitably punched up with cheese and pepper, makes this a welcome addition to any sideboard.

3 cups bread flour
2¹/₂ teaspoons bread machine yeast
1 cup water
¹/₄ cup fruity olive oil
¹/₄ cup freshly grated Parmesan cheese
1 tablespoon freshly ground black pepper
¹/₄ cup minced sun-dried tomatoes

Combine all the ingredients in the bread machine pan. Process on the dough setting, then remove to a lightly floured board and punch down. Cover with the bread machine pan and let the dough rest for 10 minutes, then roll it into a rough 14-inch round. Transfer the round to a piece of parchment paper generously dusted with cornmeal. Put a bowl about 4¹/₂ inches in diameter in the middle of the dough. Then, cut the dough into quarters, then eighths, and finally sixteenths, until you have sixteen even sunrays coming out from the middle of the sun. Lift the bowl from the center.

Generously dust the top of the dough with flour. Then twist

each sunray 3 times. This will give you a candycane effect on each sunray between flour and cornmeal-streaked bread.

Preheat the oven to 450° F. Slide the sun bread on the parchment onto a baking sheet and set it aside to rise until puffy, about 20 minutes. Bake for 20 to 25 minutes, until brown. Cool on a rack. Best served the day it's made.

DRIED TOMATO TIPS

To crush dried tomatoes, toss a bag of dried tomatoes into the freezer until they get brittle, then crush them by bashing them with a rolling pin.
To make Dried Tomato Butter, mix 2 or 3 cloves garlic, minced, with 1 tablespoon minced dried tomatoes; drizzle with some olive oil to moisten, then mash into a stick of butter.
Mix well with a fork. Form into a half-round by patting the mixture into the scooped-out peel of half an orange. Freeze until the butter is firm, then pop it out of the orange rind onto a plate. Allow the butter to warm a bit before serving.
Decorate with basil leaves and/or rosemary needles, if you wish.
Dried Tomato Cream makes a great sauce for poached salmon, grilled chicken, or even plain old pasta.
Simply cook a pint of heavy cream down until it begins to thicken, then add a 1-ounce package of tomato bits; 1/4 cup white wine; 1 heaping tablespoon chopped fresh basil; and 2 or 3 cloves garlic, minced.
Cook until the flavors blend, at least 10 minutes.
Adjust the seasoning with salt and pepper.
Pour this lovely pink cream over whatever you can find.
It would probably make tennis shoes delectable.

GEORGIAN KHACHAPURI

Dough Setting
Makes one 2-pound filled bread
or six hors d'oeuvre breads

In Russia, small hand-held Khachapuri sold from pushcarts on the street are the original fast food. The round soft cheese breads are kept warm over glowing charcoal embers and fuel the masses as they stand in endless lines to buy other goods.

We like to make one big bread to serve as an appetizer at parties and large gatherings. For serving 2 to 4, the small breads are perfect, and they can be stored in the freezer and thawed and warmed as needed.

DOUGH:
2¹/₂ teaspoons bread machine yeast
²/₃ cup milk
1 tablespoon honey
¹/₄ cup (¹/₂ stick) unsalted butter, at room temperature
1 large egg
¹/₂ teaspoon salt
2¹/₂ cups bread flour or all-purpose flour

CHEESE FILLING:
1 pound Monterey Jack cheese, grated
1 pound Muenster cheese, grated
¹/₄ cup minced fresh parsley
2 large eggs, lightly beaten
1 egg yolk, lightly beaten
2 tablespoons unsalted butter, at room temperature

1½ teaspoons ground coriander, or 2 tablespoons finely
  chopped fresh cilantro leaves

¼ teaspoon freshly ground black pepper

GLAZE:

1 large egg lightly beaten with 1 tablespoon milk

To make the dough, add the dough ingredients to the bread machine pan. Process on the dough setting.

For the filling, in a bowl combine all of the cheese filling ingredients and stir to mix thoroughly. Set aside.

For the large bread, grease the bottom and sides of a 10-inch round cake pan. Cut a piece of parchment or waxed paper to fit and place it in the bottom of the pan. Grease the paper, then generously sprinkle it with cornmeal. For smaller breads we use a Texas-sized muffin tin (each muffin cup being approximately 2 inches deep and 4 inches in diameter). Place muffin papers in the cups and spray them lightly with non-stick cooking spray, then sprinkle generously with cornmeal.

Turn the dough out onto a lightly floured surface. The dough will be very soft and slightly sticky. Knead it for a few seconds to remove any remaining air bubbles.

For the large bread, roll the dough out into a 15-inch circle. For the 6 small breads, divide the dough into 6 equal portions and roll each portion into an 8-inch circle. Dust the dough lightly with flour, fold it into quarters, and transfer it to the prepared pan. Unfold the dough and gently press it into the bottom of the pan or muffin cups.

Spoon the filling into the dough. Gather the overhanging dough into even folds over the filling and twist the ends slightly to form a topknot. Brush the dough with the glaze

Khachapuri cheese breads may be frozen for later use. Place in freezer bags and use within 2 months.
To use, let the breads thaw at room temperature for about 4 hours, then heat in a 350° F. preheated oven—20 to 25 minutes for the large bread and 15 minutes for the small breads.

and set it aside to rise in a warm, draft-free area for 20 minutes. Meanwhile, preheat the oven to 350° F.

Bake the dough on the middle rack of the preheated oven for approximately 50 minutes for the large loaf and 30 minutes for the small loaves, or until lightly browned. Cool in the pans for 15 minutes, then carefully remove from the pans and cool for another 15 minutes before serving.

DURUM FOCACCIA OR PIZZA CRUST

Dough Setting
Makes one 14-inch round focaccia or pizza

This recipe can be used to make a chewy focaccia with a crisp crust or a deep dish pizza. You will need to start a durum *biga* the night before you make the dough. For either the focaccia or the pizza, you will need a deep dish pizza pan—our favorite is a non-stick steel pan called Baker's Advantage by Roshco. The bread doesn't stick and neither will the cheese if it accidentally runs down the side. The black exterior absorbs enough heat to let the bread brown, and since it's nonstick, cleanup is a breeze.

We call for durum flour, which is usually used for pasta and is available in better markets. Durum flour gives this focaccia it's earthy flavor and chewiness. The oil on the bottom of the pan is what gives the crust it's crispness. We use golden durum flour, which is available from most health food stores or gourmet specialty shops or by mail order from Arrowhead Mills or King Arthur Flour (see page 307 for mail order sources).

1¼ teaspoons bread machine yeast
⅓ cup Durum Flour Biga (see page 61)
1¾ cups water
1¾ cups durum flour
1¾ cups bread flour
1½ teaspoons salt
5 tablespoons cold-pressed first-pressing extra-virgin
    olive oil
1 large clove garlic, peeled
¾ teaspoon kosher salt
1 teaspoon chopped fresh oregano leaves,
    or ½ teaspoon dried

Add the yeast, *biga,* water, flours, and salt to the bread machine pan. Process the ingredients according to your manufacturer's instructions for a dough setting. While the dough rises, oil the sides and bottom of the pizza pan with 3 tablespoons of the olive oil. Cut the garlic clove in half and rub the cut halves around the bottom and sides of the pan. Discard the garlic.

When the dough has finished its cycle, using wet hands, turn it out into the pizza pan. Press and stretch the dough to cover the bottom and sides of the pan with a ½-inch lip. Set aside in a warm place and allow the dough to rise until well puffed, about 45 minutes. Meanwhile, set a baking stone or tiles in the oven and preheat to 400° F. for 30 minutes. This recipe can also be baked on the middle rack of the oven without a stone or tiles.

Dimple the top of the dough aggressively with your fingertips. Brush it with the remaining 2 tablespoons of oil and sprinkle with the kosher salt and oregano. Place the pan on the stone or rack and bake for 20 to 25 minutes, spraying with water 3 times in the first 10 minutes (see page 74). The focaccia will be golden brown and smell of sweet olive oil when finished. Remove it immediately to cool on a rack. Can be served warm or at room temperature.

DURUM FOCACCIA PIZZA

Makes one 14-inch pizza

We like to use this focaccia as a base for our favorite pizzas.
The following is one of our favorites.

1 Durum Focaccia prepared through the dimpling and brushing
with olive oil
1 cup shredded mozzarella
1 cup shredded sharp cheddar
1½ cups favorite marinara sauce or Betty Collingwood's Famous
Marinara Red Wine Sauce (see page 172)
¾ pound sweet Italian sausages, cooked, drained, and
removed from casings, crumbled
⅔ cup Kalamata olive halves
½ cup thinly sliced sweet red onion
1½ cups white mushrooms, quartered and sautéed
in ¼ cup olive oil until tender
4 ounces goat cheese, crumbled
1 teaspoon chopped fresh oregano leaves, or ½ teaspoon dried

Preheat the oven to 425° F. Mix the mozzarella and cheddar cheeses
together. Sprinkle 1 cup of mixed cheeses over the focaccia. Spread with
marinara sauce and layer with sausage, olives, onion, and mushrooms.
Crumble the goat cheese over the top and sprinkle with the oregano.
Sprinkle with the remaining 1 cup of mixed cheeses. Bake on the middle
rack of the preheated oven for 20 to 25 minutes, or until the pizza is brown
and bubbling. Remove from the pan and serve immediately.

ITALIAN MUSHROOM AND PROSCIUTTO PIZZA

Dough Setting
Makes one 15-inch round pizza

We make this pizza every spring when wild mushrooms are plentiful. We start with wild morels from the local farmer's market and add white button mushrooms and any other wild mushrooms that look good in the produce section of the supermarket. Chanterelles, portobellos, fresh or rehydrated dried porcini—just about any combination of mushroom will taste delicious on this pizza.

SPONGE:
$2^{1}/_{2}$ teaspoons bread machine yeast
$^{1}/_{2}$ cup bread flour
$^{1}/_{2}$ cup water

DOUGH:
2 cups bread flour
$^{1}/_{2}$ cup rye flour
$^{1}/_{4}$ cup water
$^{1}/_{2}$ cup cold-pressed first-pressing extra-virgin olive oil
$^{1}/_{2}$ teaspoon salt

TOPPING:
4 tablespoons cold-pressed first-pressing extra-virgin
   olive oil
$1^{1}/_{2}$ pounds fresh mushrooms, sliced into quarters if large
Salt and freshly ground black pepper to taste

$^1\!/_4$ pound Fontina cheese, sliced thin
$^1\!/_4$ pound mozzarella cheese, sliced thin
$^1\!/_4$ pound prosciutto, julienned
2 tablespoons minced fresh Italian flat-leaf parsley
Parmesan cheese, shaved

For the sponge, add the ingredients to the bread machine pan. Process the ingredients on the dough setting until well mixed, about 5 minutes. You may need to scrape down the sides and bottom of the pan with a rubber spatula. Turn off the machine and allow the sponge to sit in the bread pan for 40 minutes.

To make the dough, add the flours, water, olive oil, and salt to the sponge in the pan. Process on the dough setting.

While the dough works, heat the olive oil in a large skillet over medium-high heat and sauté the mushrooms until they give off their liquid and are nicely browned, about 20 minutes. Season with salt and pepper and reserve. Preheat the oven to 450° F. with a baking stone in place on the middle shelf. You can also bake this pizza in a pizza pan or on a baking sheet.

When the dough has finished the dough cycle, remove it to a lightly floured surface and roll it into a 15-inch circle. Place the circle of dough on a peel lightly dusted with cornmeal, or place it in your pizza pan or on the baking sheet. Let the dough rest for 15 minutes. Lay the cheeses, mushrooms, and prosciutto over the dough.

Bake the pizza on the stone or on the middle rack for 15 to 20 minutes, until browned and bubbly. Remove from the oven and sprinkle with the parsley and Parmesan cheese. Serve immediately.

PIZZA ESSENTIALS

If you want to make baking pizza easier, you might like to try some of the pizza hardware currently on the market:

BAKING STONES
Our favorite is made by the Old Stone Oven Corporation and measures 14 × 16 inches. It's expensive (about $25), but worth it as it is peerless for making most free-form breads and gives you that professional crisp, thick crust that so many home bakers want.

PIZZA SCREEN
A heavy wire mesh screen edged with wire tape for transferring the pizza to the baking stone. This screen supports a pizza while it is being placed on a stone and aids in removal of the pizza when it is finished baking. Pizzas with sticking cheese or dripping sauce are much easier to remove with a screen under them.

CUTTING WHEEL
A cutting wheel is used to slice through pizza with ease. Make sure to choose a sharp one with sturdy handles and blade guards. A Dexter professional wheel is considered by many to be the best. It has a replaceable blade and is well worth the price.

PEPERONCINI CHEESE LOAF

Dough Setting
Makes one 1½-pound loaf

When a professional baker falls in love with a country and its people, she doesn't write a sonnet or symphony. She invents a recipe. Here's one created by a baker after a trip to Italy.

Notice how our lovesick baker mixed hard and soft wheat flours. The bread flour gives the final product lift; the soft wheat makes for a fine texture.

DOUGH:
2½ teaspoons bread machine yeast
2 cups bread flour
1 cup cake flour
2 tablespoons sugar
1 teaspoons salt
¼ cup (½ stick) unsalted butter, at room temperature
1 cup milk
1 large egg
⅓ cup drained peperoncini peppers, patted dry with paper towels, and chopped coarse

FILLING AND TOPPING:
3 tablespoons unsalted butter, at room temperature
1 large egg, whisked
⅔ cup grated sharp cheddar cheese
⅓ cup drained peperoncini peppers, patted dry with paper towels, and chopped coarse
1 tablespoon crushed dried red chilies

For the dough, add the yeast, flours, sugar, salt, butter, milk, and egg to the bread machine pan. If you are using a 1-pound machine, let the ingredients be mixed and kneaded, about 25 minutes in most machines, and then turn off the machine. Turn the dough out into a lightly greased 3-quart bowl, cover tightly with plastic wrap, and set to rise in a warm place until doubled in bulk, about 1 hour.

If you are using a 1½-pound machine, process completely on the dough setting.

Meanwhile, lightly grease a 9 × 5 × 3-inch loaf pan. When the dough has doubled in bulk, transfer it to a lightly floured surface and knead in the ⅓ cup peperoncinis. Roll the dough into a rectangle about 10 × 12 inches. Smear the surface with the butter. Paint the dough with all but 2 tablespoons of the whisked egg. Sprinkle with the cheese and then the peperoncinis, holding back a hefty pinch of each for the top. Roll up, jelly-roll fashion, beginning at the 10-inch side. Gently place the dough in the prepared pan, seam side down, and cover loosely with plastic wrap. Set to rise in a warm, draft-free place until the top of the dough is just 1 inch above the top of the pan, about 45 minutes to 1 hour. Meanwhile, preheat the oven to 375° F.

When the dough has risen, brush it with the reserved 2 tablespoons of egg to make a glaze, taking care not to allow any to run down the sides of the pan (it sticks). Make 3 deep, diagonal slashes in the top with a sharp knife or a razor blade. Sprinkle with the reserved peperoncinis, cheese, and the crushed dried red chilies.

Bake on the middle rack of the preheated oven for 35 minutes, or until evenly browned. Let the bread sit in the pan for 20 minutes to allow the cheesy center to solidify, and then turn it out onto a rack to cool completely. This bread will keep up to a week if stored in a plastic bag.

EGGS WITH OLIVE OIL, CHEESE, AND SWEET MARINARA SAUCE

Toast 4 slices of Peperoncini Cheese Loaf. Place 1 slice in the bottom of each of 4 buttered individual glass casseroles. Brush the tops with olive oil. Spread the toast with 1 tablespoon of your favorite marinara sauce. Then add 1 raw egg and set in a hot-water bath. Bake in a preheated 350° F. oven just until set, about 5 minutes. Sprinkle with grated Parmesan cheese and serve immediately.

CROSTINI AND BRUSCHETTA

What are crostini you ask? Crostini are small toasted slices of a country bread ready to be topped with spreads and various toppings to become appetizers or *merende* (see page 250). Old baguettes, heavy country breads, and chewy mixed-grain breads all make for excellent crostini.

Crostini are easily made ahead for cocktail parties when large quantities are needed. Simply place the bread slices in a single layer on an ungreased baking sheet or one lined with parchment paper or foil for easy cleanup. Preheat the oven to 375° F. and bake until lightly toasted, about 15 minutes. Store the toasts in tins and spread just before serving with the topping of your choice.

Bruschetta, thicker than crostini, has been referred to as the original garlic bread. Slices of country or sourdough bread are toasted and rubbed with fresh garlic until the clove just disappears into the bread pores, then brushed with a first-rate olive oil. Ideally, bruschetta should be grilled over a wood fire, but that's not absolutely necessary. A toaster oven, cast-iron skillet seasoned with olive oil, or a stovetop grill will work just fine. The toast can be topped with fresh, ripe tomatoes and fresh herbs, or used as a dipper for sauces such as marinara or a blend of olive oil and balsamic vinegar. Other toppings such as pestos, grilled vegetables, and cheeses are also popular. Bruschetta is an easy and excellent appetizer to make outdoors around the grill and to share with family and friends.

CROSTINI WITH ARTICHOKES AND MELTED MOZZARELLA

Makes 18 to 20 appetizers

$^1/_2$ cup (1 stick) unsalted butter, at room temperature

3 cloves garlic, peeled and minced

1-day-old baguette such as French Baguettes for a Crowd (see page 256), sliced into 18 to 20 slices

8 ounces marinated artichoke caps or hearts, drained and chopped

1 pound mozzarella cheese, cut in thin slices to fit the baguette rounds

Preheat the oven to 350° F. In a food processor, blend the butter with the garlic until smooth. Butter one side of each slice of baguette and arrange on a baking sheet in a single layer. On each slice of baguette, place 1 rounded tablespoon of artichoke. Cover with a slice of cheese. Bake until the cheese is melted, bubbly, and lightly browned, 15 to 20 minutes.

CROSTINI WITH
SUN-DRIED TOMATO TORTA

Makes 18 to 20 appetizers

1 French baguette such as French Baguettes for a Crowd or
    Épi (see page 256 or 258)
½ cup cold-pressed first-pressing extra-virgin olive oil
½ recipe Pesto Torta with Tomatoes (see page 105)
18 to 20 sprigs fresh Italian flat-leaf parsley, stems removed

Preheat the oven to 375° F. Spread the baguette slices in a single layer on a baking sheet. Brush lightly with olive oil. Bake in the oven just until they begin to take on color, 10 to 15 minutes. Remove to a rack to cool. Just before serving, spread with Pesto Torta and place 1 leaf of parsley on each toast.

CROSTINI WITH TOMATOES, BALSAMIC VINEGAR, CHEESE, AND ANCHOVIES

Makes 16 crostini

Sixteen ½-inch slices day-old baguette or country bread,
   toasted without oil or butter
12 anchovy fillets in oil, rinsed and mashed to a paste;
   or ½ cup commercial anchovy paste
6 to 8 fully ripe plum tomatoes, sliced ½ inch thick
¼ cup balsamic vinegar
½ pound finest-quality fresh mozzarella cheese
   or goat cheese
½ cup minced fresh Italian flat-leaf parsley

Preheat the broiler. Thinly spread a layer of anchovy paste on the toast. Top with 2 slices of tomato. Brush the tomato lightly with the vinegar.

   In a small bowl, mash the cheese and the parsley together. Place a tablespoon-sized dollop of cheese mixture on top of the tomatoes. Broil about 4 inches from the heat source until the cheese begins to melt and brown lightly on the edges. Serve immediately.

SAGE HEN CROSTINI

Makes 16 large crostini

16 thin slices country bread
2 tablespoons unsalted butter, plus 2 to 4 tablespoons
   melted unsalted butter, if needed
2 tablespoons cold-pressed first-pressing extra-virgin
   olive oil
$\frac{1}{2}$ cup finely chopped sweet onion
1 pound chicken livers, cleaned of greenish bits and fat
4 fresh sage leaves, minced; or 1 teaspoon dried and
   crumbled, plus fresh sage leaves for garnish
$\frac{1}{2}$ cup Marsala wine
4 teaspoons drained capers
Salt and freshly ground black pepper to taste

Preheat the oven to 400° F. Arrange the bread in a single
layer on a large baking sheet and bake until toasted and
golden, about 5 minutes.

Melt the 2 tablespoons of butter with the oil in a large
skillet. Add the onion and cook until soft. Add the chicken
livers and cook over medium-high heat for 6 to 8 minutes,
stirring frequently, until crusty and browned on the outside
and still pink inside. Stir in the minced or crumbled sage,
Marsala, and capers. Cook until the liquid is almost completely evaporated.

Preheat the broiler. Scrape the chicken livers and any
crusty bits still clinging to the pan into a large mixing bowl.
Using a pastry blender with sharp edges or 2 sharp knives,
chop the mixture fine. (Do not use a blender or food processor as the mixture will become paste.) Season with salt and

pepper. Beat by hand to a spreadable consistency, adding a little melted butter if necessary to moisten.

Spread the mixture on the toasts and run them under the broiler just to heat through, no longer than 1 minute. Garnish with fresh sage leaves and serve immediately.

BASIC BRUSCHETTA

Makes 8 to 12 appetizers

$^1/_2$ pound sourdough such as Pain au Levain or Italian
    Marketplace Bread (see page 94 or 106)
4 large cloves garlic, peeled and halved
$^1/_2$ to $^3/_4$ cup cold-pressed first-pressing extra-virgin
    olive oil
Coarse-grained salt such as kosher salt
Freshly ground black pepper

Slice the bread $^3/_4$ inch thick. Grill or toast the slices until
well browned on both sides. Working quickly, rub each piece
with the cut garlic. Place the bread on a serving tray, brush
with olive oil, and sprinkle to taste with coarse salt and
freshly ground black pepper. Serve immediately.

BRUSCHETTA
WITH FRIZZLED PROSCIUTTO

Makes 8 appetizer servings

8 slices country-style bread such as Italian Marketplace
    Bread (see page 106), cut 1/2 inch thick and halved
2 large cloves garlic, peeled and halved
1/4 cup cold-pressed first-pressing extra-virgin olive oil
1/2 pound prosciutto, sliced thin

Toast the bread and, when cool enough to handle, rub the
slices with the garlic clove and brush with the olive oil.

Preheat the broiler. Arrange the bread on a large baking
sheet and top with the prosciutto slices. Broil until the prosciutto begins to crinkle and the edges begin to curl, about
1 minute. Serve immediately.

BRUSCHETTA WITH TWO-OLIVE PESTO AND FRESH MOZZARELLA

Makes 8 large appetizers

TWO-OLIVE PESTO:

$^1/_2$ cup pitted Kalamata olives

$^3/_4$ cup pitted California black olives

1 tablespoon plus 1 teaspoon fresh lemon juice

$^1/_3$ cup freshly grated Parmesan cheese

$^1/_2$ cup fresh Italian flat-leaf parsley leaves

1 tablespoon plus 1 teaspoon drained capers

$^1/_4$ cup cold-pressed first-pressing extra-virgin olive oil

$^1/_8$ teaspoon dried thyme

Salt and freshly ground black pepper to taste

8 large slices Italian-style country bread such as
    Italian Marketplace Bread (see page 106)

$^3/_4$ pound fresh mozzarella, drained and cut into $^1/_4$-inch-
    thick slices

Paprika for garnish (optional)

8 Italian flat-leaf parsley leaves for garnish (optional)

To make the pesto, in the bowl of a food processor fitted with the steel blade, combine the olives, lemon juice, cheese, parsley, capers, olive oil, and thyme. Pulse on and off until a rough-textured puree is made. Season with salt and pepper.

Preheat the oven to 375° F. and toast the bread slices lightly, about 15 minutes. Spread with the pesto and top with 1 slice of mozzarella.

Preheat the oven to broil. Broil the bread slices about 4 to 6 inches from the heat source until the cheese is melted. Sprinkle lightly with paprika for color and add one Italian flat-leaf parsley leaf for garnish if desired. Serve immediately.

GRILLED ONION BRUSCHETTA WITH ROMESCO SAUCE

Makes two dozen appetizers

24 small sweet onions, each 2 to 3 inches long
Olive oil
One 1¹/₂-pound country bread such as Italian Marketplace
    Bread (see page 106), or 2 large baguettes such as
    French Baguettes for a Crowd (see page 256), cut into
    twenty-four ³/₄-inch-thick slices, halved and toasted well
    on both sides
Salt and freshly ground black pepper to taste

SAUCE:
1 teaspoon dried red chili pepper flakes
2 egg yolks
¹/₃ cup toasted, slivered almonds
1 red bell pepper, roasted, peeled, and seeded
1 small tomato, peeled and seeded
¹/₄ cup red wine vinegar
Juice of 1 lemon
1 cup extra-virgin cold-pressed first-pressing olive oil

Peel and slice off the root ends of the onions. Rub each onion
with a little olive oil. Place the onions over hot coals, on a gas
grill, or on a stovetop grill, turning them as they brown. Cook
until they're tender all the way through when pierced with a
fork. Meanwhile, prepare the Romesco sauce.

Place all of the sauce ingredients except for the olive oil
in the bowl of a food processor or blender and process to a

smooth paste. With the machine running, slowly add half the olive oil. With a rubber spatula, clean the sides of the bowl and continue to process adding the remaining oil.

To prepare the bruschetta, pour a small pool of sauce on each serving plate, place 2 bruschetta on top of the sauce, top each bruschetta with 1 grilled onion and flatten it slightly with the back of a spatula. Season with salt and pepper to taste and serve immediately.

8

*B*UNS, BAGELS, BAGUETTES, BREADSTICKS, BRIOCHE, AND ROLLS

Petits Pains
Classic Breadsticks
Swiss Sticks
Anise Breadsticks
Grissini Grande
Grissini Romano
Sour Yogurt–Sprouted Rye Breadsticks
The Bread of Life
Prosciutto Bread
Mount Olive Rolls
Raisin in the Rye Rolls
Milk Rolls for Meat and Cheese *Merende*
Golden Raisin Lemon Buns with Saffron
The Bagels of Paris (with 3 Variations):
    Whole Wheat Bagels
    Pumpernickel Raisin Bagels
    Egg Bagels
French Baguettes for a Crowd
The *Épi*
Stirato for the Bread Machine
Feather Bread Croissants (with a Variation)
    Pains au Chocolat
Bread Machine Brioche
Whole Olive Brioche with 2 Cheeses

PETITS PAINS
Hard Rolls

Dough Setting
Makes 6 large rolls or a dozen small ones

Technique is all for hard rolls as good as those you buy in a fine bakery. Let the bread machine do the basic mixing, kneading, and first rising of the dough, then you get the fun of shaping and raising the rolls themselves. This is a 4-rise process. The flavor is well developed and the crust will be hard on the outside, while inside the rolls will be soft and flavorful.

1 tablespoon plus 2 teaspoons bread machine yeast
3 cups bread flour
1 cup gluten flour
1 teaspoon sugar
1 1/2 teaspoons salt
1 1/2 cups water
1 egg white whisked with 1 teaspoon spring water for glaze

Add the yeast, flours, sugar, salt, and water to the bread machine pan and process on the dough setting. Once the cycle is complete, remove the dough to a lightly floured surface and knead it by hand for a few seconds, then form into a tight ball. Cover with the bread machine pan and let the dough rest for 15 to 30 minutes.

Now, form the rolls. Cut the dough into 6 equal pieces. Roll the pieces into tight balls and place them on a peel covered with parchment paper. Let the rolls rise, uncovered, until almost doubled in bulk.

Note that the tops are now crusty and dry. Flatten each ball and fold it in half, the crusty side in. Roll the dough between the palms of your hands, forming a torpedo-shaped *petit pain* (see page 81), about 5½ × 1½ inches, tapering both ends. Transfer the rolls back to the parchment and raise again, uncovered, until almost doubled in bulk.

Meanwhile, preheat the oven to 425° F., with the baking stone in place on the middle rack, for at least 30 minutes. Once the rolls have risen, make a deep slash about 4 inches long down the center of each. Brush gently with the egg white glaze, then shovel the parchment and rolls onto the baking stone. Bake for 20 minutes, or until the rolls have turned golden brown. Spritz the oven with plain water 6 or 7 times during the first 10 minutes of baking (see page 74) for the best possible crust. Cool on a rack.

SPINACH AND STRAWBERRY SALAD

Serves 10 as a first-course salad

This beautiful salad is a feast for the eyes as well as for the heart.
Rich in vitamin C and iron, and high in fiber,
it should be in everyone's recipe file.
We think it's beautiful when served in the garden
for a bridal shower or with red strawberry hearts
on a beautiful emerald background for Valentine's Day.
If strawberries are available in your market in the winter, why not try
it for Christmas—a red and green salad on clear glass salad plates.

SALAD:
2 tablespoons unsalted butter
$^2/_3$ cup sliced almonds
1 pound spinach, washed, trimmed of stems and torn into bite-sized pieces
1 pint fresh strawberries, stemmed and sliced like hearts

DRESSING:
2 tablespoons lightly toasted sesame seeds
1 tablespoon poppy seeds
$^1/_2$ cup sugar
2 teaspoons minced red onion
$^1/_4$ teaspoon paprika
$^1/_4$ cup cider vinegar
$^1/_4$ cup white wine vinegar
$^1/_2$ cup vegetable oil

Melt the butter in a small skillet and sauté the almonds until lightly browned and toasted.
Remove from the heat and set aside to cool.
In a large salad bowl, combine the spinach and strawberries. Toss to mix. For the dressing,
toast the sesame seeds in the microwave (about 3 minutes on high), or shake them over medium
heat in a dry skillet until lightly browned. In a jar with a tight-fitting lid, combine the
sesame seeds, poppy seeds, sugar, onion, paprika, vinegars, and oil. Shake well.
To serve, $1^1/_2$ cups of spinach-strawberry salad on each plate
and sprinkle with a tablespoon of almonds.
Spoon the dressing over the top and serve immediately.

CLASSIC BREADSTICKS

Dough Setting
Makes 20 breadsticks as thick as your thumb

Make these breadsticks as thick as your thumb, or as fine as a shoelace, depending on your preference. Whatever the diameter, the flavor's the same: wheaty, snappy with salt, and rich with olive oil.

3 cups bread flour
1 teaspoon salt
2 teaspoons olive oil
1 teaspoon sugar
$1/4$ cup nonfat dry powdered milk solids
$2^1/_2$ teaspoons bread machine yeast
$1^1/_8$ cups water
1 egg white whipped with 1 tablespoon warm water

Combine all the ingredients except the egg white in the bread machine pan and process on the dough setting.

When the cycle is completed, transfer the dough to a lightly floured surface, punch it down, and pinch it into about twenty equal pieces. Roll each piece into a ball, cover with plastic, and allow it to rest 10 minutes. Then, on a lightly floured surface, shape the balls into pencil shapes about 14 inches long, rolling them under the palms of your hands.

Coat a 14 × 16-inch baking sheet with cornmeal, then arrange the breadsticks on the sheet, sides not touching. Cover with plastic wrap and set aside to rise for about 20 minutes.

Meanwhile, preheat the oven to 400° F. Just before baking, brush the breadsticks with the foamed egg white. If you wish, finish with seeds of your choice (see box), or with kosher salt. Bake until golden brown, about 15 minutes. Cool on a rack.

FINISHING YOUR BREADSTICKS:
RUFFLES AND FLOURISHES

Learn to make classic breadsticks and you can create a variety of finishes
simply by changing the toppings. Brush the breadsticks with a little egg
white frothed up with a tablespoon of water, then sprinkle on any of these
seeds, seasonings, or herbs before baking.

Mix together $1/3$ cup sesame seeds and 3 tablespoons *each* cuminseed and
poppy seeds. Roll the breadsticks in this mixture to coat all over, then place
on a baking sheet that's been thoroughly spritzed with cooking spray.

Sprinkle breadsticks with kosher or Margarita salt.

Sprinkle red pepper flakes over all sides of the breadsticks.

Sprinkle breadsticks with fennel, dill, flax, sesame, black sesame, poppy,
caraway, cumin, or a mixture thereof.

Sprinkle maple sugar or turbinado sugar on plain breadsticks.

Add a tablespoon of sugar to the dough, then sprinkle sweet breadsticks
with equal parts sugar and cinnamon.

SWISS STICKS

Dough Setting
Makes 10 breadsticks

A wintry night, snowy mountain peaks, a dinner after skiing. Make these triple-seeded Basel breadsticks and serve them with a cauldron of Hot Beer and Cheese Soup (see sidebar, page 233).

2 cups whole wheat flour
1 cup bread flour
$\frac{1}{2}$ teaspoon salt
$2\frac{1}{2}$ teaspoons bread machine yeast
2 tablespoons mild olive oil
1 tablespoon honey
$1\frac{1}{8}$ cups water
$\frac{1}{3}$ cup sesame seeds
3 tablespoons *each* cuminseed and poppy seed
1 large egg white

Place the flours, salt, yeast, oil, honey, and water in the bread machine pan and process on the dough setting.

While the dough works, combine the sesame, cumin, and poppy seed. Once the cycle is completed, lift the dough to a lightly floured surface and punch it down. Turn the bread machine pan on top of the dough and let it rest for 10 minutes. Now pat the dough into a 10 × 6-inch rectangle. Cut into ten 6-inch strips and let them rise until puffy, about 25 minutes.

Preheat the oven to 375° F. Line 2 large baking sheets with parchment paper. Whip the egg white until frothy and brush it evenly over the breadsticks. Place the mixed seeds on a piece of waxed paper. Pull each breadstick into a 12-inch length and roll it in the seeds to cover evenly. Twist the stick 3 or 4 times, then place it on the baking sheet. Repeat, placing the sticks about 2 inches apart on the baking sheets.

Bake in the preheated oven until the sticks are brown and crusty, about 25 minutes. Cool the breadsticks on a rack. To store, place in an airtight tin.

HOT BEER AND CHEESE SOUP

2 quarts water
1 pound smoked ham
1 medium yellow onion, chopped
$^3/_4$ teaspoon freshly ground black pepper
$^1/_2$ cup vegetable oil
1 cup all-purpose flour
2 cups whole milk
$^3/_4$ cup beer
12 ounces sharp cheddar cheese, grated
$^1/_4$ cup chopped fresh parsley, for garnish

In a large soup pot, combine the water, ham, onion, and pepper.
Bring to a boil, then reduce the heat and simmer for about 1 hour.
Skim fat and discard.
Meanwhile, in a cast-iron skillet, make a roux using oil and flour:
Heat the oil over medium heat, stir in the flour, and cook, stirring, until the mixture is a rich, golden brown.
Then stir in the milk slowly until you have a thick, smooth sauce. Pour this into the hot stock. Add the beer and blend until smooth. Off the heat, stir in the cheddar cheese until it melts. Serve in soup bowls, garnished with parsley.

ANISE BREADSTICKS

Dough Setting
Makes two dozen medium breadsticks

The bite of anise in a crunchy breadstick makes an ideal accompaniment to potato soup or a good marinara sauce.

3^1/$_2$ cups bread flour
2 tablespoons granulated sugar
^{3}/$_4$ teaspoon salt
2^1/$_2$ teaspoons bread machine yeast
1^1/$_8$ cups water
1 tablespoon fruity olive oil
1 tablespoon brandy
^{1}/$_2$ teaspoon vanilla extract
1 tablespoon plus 1 teaspoon aniseseed
Turbinado sugar for sprinkling

Place all the ingredients except turbinado sugar in the bread machine pan and process on the dough setting. Then remove the dough and punch it down. Knead a moment on a lightly floured surface, then roll into a 16 × 6-inch rectangle. Cover with plastic and let it rest for 5 minutes or so. Meanwhile, preheat the oven to 400° F. Spritz 2 baking sheets with cooking spray.

Cut the dough into twenty-four 6-inch strips. Stretch each strip to about 15 inches, then place the strips on prepared baking sheets, sides not touching. Cover and set aside to rise until puffy, about 15 minutes.

Just before baking, spritz the breadsticks with water and sprinkle with turbinado sugar. Bake in the preheated oven for 10 minutes then rotate the baking sheets. Spray again with water and continue baking for about 5 minutes more, until the sticks are golden brown. Cool on a rack. Store in airtight tins.

COLD POTATO SOUP

Makes 2 quarts

1 pound russet potatoes, peeled and
chopped
1 leek, cleaned and chopped
6 cups chicken stock
Salt and white pepper to taste
2 cups crème fraîche
3 tablespoon minced fresh chives

Place the potatoes, leek, and chicken stock in a large soup pot and boil hard until the potatoes are tender, about 15 minutes. Puree in a blender or food processor, then adjust the seasoning with salt and white pepper. Stir in the crème fraîche, cover, and refrigerate. Serve cold, garnished with chives.

GRISSINI GRANDE

Dough Setting
Makes 16 big breadsticks

Big, soft breadsticks terrific for dipping into fresh Roma tomato sauce. A fine accompaniment to pastas.

1 tablespoon plus 2 teaspoons bread machine yeast
3 cups bread flour
1 tablespoon sugar
3 tablespoons fresh herbs of your choice, such as basil,
    oregano, Italian flat-leaf parsley, sage
1/4 cup olive oil
1 cup water
1/2 teaspoon salt
1 large egg beaten until frothy with 1 tablespoon water
Kosher salt, sesame or poppy seeds for sprinkling on top

Place the yeast, flour, sugar, herbs, oil, water, and salt in the bread machine pan and process on the dough setting.

Once the cycle is complete, remove the dough to a lightly floured board and form into a tight ball. Cover with the bread machine pan and let the dough rest for 10 minutes.

Meanwhile, preheat the oven to 350° F. Spritz 2 large baking sheets with cooking spray, or cover them with parchment paper. Cut the dough into 16 equal-sized pieces.

Roll each piece into a 20-inch-long rope. Place the sticks on the prepared baking sheets, sides not touching, and set aside to rise until puffy, about 15 minutes. Brush with frothy egg white and sprinkle with salt or seeds. Bake until golden brown, about 30 to 35 minutes. Cool on the baking sheet for 5 minutes, then transfer to a rack. Serve warm or at room temperature. Great with marinara sauce.

SIMPLE MARINARA

Makes 1 pint

Italian restaurants sometimes offer breadsticks
with a marinara sauce for dipping. Here's a simple version.

2 tablespoons fruity olive oil
4 cloves garlic, peeled and minced
1 small onion, minced
1 tablespoon dried rosemary
1 (16-ounce) can tomatoes and their juice, chopped coarse
$1/2$ teaspoon sugar
Salt and freshly ground
black pepper to taste
$1/4$ cup chopped fresh basil

In a medium saucepan, heat the oil and sauté the garlic, onion, and
rosemary over medium heat until the onion turns clear. Add the tomatoes
and their juice. Stir in the sugar, and salt and pepper. Boil gently uncovered,
about 10 minutes, then stir in the basil. Cover and let it stand for at least
30 minutes. It's even better the second day.
Store, covered, in the refrigerator.

GRISSINI ROMANO

Dough Setting
Makes 56 pencil-thin breadsticks

Standing in a glass on the table of many Italian restaurants is a bunch of pencil-thin breadsticks: crisp, bright with Romano cheese, they're a meal in themselves.

2$\frac{1}{2}$ teaspoons bread machine yeast
3 cups bread flour
1 teaspoon salt
$\frac{3}{4}$ cup freshly grated Romano cheese
$\frac{1}{4}$ teaspoon cayenne pepper
1 teaspoon sugar
$\frac{1}{4}$ cup nonfat dry powdered milk solids
1$\frac{1}{8}$ cups water
2 teaspoons olive oil
1 egg white whipped with 1 tablespoon warm water

Combine all the ingredients except the egg white and $\frac{1}{4}$ cup of the Romano cheese in the bread machine pan and process on the dough setting. Remove the processed dough to a lightly floured surface and punch it down.

Divide the dough into two equal pieces. Roll each piece into a 10 × 14 × $\frac{1}{4}$-inch rectangle. Cover with plastic wrap and allow it to rest for 10 minutes. Then, cut it into 10 × $\frac{1}{2}$-inch strips. Roll each strip between the palms of your hands into long pencil lengths.

Coat a 14 × 16-inch baking sheet with cornmeal, then arrange the breadsticks on the sheet, sides not touching. Cover with plastic wrap and set aside to rise for about 20 minutes.

Meanwhile, preheat the oven to 375° F. Just before baking, brush the breadsticks with foamed egg white. Finish with the remaining ¼ cup of grated cheese. Bake until golden brown, about 15 minutes. Cool on a rack. Store in airtight tins.

SUMMER GARDEN ANTIPASTO

Good only when summer tomatoes are at their sweetest. Combine these with slices of salami, pickled peppers, and breadsticks for a fine summer antipasto served with a glass of gutsy red wine. Come to think of it, on hot nights this is all we want for dinner.
With maybe a little gelato to finish.

3 large beefsteak tomatoes,
sliced ¼ inch thick
1 green bell pepper,
seeded and finely chopped
1 yellow bell pepper,
seeded and finely chopped
Salt and freshly ground black
pepper to taste
½ pound provolone cheese, sliced thin
1 cup Italian bread crumbs

Preheat the oven to 350° F. Spritz a deep 2-quart baking dish with olive oil cooking spray. Then layer in a third *each* of the tomatoes, peppers, salt and pepper, and cheese slices. Top with a third of the crumbs. Repeat twice, finishing with crumbs. Cover and bake for about 30 minutes, or until the mixture is bubbly and hot throughout.

SOUR YOGURT–SPROUTED RYE BREADSTICKS

Dough Setting
Makes 16 large breadsticks

Rye breadsticks just beg for a pot of borscht or perhaps a cheese fondue. Make them a couple of days after you remembered to sprout the rye berries.

1 tablespoon bread machine yeast
2½ cups bread flour
1 cup medium rye flour
1 tablespoon yellow cornmeal
1 teaspoon salt
1½ tablespoons sugar
¾ cup plain nonfat yogurt
½ cup water
3 tablespoons butter or margarine
1½ teaspoons caraway seeds, plus extra for topping
   (optional)
½ cup sprouted rye berries (see sidebar, page 241)
1 large egg white mixed with 1 tablespoon water for a wash
Kosher salt (optional)

Combine the yeast, flours, cornmeal, salt, and sugar in the bread machine pan. Add the yogurt and water, then the butter. Process on the dough setting. Once the cycle is completed, remove the dough from the machine and knead in the caraway seeds and rye berries.

Remove the dough to a generously floured board and

form it into a ball. Turn the bread machine pan over the dough and let it rest while you prepare the baking sheets.

Spritz 2 large baking sheets with cooking spray or cover them with parchment paper. Preheat the oven to 400° F. Divide the dough into 16 equal-sized pieces. Roll each piece into a rough ball and set aside, covered, until nearly doubled in bulk, 20 to 30 minutes.

Roll each piece into a 20-inch-long rope. Place the breadsticks on the prepared baking sheets, sides not touching. Set aside in a warm place and allow the sticks to rise until puffy, about 15 minutes.

Just before baking, lightly brush each breadstick with the frothy egg white wash. Sprinkle with additional caraway seeds or with kosher salt, if desired. Bake on the middle rack of the preheated oven for 20 minutes, or until lightly browned. Cool for 5 minutes on the baking sheet, then remove to a rack. Serve warm or at room temperature. Store in airtight containers or plastic bags.

To sprout rye or wheat berries, wash the dried berries in cold water, then place in a glass jar, cover loosely, and set in a dark cabinet for a day or two. You'll see the tiny hairlike sprouts beginning to appear. If you're not ready to use the sprouts that day, cover with plastic wrap and refrigerate up to 2 days before using in a bread recipe.

THE BREAD OF LIFE

Dough Setting
Makes 6 large rolls

ITALIAN TART GREEN SALAD WITH PINE NUTS, PROSCIUTTO, AND SIZZLING GARLIC DRESSING

Makes 8 servings

Making a great salad has never been so easy as it is now with the availability of washed, mixed greens in your supermarket's produce section.
Our favorite brand, Fresh Express, sells washed greens in 10- or 14-ounce bags. Each combination has a different name (Euro-Mix, Italian Delight, Mesclun) but our favorite is the Italian Mix of radicchio, romaine, red-leaf lettuce, and curly endive. If you can't find Italian Mix for this recipe, substitute 10 cups of mixed red-leaf, romaine, radicchio, and a little curly endive.

1 small red onion, sliced into thin rings
$1/3$ cup red wine vinegar
2 (14-ounce) bags Fresh Express Italian Salad mixed greens,
or 10 cups of your own mixed greens, including romaine, radicchio, red-leaf lettuce and curly endive
1 cup lightly packed fresh Italian flat-leaf parsley leaves (do try to use this as opposed to the curly leaf; it makes a big difference)
4 whole green onions, sliced thin
$1/2$ cup pine nuts
1 cup shaved Parmesan cheese (do this with a vegetable peeler)
$1/4$ pound thinly sliced prosciutto, julienned

The Bread of Life has long been the blessing bread used at wedding feasts throughout much of Italy. The embracing limbs of the two pieces of dough make a beautiful visual statement that is a celebration of life.

We want to point out that even though the recipe makes only 6 rolls, they are large, and one is approximately twice the size of an average dinner roll. So much of the dough is exposed to the hot oven air that the entire roll is crisp, with very little soft crumb, thus making it an excellent salad accompaniment.

SPONGE:
Pinch bread machine yeast
$1/4$ cup plus 2 tablespoons bread flour
$1/4$ cup plus 2 tablespoons water
$1/2$ teaspoon olive oil

DOUGH:
$1/2$ teaspoon bread machine yeast
$1 1/2$ cups bread flour
$1/2$ cup soft-wheat cake flour
$1/2$ cup plus 1 tablespoon water
$3/4$ teaspoon salt
2 tablespoons olive oil

Combine the sponge ingredients in the bread machine pan and process on the dough cycle until the sponge is well combined, about 5 minutes on most machines. Turn off the machine and let the sponge sit in the pan for at least 12 hours or as long as 24.

Add the dough ingredients to the sponge in the pan. Process on the dough setting. Let the dough sit in the machine for an hour after the cycle is finished. Meanwhile, cover 2 large baking sheets with parchment paper and sprinkle the paper liberally with cornmeal.

Turn the dough out onto a lightly floured surface and, with floured hands, divide it into 6 equal-sized balls. Let the dough rest for 5 minutes to relax the gluten. Roll each piece of dough into a thin 6-inch square. Cut each square diagonally into two pieces. Gently stretch each triangle of dough point to point and wide end to point. Starting at the wide side, roll each triangle tightly. The dough will look like tightly curled croissants. Place two pieces of dough together and squeeze to seal in the middle. Place the roll on the prepared baking sheet and curve each of the 4 limbs slightly to look somewhat like a cursive letter H.

Cover the rolls with plastic wrap and let them rise in a warm, draft-free place for approximately 45 minutes. Meanwhile, preheat the oven to 350° F. Bake the rolls on the middle shelf for 30 to 35 minutes, or until they're golden brown. Remove from the baking sheet to a rack to cool and serve at room temperature.

SALAD DRESSING:

⅓ cup cold-pressed first-pressing extra-virgin olive oil
4 cloves garlic, peeled and minced
2 tablespoon balsamic vinegar
2 tablespoons red wine vinegar
1 teaspoon brown sugar
Salt and freshly ground black pepper to taste

To make the salad, mix the onion with the red wine vinegar and set aside. Mix the greens and the parsley in a large salad bowl. Layer the green onions, pine nuts, cheese, and prosciutto on top. Refrigerate. To make the dressing, cook the olive oil and garlic in a small pan over medium heat for about 5 minutes, or just until the garlic starts to take on color. Quickly add the vinegars and boil for 1 minute. Stir in the brown sugar and cook for an additional minute. Cool for 5 minutes and add salt and pepper. Drain the red onion and add to the top of the salad bowl. Pour the hot dressing over all and toss. Serve immediately on clear glass salad plates and set 1 Bread of Life roll on the top if you like.

The Bread of Life

PROSCIUTTO BREAD

Dough Setting
Makes one dozen rolls or 1 baguette

The next time you're serving the traditional continental breakfast of fruit, bread, and cheese, add a dozen of these rolls or a baguette to the breadbasket. The salty, rosy prosciutto plays nicely against the yeasty richness of the bread. Served with cantaloupe, honeydew, or even watermelon this bread can't be beat.

DOUGH:
1½ teaspoons bread machine yeast
2 cups bread flour
1 tablespoon instant nonfat dry milk solids
1 teaspoon salt
1 tablespoon unsalted butter
⅔ cup water
1½ cups chopped prosciutto ham

GLAZE:
1 egg, lightly beaten

Add the yeast, flour, dry milk, salt, butter, and water to the bread machine pan. Process on the dough setting. Meanwhile, dust a baking sheet with cornmeal.

Remove the dough from the machine to a lightly floured surface, divide it into 12 equal balls, and let it rest for 10 minutes.

Flatten each ball into a 4- to 5-inch circle. Place 2 tablespoons chopped prosciutto on one side of each circle. Roll up the circle from the ham side to make a miniature baguette;

seal well by wetting the edges, then pinching them shut. Roll the baguettes so that the seam is on the bottom.

With a sharp knife, make 3 shallow diagonal cuts in the dough. Place on the prepared baking sheet. Cover lightly with plastic wrap and set aside to rise in a warm, draft-free place until the dough has just about doubled, about 40 minutes. Meanwhile, preheat the oven to 350° F.

Brush the rolls with the beaten egg and bake on the middle shelf of the preheated oven for 15 to 20 minutes, or until golden brown.

Remove the rolls to a rack to cool. Wrap in plastic wrap to store. These can be frozen for up to a month, then reheated in a toaster oven for 10 to 15 minutes.

To form 1 large baguette, roll the dough into a rectangle about 10 × 16 inches. Spread the prosciutto evenly over the surface, leaving a 1-inch rim. Wet the rim, fold the baguette in half, lengthwise, and pinch the seam shut. Roll the loaf onto a cornmeal-dusted baking sheet so that the seam is on the bottom. Make diagonal slashes with a razor blade, at a 45° angle along the length of the bread. Let rise until doubled in bulk, then bake for 25 to 30 minutes, or until the baguette is golden brown.

MOUNT OLIVE ROLLS

Dough Setting
Makes one dozen rolls

Once a common midafternoon snack throughout much of Italy, these rolls are now finding fans in American homes as well. We like to surprise people by adding them to the breadbasket along with a *Pain au Levain* (see page 94) and watch their eyes light up when they hit the unexpected salty little black bits of olive.

This dough is a little sticky, and one of the easiest ways we've found to work with sticky doughs is to wet your hands well before touching the dough and occasionally thereafter. Diana shapes these rolls on her countertop by the sink and lets a little trickle of water run continuously so that she can keep wetting her hands.

DOUGH:
1¼ cups spring water
½ cup Italian Winter *Biga* for Rolls and Wheat Breads
   (see page 60)
¾ teaspoon bread machine yeast
2¾ cups bread flour
½ cup whole wheat flour
1½ teaspoons salt
⅔ cup Kalamata olive halves

These rolls also make great little sandwiches filled with provolone and a good salami flavored with garlic or Parmesan. There are no substitutes for the Kalamata olives in this recipe. Our favorite brand is Peloponnese from Greece. They sell their olives in 4.5-ounce jars in our local deli at the supermarket and they are PITTED!! So now they're even easier to work with.

Add ¼ cup of the spring water and the *biga* to the bread machine pan. With a rubber spatula, stir and chop the *biga* into chunks for about 1 minute. Then add the remaining cup of water, the yeast, flours, and salt to the bread pan. *If you are using a 1-pound machine,* let the ingredients be mixed and kneaded on the dough setting. Then turn off the machine and remove the dough to a lightly greased 3-quart plastic or glass bowl and cover it with plastic wrap. Set the dough aside to rise until tripled in bulk, 3 to 4 hours.

If you are using a 1½-pound machine, process the ingredients according to the manufacturer's instructions for a dough setting. Then leave the dough in the machine to rise for an additional hour, or until tripled in bulk.

Meanwhile, cut a piece of parchment paper to match the dimensions of your baking stone or tiles. Place the parchment paper on a wooden peel or a rimless baking sheet. Sift or toss a light blizzard of flour over the parchment paper. These rolls can also be baked on a heavy baking sheet that has been lightly greased and lightly dusted with cornmeal; however, the baking stone or tiles is preferred.

Also, lightly spray a smooth work surface with water and wet your hands. Turn the dough out of the bowl or bread machine pan onto the wet work surface. Gently knead the olives into the dough. Wet your hands as necessary to keep the wet dough from sticking to your hands. Pull the dough into 12 equal pieces. Pull and tuck each piece into the middle to form a tight ball. Place the balls on the prepared parchment or baking sheet and sift the tops lightly with flour. Cover with a tent of aluminum foil that will not touch them as they rise, and set them aside until doubled, about 1 to 1¼ hours.

Thirty minutes before baking, heat the oven with the baking stone or tiles in place to 425° F. When the rolls have doubled, carefully slide the baking stone on the rack toward you a little bit so that you can slide the parchment paper with the rolls onto the stone. Slide the stone back into the oven and bake the rolls for 25 to 30 minutes, or until they're golden. The parchment paper does not need to be removed. Alternatively, the rolls on the baking sheet will bake for 25 to 30 minutes, or until the crusts are golden.

One of our favorite ways to serve bread *without* butter is to pool about ½ cup best-quality olive oil on a white saucer and then pour about 2 tablespoons first-rate balsamic vinegar into the middle of the oil. Pass the rolls and let everyone tear off a chunk and dip it into the oil and vinegar. Instant antipasto!

RAISIN IN THE RYE ROLLS

Dough Setting
Makes a dozen rolls

Raisins contain sugar and are naturally covered with yeast, which almost always makes them a welcome addition to bread dough that is started with a sponge. First the sugars feed the yeast in the dough; then the raisins' own yeast gives it a little extra lift.

The recipe can be stretched to make 15 rolls or rolled into a ball to make 1 large round *boule.*

1¼ cups spring water
½ cup Italian Winter *Biga* for Rolls and Wheat Breads (see page 106)
¾ teaspoon bread machine yeast
2¾ cups bread flour
½ cup rye flour or whole wheat flour
1½ teaspoons salt
⅔ cup raisins, soaked in water for 30 minutes if they are hard

Add ¼ cup of the spring water and the *biga* to the bread machine pan. With a rubber spatula, stir and chop the *biga* into chunks for about 1 minute. Add the remaining cup of water, the yeast, flours, and salt to the bread pan.

If you are using a 1-pound machine, let the ingredients be mixed and kneaded on the dough setting. Turn off the machine and remove the dough from the bread machine pan to a lightly greased 3-quart plastic or glass bowl and cover with plastic wrap. Set aside to rise until tripled in bulk, 3 to 4 hours.

If you are using a 1½-pound machine, process the ingredients on the dough setting, turn off the machine, and let the dough rise in the machine for an additional hour or until tripled.

While the dough rises, cut a piece of parchment paper to match the dimensions of your baking stone or tiles. Place the parchment paper on a wooden peel or rimless baking sheet. Sift or toss a light blizzard of flour over the parchment paper. These rolls can also be baked on a heavy baking sheet that has been lightly greased and dusted with cornmeal; however, the baking stone or tiles is preferred.

Lightly spray a smooth work surface with water and wet your hands. Turn the dough out of the bowl or bread machine pan onto the wet surface. Gently knead the raisins into the dough. With wet hands, divide the dough into 12 equal pieces. Pull and tuck each piece into the middle to form a tight ball. Place the balls on the prepared parchment or baking sheet and sift the tops of the balls lightly with flour. Cover with a tent of aluminum foil that will not touch them as they rise, and leave them until doubled, about 1 to 1¼ hours.

Thirty minutes before baking, heat the oven with the baking stone or tiles in place to 425° F. When the rolls have doubled, carefully slide the baking stone out a little bit so that you can slip the parchment paper with the rolls onto the stone. Slide the stone back into the oven and bake the rolls for 25 to 30 minutes, or until golden. The parchment paper need not be removed during the baking period. Alternatively, the rolls on the baking sheet will bake for 30 to 35 minutes, or until the crusts are golden. Remove the rolls to racks to cool and peel off any paper that might have stuck to the bottoms.

TRY CHEESES AS A SPREADABLE

Raisin in the Rye Rolls are wonderful plain or with just a smear of butter; however, to really gild the lily, mash 4 ounces goat cheese, fresh mozzarella, or Stilton with 2 or 3 tablespoons fresh cream or crème fraîche. Split the roll, spread with 1 tablespoon of the cheese mixture, and sprinkle with additional moist raisins. Eat immediately or run under the broiler until the cheese begins to brown around the edges. Cool 2 minutes and eat immediately.

MILK ROLLS FOR
MEAT AND CHEESE *MERENDE*

Dough Setting
Makes 10 large rolls

The Italian people may derive even more pleasure from eating than cookbook authors, hence they have a tradition of eating not 3 meals a day but 5. The 2 small meals they squeeze in between breakfast, lunch, and dinner are called *merende.*

We developed these rolls to accompany favorite meat and cheese *merende* combinations—salami and provolone, goat cheese and grilled chicken with arugula—or as a nice foil for fried calamari with garlic mayonnaise and a fresh squeeze of lemon.

These rolls keep well for 4 or 5 days if stored in a plastic bag and also make great sandwich rolls for almost any American sandwich from cheeseburgers to turkey with stuffing and a dab of cranberry sauce.

2 tablespoons bread machine yeast
3 cups bread flour
1 tablespoon sugar
1½ teaspoons salt
2 tablespoons vegetable oil
2 large eggs
½ cup water
½ cup milk
Sesame seeds for sprinkling on top (optional)

Combine the yeast, flour, sugar, salt, oil, 1 egg, the water, and milk in the bread machine pan. *If you are using a 1-pound machine*, let the ingredients be mixed and kneaded, about 25 minutes in most machines, and then turn the machine off. Turn the dough out into a lightly greased 3-quart bowl and cover tightly with plastic wrap. Set the dough aside to rise in a warm place until doubled in bulk, about 1 hour.

If you are using a 1½-pound machine, process completely on the dough setting.

Lightly grease a large baking sheet. Turn the risen dough out onto a lightly floured surface and form the dough into 10 tight, smooth, equal balls, each about the size of a golf ball. Cover the rolls with a tent of heavy-duty aluminum foil, making sure the rolls will not expand and touch the foil. Set the rolls aside to rise until doubled in bulk, about 1 hour. Twenty minutes before baking, preheat the oven to 375° F.

When the rolls have doubled in bulk, remove the foil, whisk the remaining egg well, and brush the rolls lightly with the egg. Sprinkle with sesame seeds, if desired. Bake on the middle rack of the preheated oven for 18 to 20 minutes, or until golden brown. Remove the rolls from the baking sheet to cool on a rack. When completely cool, split and fill with your favorite filling. These rolls keep well stored in a plastic bag for up to 1 week.

OIL, VINEGAR,
AND HERB DRESSING
FOR SOPHISTICATED BREADS

Makes 1¼ cups

Use this dressing for Milk Rolls, olive rolls, or grinder or sub breads when you want a change of pace from mayonnaise or other traditional condiments.

½ cup olive oil
2 medium cloves garlic,
peeled and minced
½ small onion, minced
½ teaspoon freshly ground black pepper
Juice of 2 medium lemons,
or ⅓ cup red wine vinegar
Zest of 1 lemon, minced
1 teaspoon dried oregano
¼ teaspoon red pepper flakes
1 tablespoon freshly grated
Parmesan cheese

Combine all the ingredients in a container with a tight-fitting lid and shake well. Set aside for 4 hours to allow the flavors to blend. Sprinkle on Milk Rolls or your own favorite rolls before adding fillings. This keeps well in the refrigerator for up to 2 weeks.

GOLDEN RAISIN LEMON BUNS WITH SAFFRON

Dough Setting
Makes 10 rolls

Tart minced lemon zest, golden raisins, saffron, and candied lemon peel make these rolls beautiful to behold. We usually save these for Christmastime, when candied lemon peel is most readily available. Serve them with tea and lemon marmalade or lemon curd for an afternoon snack.

SPONGE:

1/3 cup cold milk
Zest of 1 lemon, minced
2 teaspoons bread machine yeast
2 teaspoons sugar
1/2 cup bread flour

DOUGH:

1/4 cup sugar
2 large eggs
1/4 cup (1/2 stick) unsalted butter, at room temperature
1 1/2 cups bread flour
1/2 teaspoon salt
1/2 teaspoon saffron threads (optional)
3/4 cup golden raisins
1/3 cup candied lemon peel

GLAZE:

1 egg white

To make the sponge, pour the milk into a 1-cup glass measure. Add the lemon zest. Heat on High in the microwave for 30 seconds. Set aside for 15 minutes to let the lemon peel release its essence and oils into the milk. Meanwhile, add the yeast, sugar, and flour to the bread machine pan. After 15 minutes, add the milk and lemon zest. Process on the dough setting until the sponge is well combined, about 5 minutes on most machines. You may need to stop the machine and scrape down the sides and bottom of the pan with a rubber spatula. Turn off the machine and let the sponge sit in the pan for 30 minutes, or until doubled in bulk.

To make the dough, add the sugar, eggs, butter, flour, salt, and saffron, if using it, to the sponge in the pan. Process on the dough setting. At the end of the dough setting, add the raisins and lemon peel and process again on the dough setting just long enough for the machine to knead in the raisins and the lemon peel, about 5 minutes on most machines.

While the dough works, line a large baking sheet with parchment paper, or lightly grease it with shortening, and set aside. Lightly spray a smooth work surface with water and when the raisins and peel are kneaded in completely, turn off the machine and turn the dough out onto the wet surface. With wet hands, divide the dough into 10 equal balls and place them on the baking sheet. Cover with plastic wrap and let them rise until nearly doubled, about 1 1/2 to 2 hours.

Meanwhile, preheat the oven to 400° F. and lightly whisk the egg white. When the rolls are puffy and nearly doubled in size, brush them with the egg white. Bake on the middle rack of the preheated oven for 18 to 20 minutes, or until they're golden brown. Remove from the baking sheet to cool on a rack for 10 minutes. Serve warm.

METHODS FOR ADDING FRUIT

Most of our recipes direct you to add the fruit at the end of the kneading cycles, either by hand or by turning the machine back on. This is to keep the bread machine from grinding the fruit into an indistinguishable puree.
If your bread machine has a raisin bread setting, use it for adding fruits and nuts.

THE BAGELS OF PARIS

Dough Setting
Makes 8 bagels

We found that the American palate prefers a bagel not as hard and brown as the Parisian version, so we turned down the heat to make these shiny, golden bagels with a perfect crust-to-chew ratio.

Don't substitute another kind of salt for the kosher salt, and don't substitute sugar for the malt syrup; the flavor will not be the same. Malt syrup can be purchased in health food shops and some specialty grocery stores. Also, this recipe works well using the delayed start timer for the dough setting if your machine has one. After removing the dough from the pan, fresh, hot bagels can be on the table in 40 minutes.

DOUGH:

4 teaspoons bread machine yeast

3½ cups bread flour

3 tablespoons sugar

2½ to 3 teaspoons kosher salt (2½ teaspoons will allow a little sweeter taste to emerge, 3 teaspoons will be traditional)

1⅓ cups water

BOILING WATER:

2 tablespoons malt syrup

2 quarts water

Combine all of the ingredients for the dough in the bread machine pan and process according to the manufacturer's instructions for a dough setting, or you can remove the dough and shut off the machine after the dough has had a chance to rise for 1 hour.

Meanwhile, bring the malt syrup and water to a boil in a 4-quart pan. Preheat the oven to 425° F., lightly grease a large, heavy baking sheet, and sprinkle it lightly with cornmeal. When the machine has completed the dough cycle, remove the dough from the bread pan to a lightly floured surface and knead several times to deflate any air bubbles.

Pinch off 8 equal pieces of dough and form them into balls. Flatten the balls slightly on the floured work surface and, with your thumb, poke a hole in the middle. Pull and stretch the dough until it is roughly the size of a donut.

Adjust the heat under the boiling water so that the water is just at a low boil. Gently drop 4 of the bagels into the water and allow them to boil for 30 seconds. Using a skimmer, turn the bagels and boil for an additional 30 seconds. Remove from the water to drain on a clean towel. Repeat with the remaining 4 bagels. Place the boiled, drained bagels on the prepared baking sheet and bake in the preheated oven for 11 minutes. Working quickly but carefully, remove the baking sheet from the oven and turn the bagels over (this is very important or the bagels will not have the right crust-to-chew ratio). Return to the oven and bake an additional 11 minutes.

After 22 minutes, the bagels will be lightly browned and shiny; if not, continue baking for an additional minute or so, watching carefully so they do not burn. Remove the bagels from the baking sheet to cool on a rack for at least 10 minutes. These bagels are best eaten the day they are made, but they may be stored in a plastic bag for up to 36 hours.

Slice in half and serve with cream cheese, thinly sliced lox, 1 slice of ripe tomato, capers, thinly sliced red onion, and a squeeze of fresh lemon juice for a delectable deli-style lunch.

BAGEL VARIATIONS

WHOLE WHEAT BAGELS
Reduce the bread flour to 2 cups and add 1½ cups whole wheat flour. Whole wheat bagels may need to bake 4 minutes longer.

PUMPERNICKEL RAISIN BAGELS
Use 1¼ cups water or cold, strong coffee in place of the 1⅓ cups water for the dough. Replace 1 cup of bread flour with 1 cup of medium-ground rye flour. Also add to the bread pan 1 ounce unsweetened chocolate, melted; 2 teaspoons caraway seeds; and 2 tablespoons molasses. After the machine has finished the dough setting, add ⅓ cup dark raisins and process on the dough setting just long enough for the raisins to be kneaded in, about 5 minutes. Proceed with the recipe as written.

EGG BAGELS
Reduce the water for the dough to 1 cup plus 1 tablespoon. Add 1 large egg to the bread pan along with the other ingredients.

FRENCH BAGUETTES
FOR A CROWD

Dough Setting
Makes three 17-inch baguettes

We wanted to take the 1-pound machine to the limit and create a French baguette recipe that would serve at least 12 people. This recipe makes three baguettes, one of which can easily be sliced $1/2$ inch thick and served with your favorite spread for appetizers. That still leaves 2 loaves to be served with dinner. If you need to serve more people, 24 for instance, just run 2 batches, one behind the other, and let them rise together in a very large bowl.

$2^1/_2$ teaspoons bread machine yeast
$1^1/_2$ cups water, at room temperature
$3^1/_2$ cups bread flour
2 teaspoons salt

Combine all the ingredients in the bread machine pan and process on the dough setting just until mixed and kneaded. Both the 1- and $1^1/_2$-pound-size bread pans will have to be emptied into a large, lightly greased bowl and covered tightly with plastic wrap. Set the dough aside in a warm place until tripled in size, about 3 hours.

Remove the plastic wrap and, with wet hands, lightly punch the dough down. Cover again with plastic wrap and allow to rise again until doubled, about 1 hour.

Sift flour lightly over your work surface and, with floured hands, turn the dough out onto the work surface. Divide the dough into three equal pieces and let it rest for 5 minutes.

Meanwhile, cover a large baking sheet with parchment paper or grease it lightly.

With floured hands, roll each piece of dough into a cylinder 17 inches long, or however long you want the finished length to be. With the side of your palm, hit the cylinder all the way down the back to form a crease. Pinch the crease closed and taper the ends of the loaf. Lay the baguettes on the prepared baking sheet leaving at least 2 to 3 inches between each one. Lightly mist the dough with water and cover loosely with plastic wrap. Place in a warm, draft-free place to rise until the baguettes are 1½ times their original size, 1½ to 2 hours. Thirty minutes before the estimated baking time, preheat the oven to 450° F.

Press the dough of one baguette lightly with your finger; if it feels springy and has not dried out and formed a crust, leave it alone, if you can feel a dry crust, gently roll and turn the baguette over so that the soft bottom crust, which has been against the baking sheet, is now on the top.

Slash the baguettes diagonally with a razor or a sharp knife 3 times along the length, making sure not to cut more than ½ inch deep.

Lightly mist the dough with water and place the baking sheet on the middle rack of the preheated oven, quickly spray the oven floor several times (see page 74), and shut the door. Spray 3 more times every 3 minutes for a total of 4 sprays in 9 minutes. Bake for 25 minutes, or until the breads are nicely browned. Remove immediately to a rack to cool to room temperature, about 2 hours. This bread is best eaten the day it's made, or frozen for later use. To reheat frozen bread, place the baguette on a baking sheet and place in a preheated 375° F. oven for about 25 minutes, or until hot and crisp.

THE SHAPE OF THINGS TO COME

French Baguettes for a Crowd
makes approximately 4 cups of dough,
which will make the following different
rolls and loaves:

1 large round or oval *pain de campagne*
3 round *boules,*
each about 8 inches in diameter
20 round or oval *petits pains*
18 round rolls with a slashed
split in the middle, *pistolet*

THE *ÉPI*

Dough Setting
Makes one 14-inch loaf

The *Épi* is one of the prettiest breads available in the bakery and is easily made at home. Shaped like a stalk of wheat, the finished loaf is extremely crusty because an enormous amount of its surface is exposed directly to the hot oven air.

French bread flours are usually much softer than either the bread flour or the all-purpose flour used in the United States. The percentage of protein in French flours usually runs somewhere between 7 and 9 percent, compared with an average of 10 to 12 percent for our flours. The more protein, the stronger the gluten web that is formed, and so the sturdier the crumb. We've combined organic cake flour with all-purpose flour to best approximate the French. Our *Épi* has a very crunchy, firm crust enclosing an almost cottony crumb.

1¼ teaspoons bread machine yeast
1¾ cups cake flour
¼ cup all-purpose flour
¾ teaspoon salt
¾ cup water

For two 14-inch loaves

2½ teaspoons bread machine yeast
3½ cups cake flour
½ cup all-purpose flour
1½ teaspoons salt
1½ cups water

Combine all the ingredients in the bread machine pan. Process on the dough setting. Meanwhile, line a baking sheet (a large baking sheet if you're making 2 loaves) with parchment paper.

When the cycle is finished, remove the dough from the bread pan to a lightly floured surface and roll the dough in a little additional flour to make the handling easier.

(Cut the dough in half if you are making 2 loaves.) Form the dough into a 14-inch-long baguette. Place it on the prepared baking sheet and allow it to rest for 25 minutes. Meanwhile, preheat the oven to 400° F.

With a pair of clean kitchen shears, make diagonal cuts, three quarters of the way through the dough and about 2 inches apart, all down the length of the baguette. Pull the pieces to opposite sides and pinch the ends of each piece to make them extremely pointy.

Mist the dough with water from a spray bottle and bake on the baking sheet set on the middle rack of the preheated oven for 1 hour, misting with water about every 15 minutes (see page 74). The loaves will be a medium-to-dark shade of brown with a hard, shell-like crust. The misting creates a hard crust and keeps the bread from burning in such a hot oven for such a long period of time. Remove the *épi* from the baking sheet to cool on a rack.

The finished Épi

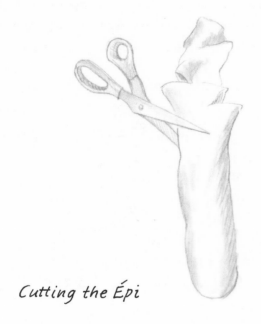

Cutting the Épi

STIRATO
FOR THE BREAD MACHINE

Dough Setting
Makes two 17-inch baguettes

Stirato is the longest of the Italian baguettes. The dough is very wet and easy to work with as long as you keep your hands and a smooth work surface wet. We use our counter next to the sink with a small stream of water running so that we can wet our hands occasionally. This is a good way to treat any extremely wet dough, since it can't stick to wet hands or a wet counter.

Stirato can be stretched as long as your oven can accommodate. We use a 17-inch baking sheet, which is about all that most home ovens can hold.

The texture of the *Stirato* differs from that of other baguettes. It's chewy, with large air bubbles, and the interior crumb appears stretched instead of having the normal close cell structure. Split lengthwise and filled with toppings such as caponata or grilled vegetables, the bread is beautiful and serves quite a crowd without a lot of fuss.

2½ teaspoons bread machine yeast
3 cups bread flour, plus 2 tablespoons for the finish
1 teaspoon sugar
1¾ cups water
1 teaspoon salt

Add the yeast, 3 cups bread flour, sugar, water, and salt to the bread machine pan and process on the dough setting just until mixed and kneaded. Empty the dough into a large, lightly greased bowl and cover tightly with plastic wrap. Set aside in a warm place until tripled in size, about 2 hours.

When the dough has tripled in bulk, lightly spray a smooth work surface with water and, with wet hands, turn the dough out onto it. Lightly punch it down and divide the dough into two equal pieces. Form each piece into a baguette about 12 inches long. Let the dough rest on the work surface for 30 minutes. Meanwhile, line a large baking sheet with parchment paper, or grease it lightly.

After 30 minutes, stretch the baguettes to about 17 inches long and lay them on the prepared baking sheet. Let them rise for another 20 minutes. Meanwhile, preheat the oven to 450° F. Lightly sift the baguettes with about 2 tablespoons of flour and place them, on their baking sheet, on the middle rack of the preheated oven. Immediately turn the heat down to 400° F. and bake for 25 to 30 minutes, or until golden brown. Remove from the baking sheet to cool on a rack. These baguettes are best eaten the day they are made.

CAPONATA

Makes 5 to 10 servings

Although this doesn't take long to put together, it tastes best
if it's allowed to stand overnight in the refrigerator.
Make it the day before you want to serve—if you can wait that long.
Serve with *Stirato* or your favorite baguette.

2 medium eggplants, 1 peeled and 1 trimmed of the stem but not peeled
2 tablespoons salt, plus extra to taste
1 pound canned Italian plum tomatoes, drained, or 1 pound fresh Italian
plum tomatoes, peeled (2 cups chopped)
1 ½ cups cold-pressed first-pressing extra-virgin olive oil or to taste
1 medium sweet yellow onion
1 medium sweet red onion
2 large ribs celery
2 large cloves garlic, peeled and chopped
¼ cup minced fresh Italian flat-leaf parsley
½ cup chopped black olives
2 tablespoons capers, drained
¼ cup red wine vinegar
2 tablespoons water
1 tablespoon brown sugar
2 tablespoons tomato paste
Freshly ground black pepper to taste
2 tablespoons pine nuts

Chop the eggplant into large chunks and salt it generously. Put the eggplant in a colander and, using your hands, toss it together with the 2 tablespoons salt. Set the colander over a plate and allow the eggplant to drain for 45 minutes or up to 2 hours. This will help remove any bitterness it might contain. After the draining period, rinse the eggplant well under cold running water to rid it of excess salt and juices.

Pour the eggplant into a lightly greased microwavable bowl. Cover the bowl, and cook on High for 10 minutes or until the eggplant is easily pierced with a fork.

Alternately, the eggplant can be roasted in the oven. Preheat the oven to 375° F. and lightly grease a large baking dish. Add the eggplant and roast, uncovered, for 35 to 45 minutes, or until tender when pierced with a fork.

Meanwhile, chop the tomatoes in the food processor fitted with the steel blade, then set them aside.

In a medium-sized saucepan, heat ½ cup of the olive oil. While it's heating, finely chop both onions and then the celery in the food processor.

Sauté the onions in the olive oil until they are soft but not brown. Stir in the celery and garlic. Continue cooking for 5 minutes over medium heat, stirring until everything is soft and tender.

Add an additional ½ cup of olive oil and the eggplant to the onion mixture and cook over medium heat just until heated through. Mix in the parsley, olives, capers, vinegar, water, brown sugar, and tomato paste. Stir until thoroughly mixed.

Cover and cook over medium heat, stirring frequently, for 15 minutes, adding additional olive oil if needed to prevent sticking.

Try not to beat the mixture into a soupy consistency, the vegetables should retain their shape as much as possible. Season with salt and pepper.

Remove from the heat and cool to room temperature. Cover and refrigerate for at least 24 hours to allow the flavors to blend.

To serve: Spoon the caponata into a clear glass bowl and sprinkle with pine nuts. Serve with plain or toasted *Stirato* or baguette slices.

FEATHER BREAD CROISSANTS

Dough Setting
Makes a dozen croissants

When we began to make croissants, our goal was to make the flakiest, lightest roll ever created. Naysayers insisted, "No way in a bread machine, the machines will overknead and develop the gluten." Well, hadn't they ever heard of the on and off button! With croissants, we use the machine only to mix the dough, not to knead it. Then we turn the machine off and let the dough rise in the pan.

With croissants, less is more. Add as little extra flour as possible to keep the dough manageable and, other than the folding process, handle it as little as possible. You will be rewarded with a most sublime pastry, full of blistered, buttery bits that flake and are crisp.

2 teaspoons bread machine yeast
2¼ cups all-purpose flour (do not use bread flour)
2 teaspoons salt
2 tablespoons instant nonfat dry milk solids
1 tablespoon sugar
⅞ cup water
1 stick unsalted butter
1 large egg beaten with 1 tablespoon water for glaze

Add the yeast, flour, salt, dry milk solids, sugar, and water to the bread machine pan and place in the machine. Process the ingredients on the dough setting until well incorporated, with no dry ingredients clinging to the sides of the pan, about 10 minutes on most machines. After the dough has been mixed, turn off the machine and let the dough rise in the machine until doubled, about 1½ hours.

Meanwhile, place the stick of butter between 2 layers of plastic wrap or waxed paper. With your fingers, flatten and shape the butter into a 6-inch square that is about ⅓ inch thick. Chill for at least 15 minutes. The butter must be the consistency of vegetable shortening when you use it. If it is too hard, it will tear the dough; if it is too soft, it will ooze out the sides. Warm it or chill it accordingly.

When the dough has doubled in volume, turn it out onto a well-floured surface. With floured hands, press the dough into a 13-inch square. Unwrap the chilled butter and place it diagonally in the center of the dough square. Bring the corners of the dough over the butter to meet in the center (it will look like an envelope). Press the center and edges of the dough to flatten and seal in the butter.

Using a lightly floured rolling pin, roll the dough into an 18 × 9-inch rectangle. Do not press too firmly. If you do, the butter will ooze out or the dough will tear (if it does tear, just

Rolling the croissant

pinch to patch). Fold one 9-inch end of the dough rectangle over the center third of the dough. Fold this over the remaining third. Roll the dough out again into an 18 × 9-inch rectangle. Fold it as before to form the 3 layers and place in a plastic bag or wrap loosely in plastic wrap. Refrigerate the dough for 30 minutes and then repeat the rolling, folding, and chilling process twice more. Refrigerate the dough overnight after the last folding.

To cut and shape the croissants, cut the dough in half. Wrap one half in plastic and return it to the refrigerator while you work with the other half. Roll the dough out on a lightly floured surface to a 13-inch circle. Cut it into 6 wedges. Gently pull the base of each wedge to a width of about 6 inches and the length of each wedge to about 7 inches. Starting from the base, roll up the wedge. Place the croissant, top-point underneath, on a heavy-duty baking sheet. Curve and bring the base points toward the center to form a crescent. Roll and shape all the croissants, placing them 2 inches apart on the baking sheet.

A croissant ready for baking

Brush the croissants lightly with the egg glaze. Then, allow them to rise in a warm place until light and puffy, about 1½ hours. Meanwhile, preheat the oven to 400° F. Brush the croissants with the egg glaze one more time right before putting them in the oven. Bake for 15 minutes, or until they are golden brown. Remove the croissants from the baking sheet to cool on a rack. Serve warm, with jam or your favorite sandwich filling.

Making a chocolate croissant

PAINS AU CHOCOLAT
Chocolate Croissants

Chocolate Croissants are a Parisian variation of plain croissants.
Sweet and simple.
Prepare the croissant dough as directed. After you cut it in half, roll each half into a 14 × 12-inch rectangle on a lightly floured surface. Cut each half into six 7 × 4-inch rectangles. Break apart three 1.45-ounce bars of semisweet or dark chocolate to make 12 rectangles, each about 3 × 1 ½ inches. Place one piece of chocolate lengthwise along one short end of each piece of dough. Roll to enclose the chocolate completely and press the edges to seal. Place the croissants, seam side down, on a large baking sheet. Proceed to glaze and bake as directed.

BREAD MACHINE BRIOCHE

Dough Setting
Makes a dozen rolls

The rich, buttery bread of France is called *brioche.* It can be hard to handle, a little sticky and greasy, a dough that's mixed best in the bread machine. All that's left for the cook is the shaping.

Sometimes these breads can be cantankerous when it comes to rising, just give them plenty of time in a warm spot or place them, covered, in direct sunlight until they have reached the top of the pan.

2 teaspoons bread machine yeast
3 cups bread flour
2 tablespoons water
3 large eggs
2 tablespoons plus 1 teaspoon sugar
$^1/_2$ teaspoon salt
$^3/_4$ cup (1$^1/_2$ sticks) unsalted butter, cut into small pieces
1 egg yolk whisked with 1 tablespoon cold water for glaze

Combine all the ingredients except the glaze in the bread machine pan. Process on the dough setting. Meanwhile, lightly butter a dozen brioche molds or custard or muffin cups.

Remove the processed dough to a lightly floured surface and knead it briefly to remove any remaining air bubbles. Pinch off about $^3/_4$ cup of the dough and set it aside. Divide the remaining dough into 12 equal pieces.

To shape brioches, shape each piece of dough into a golf ball–sized ball. Place each ball of dough into the mold. Then roll the reserved dough into a dozen marble-sized balls. Using your thumb, make a deep indentation in the top of each larger dough ball and firmly press the smaller ball on top.

These rolls are perfect for the holidays and for large gatherings because they reheat well. To reheat, wrap the rolls in aluminum foil and place them in a preheated 350° F. oven for 10 minutes.

Cover the molds lightly with waxed paper and raise the rolls in a warm, draft-free place until doubled in bulk, about an hour. Meanwhile, preheat the oven to 425° F.

When the rolls have risen, brush them lightly with the egg yolk glaze, taking care that it doesn't slip into the mold (it sticks).

Bake the brioches for 12 to 15 minutes, until puffed and browned, then reduce the oven temperature to 350° F. and bake for 10 minutes more.

Remove the brioches from the oven and let them cool in the pans about 5 minutes before removing to a rack. Wrap in foil to store.

WHOLE OLIVE BRIOCHE
WITH 2 CHEESES

Dough Setting
Makes 1 large brioche

A bread so rich and colorful can be a meal in itself when served with the Italian Tart Green Salad with Pine Nuts, Prosciutto, and Sizzling Garlic Dressing (see page 242) and a fine wine such as a Pinot Noir from Oregon. Diana serves it grilled and floating in a scarlet pool of Betty Collingwood's Famous Red Wine Marinara Sauce (see page 172). However you decide to serve it, family and friends alike will be asking for the recipe.

2^1/$_2$ teaspoons bread machine yeast
^{1}/$_4$ cup water
2 large egg yolks
3 large eggs
^{1}/$_2$ cup olive oil
2^1/$_2$ cups bread flour
1^1/$_2$ teaspoons salt
4 ounces Parmesan cheese, freshly grated
1 ounce Pecorino Romano cheese, freshly grated
^{1}/$_2$ cup Kalamata olive halves
1 large egg, lightly beaten, for glaze

Combine all ingredients except the olives and the egg for glazing in the bread machine pan. Process according to the manufacturer's instructions for a dough setting. After the cycle is completed, leave the dough in the bread pan in the machine for an additional hour.

Meanwhile, lightly oil the entire surface and curves in a 2-quart brioche pan. Turn the dough out onto a lightly floured surface and gently knead in the olives. Pinch off a piece of dough about the size of a golf ball. Form each piece into a tight ball. Place the large ball in the oiled brioche pan and, with your thumb, make an indentation on top. Place the smaller ball in the indentation. Cover the brioche pan with plastic wrap or foil and allow the bread to rise three quarters of the way up the sides of the pan, anywhere from 2½ to 4 hours.

Meanwhile, preheat the oven to 425° F. Brush the top of the brioche dough with 2 tablespoons of the beaten egg, being careful not to let the egg run down the side of the pan, where it will stick when baking. Discard the rest of the egg. Bake the broiche on the middle rack of the preheated oven for 40 to 45 minutes, or until it forms a deep, shiny brown crust. Let the bread cool in the pan on a rack for 20 minutes, then unmold and cool completely on the rack.

OLIVE OILS

We love the taste of olive oils. We used the plural here because we believe that each olive oil has a taste all its own, and you may need several varieties of oil for different purposes. We don't usually fry with olive oil because its flavor can be overpowering, but when we do, we find that a pure light grade or an olive oil/vegetable oil blend is satisfactory. We reserve heavier-bodied and flavored cold-pressed extra-virgin imports for bread-baking, grilling bland vegetables, topping focaccias, drizzling over soups and pasta, and for spreading on crostini before grilling and adding toppings.

9

Sweet, holiday, and dessert breads

Panettone with Date and Nut Chunks
Pane alla Cioccolata
Austrian Braid (with a Variation)
    Pain des Trois Saisons
Tsoureki
French Country Bread with Fruit and Nuts
Pane all'Uva di Noci
Pao Doce
Chocolate-Cranberry Gugelhupf
Stollen
Apple-Apricot Crumb Kuchen
Golden Greek Hot Cross Buns
French Bread with Apples and Walnuts
Scottish Black Bun
Potica

PANETTONE
WITH DATE AND NUT CHUNKS

Dough Setting
Makes two 1½-pound breads

Tall and domed (it's baked in a special panettone mold or a coffee can), panettone is the most spectacular Italian Christmas bread. It's perfect slathered with mascarpone for tea or toasted for breakfast and served with a steamy cappuccino.

DOUGH:

2½ teaspoons bread machine yeast

3 cups bread flour

⅓ cup water

2 large eggs plus 2 large egg yolks

½ cup (1 stick) plus 2 tablespoons unsalted butter, at
    room temperature

½ cup sugar

2 teaspoons honey

1 teaspoon vanilla extract

½ teaspoon salt

FILLING:

¾ cup golden raisins

¼ cup chopped candied orange peel

¼ cup chopped candied citron

PANETTONES AS GIFTS

With all the jazzy gift wrapping paper that is now available, you have an endless supply from which to choose for wrapping and presenting panettones. Among our favorites are the clear cellophane bags that are available at craft stores and come in large sizes. The clear bag allows the bits of color in the bread to show through, and all you do is simply slip the cooled bread into the bag and tie it with a colorful ribbon.
Or you can wrap the cooled bread in a collar of colored waxed pape (available from Williams-Sonoma) and tie it with raffia or twine. Panettones can also be baked in buttered, clear glass, 8-cup, wide-mouthed mason jars. Tie a bow around the top of the cooled bread still in its jar and add a sprig of holly. Attach a pretty label, the recipe, or a thoughtful poem for a memorable gift.

2 teaspoons minced orange zest
2 teaspoons minced lemon zest
1/2 cup chopped dates
2/3 cup coarsely chopped walnuts
2 tablespoons bread flour

Combine all the dough ingredients in the bread machine pan. *If you are using a 1-pound machine,* let the ingredients be mixed and kneaded, then turn off the machine and transfer the dough to a 3-quart plastic or glass bowl and cover with plastic wrap. Set aside to rise until tripled in bulk, 3 to 4 hours.

If you are using a 1 1/2-pound machine, process the ingredients according to the manufacturer's instructions for a dough setting. Turn off the machine and let the dough rise in the machine for an additional hour, or until tripled in bulk.

Meanwhile, butter two 1-pound 10-ounce coffee cans or two 8-cup panettone molds and cut 2 parchment-paper circles to fit the bottom of the cans or molds. Press the paper onto the bottom of the cans or molds and lightly butter the paper.

In a large mixing bowl, combine the filling ingredients except the flour. Sprinkle with the flour and toss to coat thoroughly.

After the dough has risen, remove it to a lightly floured surface and knead several times to deflate any air bubbles. Divide the dough into four equal pieces. Flatten each piece into a disk and sprinkle each disk with one quarter of the filling. Using the palms of your hands, press the filling into the dough until it won't hold any more. Fold each disk in half and flatten again. Sprinkle with any filling that remains on the floured surface. Again press the filling into the dough.

After the filling has been incorporated into the dough, flatten two pieces of dough into disks and lay one piece on top of the other. Press the two together and gather the edges into the center to form a tight ball. Repeat with the remaining two pieces of dough. Slip the balls of dough into the prepared cans or pans. Cover with plastic wrap and place in a warm spot to rise just to the top of the can or mold, approximately 2 to 3 hours. Meanwhile, preheat the oven to 400° F.

Just before baking, cut an X in the top of each loaf. Bake on the middle rack of the preheated oven for 10 minutes, reduce the heat to 375°, and bake for an additional 40 to 50 minutes, or until a tester inserted into the middle of the panettone comes out clean. Cool completely in the cans or pans, then unmold onto a rack. The bread keeps best if stored in a plastic bag.

PANE ALLA CIOCCOLATA
Chocolate Bread
(that's better than cake)

Regular Bake Cycle or Light Crust Cycle
Makes one 1-pound loaf

Not too sweet, heaven with a smear of mascarpone cheese and a cup of *caffe latte*, this bread can be made easily in the bread machine. If you wish, however, you can shape it the Italian way, into a round free-form loaf, place it on parchment paper, and bake it on a stone. We used Pernigotti Cocoa from Williams-Sonoma for the deepest mahogany color and richest chocolate flavor. Buy the best-quality chocolate chips as well. In our market, these are Guittard. You can also use an equal measure of chocolate squares: 3 ounces, or 3 squares, equals $^{1}/_{2}$ cup chocolate chips. If you use squares, chop them up in the food processor first, pulsing until you have bits about the size of chocolate chips, or shave them with a knife into the dough. Droste, Lindt, Tobler, Ghirardelli, and Guittard are all top-quality chocolates for use in baking.

Set your machine for "light crust" to prevent overbrowning.

For an easy frosting, pull the bread out of the machine the moment it's completed baking and top it with chocolate chips. They'll melt and you can smear them over the top for a gorgeous chocolate glaze.

$1^{1}/_{4}$ teaspoons bread machine yeast
$2^{1}/_{4}$ cups bread flour
$^{1}/_{4}$ cup sugar
3 tablespoons Dutch process unsweetened cocoa
$^{3}/_{4}$ teaspoon salt
$^{3}/_{4}$ cup plus 1 tablespoon water

1 large egg yolk

1½ teaspoons unsalted butter

½ cup best-quality semisweet chocolate chips

Combine all the ingredients in the bread machine pan and process on the regular bake or the light crust cycle.

For one 1½-pound loaf

2 teaspoons bread machine yeast
3 cups bread flour
⅓ cup sugar
¼ cup Dutch process unsweetened cocoa
1 teaspoon salt
1⅛ cups plus 1 tablespoon water
1 large egg yolk
1 tablespoon unsalted butter
¾ cup best-quality semisweet
chocolate chips

AUSTRIAN BRAID

Dough Setting
Makes 1 large braid

Slather jam on this lemony rich bread and you'll understand how the Austrians came to be famous for their baking.

2¹/₂ teaspoons bread machine yeast
3 cups bread flour
¹/₂ teaspoon salt
3 tablespoons sugar
¹/₄ cup (¹/₂ stick) unsalted butter, cut up
³/₄ cup warm milk
¹/₂ teaspoon vanilla extract
1 teaspoon grated lemon zest
1 large egg plus 1 large egg yolk
1 egg yolk whisked with 1 tablespoon water for glaze

Place all the ingredients except the glaze in the bread machine pan and process on the dough setting.

When the cycle is completed, remove the dough to a lightly floured surface and knead a moment, forming a ball. Turn the bread machine pan over the dough and let it stand for 5 to 15 minutes. Now, divide the dough into three equal pieces. Roll each piece into a 12-inch strand, then form into a braid beginning in the middle (see page 77). Lay the strands on top of each other like the spokes of a wheel, then braid each end, starting from the middle and moving outward.

Spritz an 8 × 4 × 2-inch loaf pan with cooking spray and place the braid in the pan, tucking the ends under. Place the loaf in a warm, draft-free place to rise until it's over the top of the pan by about 1 inch, about 30 minutes. Preheat the oven to 375° F. Just before baking, brush the loaf with the egg glaze.

Bake on the middle rack of the preheated oven until the bread is golden brown and done, 35 to 40 minutes. Spritz the oven 3 or 4 times with plain water during the first 5 minutes of baking (see page 74). Turn the loaf out of the baking pan to cool on a rack. Serve warm. Store in plastic wrap.

PAIN DES TROIS SAISONS
THREE SEASONS BREAD

Create a Viennese-style bread by making the above dough, leaving out the lemon zest, but adding instead a mixture of raisins, walnuts, and hazelnuts, about ¼ cup of each. Knead these into the dough by hand at the end of the dough cycle, then form the dough into a tight ball and turn the bread machine pan over it to rest for 10 to 20 minutes. Form the loaf into a long oval and place it on a parchment-covered baking pan to rise a final time. Score the top in deep angular slashes about 1 inch apart just before baking. Brush with the egg yolk glaze just before baking, as directed above. Spritz the oven several times during the first 10 minutes of baking. The finished bread will have a golden brown crust and a moist, pale tan crumb. Cool on a rack and store in a paper bag.

TSOUREKI
Braided Greek Easter Bread

Dough Setting
Makes 1 large braid

Brian Dupnik showed us how to blow gold flakes through a straw to gild this bread so that it had not only the traditional dyed Easter egg nestled inside, but an edible dusting of gold flakes as well. Buy the gold from a good craft shop or from one of the mail order houses for bakers (see page 307). You'll have a bread fit to celebrate the rites of spring, one whose color will rival those of nature's show.

1 cup milk
4 cups bread flour
2$^1/_2$ teaspoons bread machine yeast
$^2/_3$ cup sugar
$^1/_2$ cup chopped almonds, plus 2 tablespoons
    slivered almonds
$^1/_2$ teaspoon salt
Zest of $^1/_2$ orange
1 teaspoon ground aniseseed
2 tablespoons olive oil
2 large eggs
3 large hard-cooked and dyed Easter eggs to nestle
  in the top
1 egg yolk whisked with 1 tablespoon water for glaze
14-karat gold flakes to decorate the bread

Place the milk, half the flour, and the yeast in the bread machine pan and process on the dough setting. Meanwhile, toss the remaining flour with the sugar, chopped almonds, salt, orange zest, and aniseseed. Once the dough cycle is completed, add the flour mixture, olive oil, and eggs. Process again on the dough setting.

Once the second cycle is completed, remove the dough to a well-floured surface. Punch down and form into a ball. Cover and let the dough rest for 15 minutes. Now, divide the dough into three parts. Roll each piece into a 15-inch-long rope. On a piece of parchment paper crisscross the strands of rope forming the spokes of a wheel, and braid the bread, working from the center to the ends. Pinch the ends together and turn under. Embed the dyed eggs in the folds of the braid. Cover and let the dough rise until doubled in bulk, about 1 hour.

Meanwhile, preheat the oven to 375° F. Once the dough has risen, brush it lightly with the egg wash. Sprinkle the top of the loaf with edible 14-karat gold flakes. Sprinkle with the slivered almonds. Bake in the preheated oven for 40 to 45 minutes or until golden brown. Cool on a rack. Store in a brown bag for up to 3 days.

You don't have to buy an Easter egg dying kit to dye Easter eggs. Just add a few drops of food coloring to custard cups, add a tablespoon of plain white vinegar and a little water. Roll the eggs around in this color for a few minutes. *Voilà,* dyed eggs.

FRENCH COUNTRY BREAD
WITH FRUIT AND NUTS

Dough Setting
Makes one 8-inch round free-form loaf

Adding fruit to yeast bread gives it a rich sweetness. Substitute an apple for the pear, if you wish. And walnuts taste almost as good as hazelnuts. The country cooks of France made making-do an art. Use your bread machine and you can become a bread artist too.

½ cup whole hazelnuts
¾ cup water
½ cup chopped dried pears
1 medium ripe pear, peeled, cored, and chopped to make 1
    cup fruit with juice
2 cups bread flour
2½ teaspoons bread machine yeast
¾ cup medium rye flour
¼ teaspoon ground ginger
¾ teaspoon salt
1 large egg
1 tablespoon unsalted butter or margarine
3 tablespoons mild honey
1 large egg, lightly beaten, for glaze

Place the nuts on a microwavable dish, and microwave at 100 percent power for 1 minute. Stir, then microwave for 1 more minute. Quickly remove them to a clean tea towel, enclosing them completely, and set them aside to steam.

Combine the water and dried pears in a 1-quart liquid

glass measure and microwave on 100% power for 90 seconds. (Alternatively, boil on the stovetop in a small pan for 3 minutes or so.) Remove from the microwave and add the chopped fresh pear. Set aside to cool a bit. Drain, and reserve the juice separately.

In the bread machine pan, combine 1 cup of bread flour, the yeast, and the cooled fruit. Process on the dough setting. Then add the remaining bread flour, the rye flour, ginger, salt, egg, butter, and honey. Process again on the dough setting, adding a tablespoon or so of the reserved fruit liquid *only* if the dough seems too stiff (it should be quite soft after a few moments' kneading).

When the second dough cycle is completed, lift the dough from the pan and form it into a ball. Turn the bread machine pan over it and allow it to rest for 5 to 15 minutes. Rub the skins off the reserved hazelnuts (no need to worry if you've substituted walnuts), chop them, and knead them into the dough. Now form the dough into an 8-inch, high round ball and place it on a parchment-covered baking sheet. Set it aside to rise in a warm, draft-free place until almost doubled in bulk, about 30 minutes.

Preheat the oven to 350° F. Just before baking, glaze the top of the loaf with beaten egg and slash it in a tic-tac-toe pattern, holding the knife or razor at a 45° angle. Bake on the middle rack of the preheated oven until the bread is golden, about 45 minutes. Cool on a rack. Serve warm, with Gorgonzola if you like. Makes great toast for breakfast. Store in plastic wrap.

CHANTILLY CREAM

Makes 1 cup

Sunday Brunch calls for excess. Slather Chantilly cream onto your toasted bread and serve it with slices of fresh pear or apple.

1 cup crème fraîche
3 tablespoons superfine sugar
1 tablespoon vanilla extract

Whip the crème fraîche with the sugar and vanilla until it forms soft peaks. Cover and refrigerate.

PANE ALL'UVA DI NOCI
Country Bread with Raisins and Walnuts

Dough Setting
Makes one 10-inch round free-form loaf

Make a bread machine *biga* the night before, then finish this fine raisin-walnut bread using the dough setting of the bread machine the next day. Shape it in a classic disk shape, dust with flour, finish with a tic-tac-toe pattern, and bake on a stone. This is the best of the new and old worlds.

1 tablespoon bread machine yeast

2 cups bread flour

1 teaspoon sugar

1½ cups spring water, at room temperature

3 tablespoons gluten flour

1 cup whole wheat flour, plus extra flour for
   dusting the top

¼ cup rolled oats

½ cup medium rye flour

2 teaspoons salt

3 tablespoons raisins

⅓ cup coarsely chopped English or black walnuts

Make a bread machine *biga* by combining in the bread machine pan the yeast, 1 cup of the bread flour, the sugar, and ¾ cup of the warm spring water. Process on the dough setting and let the *biga* stand in the bread machine overnight.

The next day, add the remaining flours, oats, and water along with the salt to the *biga* in the pan. Process on the dough setting again.

When the dough cycle is completed remove the dough to a lightly floured surface and knead in the raisins and walnuts by hand. Cover the dough with the bread machine pan and let it stand for 10 to 15 minutes.

Then form the dough into a 10-inch disk and let it rise on a cornmeal-sprinkled peel until nearly doubled in bulk. Preheat the oven to 375° F. with a baking stone in place in the lower third for about 30 minutes. Just before baking, sprinkle whole wheat flour generously onto the bread and quickly slash a tic-tac-toe pattern in the top. Give the peel a trial shake before opening the oven door, then quickly shovel the bread onto the stone, and bake until golden brown and done, about 40 minutes. Spritz the oven 5 or 6 times with plain water during the first 10 minutes of baking (see page 74). Cool the bread on a rack. Store in a brown paper bag.

PLAYING TIC-TAC-TOE WITH THE BREAD

You may wonder why breads are scored on top. It serves a couple of functions. First of all, scoring controls the final rise that the bread gets when it hits the oven and experiences that "oven spring"—as if the gases made by the yeast were saying, Ouch! Let me out of here. If the bread isn't slashed, the top is likely to be lumpy and misshapen. The tic-tac-toe pattern works particularly well on this disk-shaped bread because it keeps it puffing up straight and nice. However, we hasten to note that some people like their bread all the more artisanal and lumpy. So, if you wish, try making breads without the slashes. The second reason traditional bakers marked the tops of their loaves was to "autograph" the bread. Each bread has its own signature—the originator of each mark long since lost to the mists of culinary history. But you can invent your own mark if you wish. Why not? It's your bread. But if you're tradition-bound, mark this and other round free-form loaves with the tic-tac-toe. It's esthetically pleasing. And think what a lovely game you could have if you could just keep people from ripping into this heavenly bread to eat it.

PAO DOCE
Portuguese Sweet Bread

Dough Setting
Makes one 9-inch round coiled loaf

Although traditional Portuguese bakers bake their breads in brick ovens, we think they'd like our new age version of a very old bread.

3 cups bread flour
2¹/₂ teaspoons bread machine yeast
¹/₃ cup granulated sugar, plus extra to sprinkle on top
2 tablespoons instant nonfat dry milk solids
2 tablespoons dry mashed potato flakes
¹/₄ cup (¹/₂ stick) unsalted butter
¹/₂ teaspoon salt
¹/₂ teaspoon vanilla extract
3 large eggs, 1 held for the glaze
Zest and juice of ¹/₂ lemon
³/₄ cup water

Combine all the ingredients except the egg for the glaze and the sugar for sprinkling, in the bread machine pan and process on the dough setting. Once the cycle is completed, re-move the dough to a lightly floured surface and punch it down, adding additional flour if it seems too sticky to handle. Turn the bread pan on top of the dough and let it rest for 15 minutes, then form the loaf.

Make a coiled loaf by rolling the dough into a 30-inch-long rope. Spritz a 9- or 10-inch pie pan with cooking spray, then coil the dough into the pan, beginning at the outside edge and ending in the center. Twist the rope as you lay it in the pan.

Serve with pears and triple cream blue cheese for a fine finish to a meal.

Sprinkle the top of the loaf with granulated sugar and set the loaf aside to rise until nearly doubled in bulk, about 40 minutes. Preheat the oven to 350° F. Beat the remaining egg and brush it over the loaf. Sprinkle the top with more granulated sugar and bake in the preheated oven until brown, 25 to 30 minutes.

Pao Doce

CHOCOLATE-CRANBERRY GUGELHUPF

Dough Setting
Makes one 12-inch round

From Germany and Austria, the land of afternoon coffee and sweet yeasted cakes, comes gugelhupf or kugelhof. A Viennese specialty, the gugelhupf, a sweet fruit-filled bread, is baked in a spiral-patterned mold. Bundt pans, tube pans, and ring molds work equally well. A light chocolate-cranberry-nut mixture fills the rich buttery bread. Serve it warm as a dessert at brunch or coffeetime, smothered with Chocolate Cinnamon Butter (see sidebar, page 291).

DOUGH:
2½ teaspoons bread machine yeast
1 teaspoon granulated sugar
½ cup milk
3¼ cups bread flour
⅓ cup light brown sugar, packed
2 large eggs, plus 1 large egg yolk
5 tablespoons unsalted butter, at room temperature
1½ teaspoons vanilla extract
1 teaspoon salt
1½ teaspoons finely grated orange zest

FILLING:
6 ounces semisweet chocolate, finely chopped
½ cup dried cranberries
1 cup coarsely chopped pecans

½ teaspoon ground cinnamon
2 tablespoons confectioners' sugar for sprinkling on top

Combine the dough ingredients in the bread machine pan. Process on the dough setting just until the dough has been mixed and kneaded. Turn off the machine and remove the dough to a lightly greased 3-quart mixing bowl. Cover the bowl with plastic wrap and set it aside in a warm place. Allow the dough to rise until doubled in bulk, about 1½ hours. Meanwhile, lightly grease a gugelhupf mold, or a tube or bundt pan.

In a medium bowl, combine the filling ingredients; set aside.

Turn the dough out onto a lightly floured, smooth work surface, and knead the dough to remove any remaining air bubbles. Roll the dough into a 12-inch circle. Sprinkle the circle with half the chocolate-cranberry mixture and press the mixture into the dough with the palm of your hand. Fold the outside edge of the circle into the middle, forming a 6- to 8-inch circle. Pinch the seams together in the middle and turn the circle over. With a heavy rolling pin, roll the dough into a 12-inch circle again. Sprinkle with the remaining chocolate-cranberry mixture and repeat the folding process. Poke a hole in the middle of the circle with your thumbs and place the dough in the prepared tube or bundt pan. Cover loosely with a damp tea towel or plastic wrap, and set in a warm, draft-free place until the dough is doubled in bulk, about 1 to 1½ hours. Meanwhile, preheat the oven to 375° F.

When the dough has doubled in bulk, bake it on the middle shelf of the preheated oven for 50 minutes, or until the top is dark brown.

CHOCOLATE CINNAMON BUTTER

Makes ¾ cup

½ cup (1 stick) unsalted butter, at room temperature
½ teaspoon vanilla extract
⅓ cup confectioners' sugar
½ teaspoon ground cinnamon
2 tablespoons Dutch process unsweetened cocoa powder

In a food processor fitted with the steel blade, process the butter and vanilla extract until creamy. Add the sugar, cinnamon, and cocoa and process until smooth, about 1 minute.
To store, cover and refrigerate.
Serve at room temperature.

Let the bread cool in the pan for 10 minutes and then carefully loosen the sides of the gugelhupf from the mold with a sharp knife and turn it out onto a rack to cool completely. When cool, sprinkle lightly with the confectioners' sugar and wrap in aluminum foil to store. Serve warm, with Chocolate Cinnamon Butter. This bread can be reheated wrapped in foil and placed in a preheated 350° oven for 10 minutes.

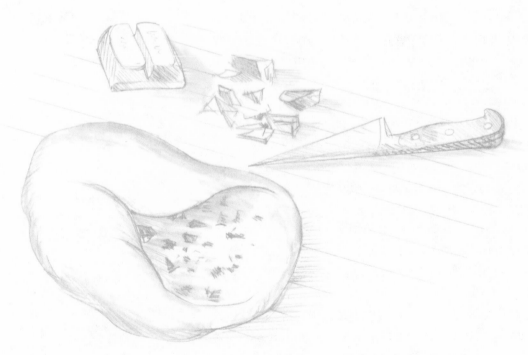

Making Gugelhupf

STOLLEN FOR THE '90S

If you're a little tired of the tried-and-true candied red cherries and green pineapple, design your own stollen using the latest in the dried fruit market. Dried cranberries, pears, and blueberries and our favorite, dried tart cherries, are available almost everywhere. Mix and match the fruits to equal 1 cup, and don't forget to vary the nuts. Pecans are wonderful with dried cherries, and hazelnuts are one of our favorites to go with dried pears.

Stollen is a wonderful bread to give as a gift, and is easily made dramatic with designer papers and tissues. A large shoe box wrapped inside and out with beautiful papers makes a good, inexpensive, ecologically correct gift wrap. Remember to wrap the lid separately so that the recipient doesn't have to tear the papers to get inside.

STOLLEN

Dough Setting
Makes one 14-inch loaf

We're pretty sure that Stollen, the German Christmas bread, is related to that all-American Yuletide favorite fruitcake—a second
cousin anyway. Loaded with candied cherries, citron, slivered almonds, and raisins, the smell of a just-baked stollen is enough to
make you start humming your favorite carol.

DOUGH:
2 teaspoons bread machine yeast
1/4 cup plus 2 tablespoons granulated sugar
3 2/3 cups bread flour
3/4 cup milk
2 tablespoons water
1 large egg
8 tablespoons (1 stick) unsalted butter, 6 tablespoons cut
    into tablespoon-sized chunks and at room temperature,
    2 tablespoons melted
1 tablespoon minced lemon zest
1/2 teaspoon salt
1/4 teaspoon almond extract

FILLING:
1/4 cup dark raisins
1/4 cup golden raisins
1/4 cup chopped candied citron
1/4 cup halved glacé cherries
1/3 cup slivered almonds
3 tablespoons rum
Confectioners' sugar for dusting

Combine all the dough ingredients *except* the melted butter in the bread machine pan. Process on the dough setting. *(If you are using a 1-pound machine,* remove the dough from the bread pan after it has been mixed and kneaded and transfer it to a 12-inch bowl. Cover with plastic wrap and set to rise in a warm place for about 2 hours, or until doubled in bulk.)

Meanwhile, combine the filling ingredients in a bowl. Mix well and allow the fruit to soak up the rum for 1 hour. Lightly grease a large baking sheet.

When the dough has doubled in bulk, turn it out onto a lightly floured surface and knead in the fruit-and-nut mixture, leaving behind any rum that has not been absorbed into the fruit. Press the dough into an 8 × 12-inch rectangle. Brush the top with half the melted butter. Bring one long side to the center of the rectangle and then the other side. Press the edge gently to keep it in place. Turn the dough over and gently place it on the baking sheet. Taper the ends of the loaf slightly into a torpedo shape (see page 81) and push the sides together to mound in the center. Brush the entire loaf with the remaining melted butter.

Cover the dough with plastic wrap and set it aside in a warm place to rise until doubled in bulk, about 1 hour. Meanwhile, preheat the oven to 375° F.

Bake on the middle rack of the preheated oven for 45 minutes, or until nicely browned. Remove the stollen from the baking sheet to cool on a rack. Discard any fruit that may have popped out and burned. When completely cool, sift with a blizzard of confectioners' sugar before slicing and serving.

APPLE-APRICOT CRUMB KUCHEN

Dough Setting
Makes two 9-inch coffee cakes

Apples and apricots top a not-too-sweet German cake with a light crumb topping. The texture of these coffee cakes is similar to that of a fine sponge cake—making it the perfect base for soaking up all of the delectable fruit juices.

DOUGH:
2½ teaspoons bread machine yeast
2¾ cups bread flour
2 tablespoons instant nonfat dry milk solids
2 tablespoons unsalted butter, at room temperature
1 teaspoon salt
1 large egg
⅔ cup water
3 tablespoons granulated sugar

APPLE-APRICOT TOPPING:
5 cups cored, peeled, and thinly sliced Granny Smith or
    other tart cooking apples (approximately 4 large apples)
1 cup granulated sugar
2 tablespoons freshly squeezed lemon juice
⅓ cup golden raisins
1 cup canned apricot halves in light syrup, drained

CRUMB TOPPING:
⅓ cup all-purpose flour

3 tablespoons granulated sugar
3 tablespoons light brown sugar
3 tablespoons unsalted butter
Lightly sweetened whipped cream (optional)

Combine all the dough ingredients in the bread machine pan. Process on the dough setting.

While the dough works, lightly grease two 9-inch cake pans and prepare your toppings. For the apple-apricot topping, combine the apples, sugar, lemon juice, and raisins in a saucepan. Cook over high heat until the apples are soft and translucent, about 10 minutes, stirring occasionally so as not to burn them. Drain the apples, discarding the liquid, and let them cool. Stir in the apricot halves.

For the crumb topping, in a bowl, mix the ingredients with a fork or pastry blender until crumbly.

Preheat the oven to 350° F. When the dough cycle is completed, remove the dough from the bread pan to a lightly floured surface and knead several times to remove any remaining air bubbles. Divide the dough in half and place each half in a prepared pan. Press the dough to the sides of the pan to cover the bottom completely. Spread half the apple-apricot topping over each dough circle. Sprinkle half of the crumb topping over the apples. Set aside in a warm, draft-free place to rest for 15 minutes.

Bake on the middle rack of the preheated oven for 30 minutes or until the edges are lightly browned. Cool the kuchen in their pans on a wire rack. Serve with lightly sweetened whipped cream, if desired.

PROCESSOR WHIPPED CREAM

Makes 2½ cups

Even though little air is incorporated into processor whipped cream, it holds its shape better than conventionally whipped cream. This makes it ideal for use in cake-top decorations. It will hold up in a pastry bag and can be used to top shortcakes well before dinner. Hold the cakes in the refrigerator until serving time, and you'll have perfect snow-capped mountaintops of whipped cream.

2 cups whipping cream, chilled
3 to 4 tablespoons confectioners' sugar

Fit the processor bowl with the steel blade. Process the cream until thickened. Add the sugar gradually, a tablespoon at a time, through the feed tube, and process until stiff. Serve, or refrigerate until serving time.

GOLDEN GREEK HOT CROSS BUNS

Dough Setting
Makes ten rolls

Hot Cross Buns are a Lenten specialty bread. Studded with plump raisins and crossed with an orange-spiked glaze, these buns will be welcome on any Lenten table.

DOUGH:
1/2 cup golden raisins
3/4 cup orange juice
2 1/2 teaspoons bread machine yeast
2 cups bread flour
1 1/2 teaspoons grated orange zest, or 1 teaspoon minced dried orange peel
1 large egg
1/4 teaspoon salt
1/4 teaspoon ground cinnamon
1/4 cup granulated sugar
1/4 cup (1/2 stick) unsalted butter, at room temperature, cut into chunks

GLAZE:
1 cup confectioners' sugar
1 tablespoon reserved orange juice
1/2 teaspoon vanilla extract

Place the raisins in a 2-cup microwavable measure and add the orange juice. Place in the microwave and heat on High for 70 seconds. Remove the raisins and juice from the microwave and set aside to rest for 10 minutes, or until the raisins are slightly plumped. Alternatively, bring the raisins and juice to a boil over medium heat. Remove from heat and set aside to steep until plump. Drain the raisins into a bowl and reserve ½ cup plus 1 tablespoon of orange juice. Set aside.

Combine ½ cup of the reserved orange juice with the remaining dough ingredients (except the raisins) in the bread machine pan and process on the dough setting. Meanwhile, lightly grease a large baking sheet.

When the cycle is finished, turn the dough out onto a lightly floured surface and knead it for a few seconds to remove any remaining air bubbles. Knead in the raisins. Form the dough into 9 or 10 equal balls and place them on the prepared baking sheet. Cover with waxed paper or plastic wrap and set the dough aside in a warm place to rise until doubled in bulk, about 1 hour. Meanwhile, preheat the oven to 350° F.

Just before baking, clip or cut a cross on the top of each bun with scissors or a sharp knife. Bake the buns on the middle shelf of the preheated oven for 20 minutes, or until golden brown. Remove to a rack to cool slightly.

Meanwhile, blend well the confectioners' sugar, the remaining tablespoon of reserved orange juice, and the vanilla for the glaze. When the buns have cooled slightly, drizzle the glaze over the cross on the top of each one. Serve warm. Place in plastic bags to store. These buns will keep for 1 week if stored in the refrigerator.

For 18 rolls

DOUGH:
1 cup golden raisins
1½ cups orange juice
3 teaspoons bread machine yeast
4 cups bread flour
2 teaspoons grated orange zest, or 1½ teaspoons minced dried orange peel
3 large eggs
½ teaspoon salt
½ teaspoon ground cinnamon
½ cup granulated sugar
½ cup (1 stick) unsalted butter, at room temperature, cut into chunks

GLAZE:
1½ cups confectioners' sugar
1½ tablespoons reserved orange juice
½ teaspoon vanilla extract

FRENCH BREAD
WITH APPLES AND WALNUTS

Dough Setting
Makes one 1½-pound loaf

This bread calls to mind Normandy in the fall, when the country-side is fragrant with the perfume of ripe apples and pressed cider. Children love this loaf slathered with fresh applesauce or apple butter. It also makes a sublime sandwich bread filled with smoked turkey or roast pork.

2 teaspoons bread machine yeast
2¾ cups bread flour
½ cup whole wheat flour
1 teaspoon salt
1½ cups sparkling apple cider or strained uncarbonated
    apple cider
1 large or 2 small cooking apples such as Granny Smiths or
    Pippins (see box)
⅓ cup coarsely chopped walnuts

Add the yeast, flours, salt, and cider to the bread machine pan and process on the dough setting until well mixed and kneaded, about 20 minutes on most machines. Remove the bread pan from the machine, cover it with plastic wrap, and place it in the refrigerator to allow the dough to rise slowly for at least 8 hours or overnight.

Remove the bread pan from the refrigerator and allow the dough to come to room temperature, about 2 hours. Remove the dough from the bread pan to a lightly floured surface and knead gently to remove any air bubbles. Let the dough rest for 5 minutes. Meanwhile, peel, core, and finely chop enough apple to make 1 cup.

Knead the apple and walnuts into the dough with the palms of your hands. Keep kneading until the apple and walnuts are distributed throughout, not just in pockets, about 5 minutes. Keep the work surface lightly dusted with flour to prevent sticking, as the apple will release moisture of its own as it is being kneaded. Lightly grease a large bowl and shape the dough into a ball. Place the dough in the bowl, cover it loosely with plastic wrap, and set in a warm, draft-free place to rise until doubled in bulk, about 2 hours.

Remove the dough from the bowl and again knead it briefly on a lightly floured surface to remove air bubbles. Dust a wooden peel heavily with cornmeal. Shape the dough into a ball and place it on the peel. Cover with plastic wrap, and allow it to rise again in a warm, draft-free place until doubled in bulk, about 1½ hours.

Meanwhile, place a baking stone or tiles on the middle rack of the oven and preheat to 450° F. for 30 minutes. With a very sharp knife or razor blade, score the top of the bread in a tic-tac-toe pattern with slashes that are ¼ inch deep.

Slide the bread onto the stone by giving the peel one or two quick jerks. Immediately spray the oven walls and floor with several squirts of water from a spray bottle. Close the door immediately and repeat the spraying procedure twice more in the first 10 minutes of baking (see page 74). Bake the bread for 15 minutes, then reduce the heat to 400° F. and bake for an additional 20 to 30 minutes, or until the loaf is a rich, dark brown and the crust is firm.

Carefully turn the bread over and thump the bottom crust with your knuckle. It should sound hollow. If not, bake for another 5 minutes or so. Remove to a rack to cool completely.

THE RIGHT APPLE

Looking for great cooking apples? Try some of these, alone or in combination, in your favorite apple breads and dishes: Stayman-Winesap, Cortland, Jonathan, Rhode Island Greening, McIntosh, Macoun, York Imperial, Northern Spy, Newtown Pippin, Yellow Transparent.

The following are considered all-purpose apples and may also be used for cooking: Rome Beauty, Baldwin, Wealthy, and Gravenstein.

SCOTTISH BLACK BUN

Dough Setting
Makes one 8-inch bun

From Scotland comes the black bun, once made only on Twelfth Night, but now available from many English bakers on New Year's Eve and throughout the year. A round of buttery rich dough is packed with dried fruits, nuts, and spices, then encased by a plain version of the same rich dough.

DOUGH:
2½ teaspoons bread machine yeast
1 cup warm water
3 cups bread flour
½ cup (1 stick) unsalted butter, at room temperature
2 teaspoons salt

FILLING:
⅓ cup slivered almonds
½ cup golden raisins
½ cup currants
¼ cup chopped candied citron
¾ teaspoon ground ginger
¾ teaspoon ground allspice
¼ teaspoon ground cloves
¼ teaspoon grated nutmeg

Combine all the dough ingredients in the bread machine pan. Process on the dough setting. While the dough works, combine the filling ingredients in a medium bowl. Mix well. Lightly grease a medium baking sheet.

At the end of the dough cycle, remove the dough from the machine to a lightly floured surface. Pinch off one third of the dough and set it aside. Gently knead the remaining dough for 1 minute to remove any air bubbles. With the palms of your hands, knead the fruit mixture into the larger piece of dough and shape it into a ball.

With a rolling pin, roll the reserved piece of dough into a circle 12 inches in diameter. Place the fruit-laden ball of dough in the middle and wrap it with the thinner piece of dough. Pinch to seal. Turn the dough over so the smooth surface is on top. Place the dough ball on the baking sheet and prick the top and sides of the ball with the tines of a fork, going completely through the outer layer but not deep into the middle ball. Let it rest for 20 minutes. Meanwhile, preheat the oven to 350° F.

Bake the bun on the middle rack of the preheated oven for 1 hour. The outside of the loaf will not rise very much, and it will be golden brown and sound hollow when tapped on the bottom. Remove from the baking sheet to cool on a rack. Slice in wedges and serve.

To freshen stale wedges of black bun, wrap the wedge in a damp paper towel and microwave for approximately 20 seconds on High. Remove from the paper towel, butter lightly, and drizzle with honey. Alternatively, you can wrap a wedge of black bun which has been spritzed with water in foil and reheat it in a preheated 350° F. oven for 10 to 15 minutes.
To freshen an entire bun, wrap the entire bun in 2 damp paper towels and place in a plastic bag. Refrigerate overnight. To reheat, remove the bun from the bag, place it on a baking sheet, and set in a preheated 350° oven for 10 minutes. Cut into wedges and, for added moisture, strength, and flavor, brush it with your favorite brandy.

POTICA
Slovenian Christmas Cake

Dough Setting
Makes 12 servings

This filled jelly roll begins with a tender dough that's difficult to handle by hand, but a whiz in the bread machine. The cake is a good keeper and makes a great gift. Wrap it in red cellophane paper and tie it with a bright bow.

CAKE:
2 tablespoons bread machine yeast
1 1/2 cups bread flour
1 cup cake flour
2 tablespoons granulated sugar
1/4 teaspoon salt
1/2 cup water
1 cup (2 sticks) unsalted butter
1/4 cup half and half
3 large egg yolks, lightly beaten

FILLING:
2 cups ground walnuts or hazelnuts
1 cup plus 3 tablespoons granulated sugar
1 teaspoon ground cinnamon
1/4 cup half and half
3 egg whites

GLAZE:

¹/₂ cup confectioners' sugar

1¹/₂ tablespoons orange juice

Combine all the dough ingredients in the bread machine pan and process on the dough setting. Generously butter a 10-inch tube pan and set it aside.

To make the filling, combine the walnuts, 3 tablespoons of the sugar, the cinnamon, and half and half in a saucepan. Set over medium heat and cook, stirring constantly, until the mixture forms a thick paste, about 10 minutes. Set aside to cool. Meanwhile, beat the egg whites until soft peaks form, then gradually add the remaining cup of sugar and continue beating until stiff peaks form. Fold the beaten egg whites into the cooled nut paste. Cover and reserve.

Once the dough cycle has completed, turn the dough out onto a lightly floured surface and divide it in half. Roll each half into a 20-inch square. Spread half the filling on one square of dough, leaving a ¹/₂-inch border around the edge. Roll up as for a jelly roll and pinch the edges together.

Place the jelly roll in the tube pan, seam side down. Spread the other half of the filling on the second 20-inch square, roll as for a jelly roll, pinch the edges together, and place this roll on top of the first one in the tube pan. Cover and set to rise in a warm, draft-free place until doubled in bulk, about 1 hour.

Preheat the oven to 350° F. When the cake has finished rising, bake it in the preheated oven for 60 to 65 minutes, or until golden brown and done. Cool in the pan on a rack for 10 minutes, then remove from the pan.

Mix the confectioners' sugar with the orange juice and drizzle this glaze over the warm *Potica* on the rack. After the glaze has firmed up, transfer the cake to a serving dish.

Grinding nuts is easy in the food processor. Add nuts to the food processor bowl fitted with the steel blade. Pulse until the nuts are ground as fine as you want them for the recipe. Don't just turn the machine on and run it or you'll have a nut paste before you know it. For the *Potica,* pulse until the nuts resemble tapioca beads.

MAIL ORDER SOURCES

You'll want to read this whole list because it's better than an old-fashioned wish book. Even though we have arbitrarily broken out the listings by category, some stores have everything. We've ranked them according to their strengths—as we see it. Answering the chicken-and-egg question for once and for all, we still say order bread first from one of these companies and you'll develop standards that will help you in your own baking adventures.

Mail order guide to specialty breads, ingredients, and baking equipment

Rustic European-Style Breads

Bread Alone (914) 657-3328
Route 28, Boiceville, NY 12412

Order bread from Dan Leader to help yourself establish some standards for rustic artisanal breads. His pain levain, peasant bread, raisin pumpernickel, and whole wheat walnut are what we try to emulate when we make a starter and use our bread machines. Dan Leader's a bread baker of the first order. His book, Bread Alone, was named the best bakery book by the International Association of Culinary Professionals for 1993, and well it should have. We recommend both Leader's breads and his book for dedicated bread connoisseurs.

New Bakery (312) 925-0064
2022 West 51st Street, Chicago, IL 60609

More versions of rye bread are baked in this fine South Chicago bakery than you could ever imagine. If you want to learn what real Russian rye is supposed to be like before you begin to bake your own, order Eugene Kniuksta's. He may sell the best pumpernickel in America. You want to learn to bake dark breads, try a batch of Eugene's and you'll develop some standards.

New Sammy's Bistro and Bakery (503) 535-2779
2210 S. Pacific Highway,   Talent, OR 97525

Here's our local source for rustic European-style breads. Charlene Rollins trained in France and returns their annually during January and February to gain new inspiration for her world-class restaurant and bakery. She'll mail out bread to you. Call and ask her what's baking today. And if you're on I-5 traveling between Seattle and San Diego, stop by for dinner. This very may well be the best place on the route.

Zingerman's (313) 663-3400
422 Detroit Street,   Ann Arbor, MI 48104

The first thing you should order is their bread. It will give you standards for fine artisan loaves of bread. Their rye bread is the best. They also sell corn flour, good Parmigiana-Reggiano Parmesan, polentas, olive oils, and other pantry items.

Flour, Grains, Meals, and Other Ingredients

Arrowhead Mills (713) 364-0730
P.O. Box 866,   Hereford, TX 79045

Stone-ground flours from organic grains. Frank Ford, a wheat farmer from Linda's home town, bucked Texas tradition and began growing grains organically. His Arrowhead products can be found in natural food stores from coast to coast. They're good. Call for the retail outlet closest to you.

Balducci's (800) 225-3822
424 Avenue of the Americas (in Greenwich Village),   New York, NY 10003

A must-see for visitors to New York, this store offers not only bakers' supplies for Italian-style breads, but also good examples of Italian breads you can taste for inspiration.

Bickford Flavors (216) 531-6006
19007 St. Clair Avenue,   Cleveland, OH 44117

For old-fashioned pure flavors to bake with, Bickford's the place. Their vanilla is the best. They also make exotic flavors including black walnut, clove, mango, and a bunch more. Call for a list.

Brewster River Mill (802) 644-2987
Mill Street, Jeffersonville, VT 05464

Stone-ground organic flours and maple syrup. Whole wheat, white bread flour, buckwheat and rye flours, as well as stone-ground cornmeal.

Brumwell's Mill and Amana Products (319) 622-3455
(back of Schanz Furniture)
Highway 6, South Amana, IA 52334

Excellent-quality yellow cornmeal, whole wheat flour, graham flour, coarse rye meal, and dark rye flour. Buckwheat flour, unbleached flour, rolled and cracked wheat. Steel-cut oats, oat bran, barley grits, and whole wheat flour. Seven-grain bread mix.

Butte Creek Mill (503) 826-3531
402 Royal Avenue N., Box 561, Eagle Point, OR 73531

Stone-ground cornmeal, 100 percent whole wheat flour, rye flour made from waterpower from Little Butte Creek diverted through millrace that activates a turbine that turns 1,400-pound millstones that grind against one another to produce superior-quality products. The store in an old barn is a great tourist attraction for those who veer off I-5 just north of the California border.

Cal-Gar Corp. (201) 691-2928
3 Fern Court, Flanders, NJ 07836

San Francisco sourdough starter is made and sold in granular form by this New Jersey company. We've used it with great success. How come you get San Francisco sourdough from New Jersey? Go figure. All we know is, it works. They also sell gluten and a bunch of chemical-free bread machine mixes.

Community Mill and Bean (800) 755-0554
267 Route 89 South, Savannah, NY 13146

Want your flour ground to order? Here you can get really fresh flour. They mill it just like you ask them to.

Dean & DeLuca (800) 221-7714
560 Broadway, New York, NY 10012

All things Italian as well as a good supply of fine bakers supplies. Gucci groceries and worth a visit when you're in New York, their perfect produce is exceeded only by their fine bakery products. They carry a wide supply of good flours and supplies for baking.

The Fowler's Mill (800) 321-2024
12500 Fowlers Mill Road, Chardon, OH 44024

Stone-ground whole wheat and buckwheat flour.

Giusto's (sold by Pamela's Products) (415) 952-4546
156 Utah Avenue, San Francisco, CA 94080

A complete line of organic bread flour as well as about forty other organic flours and meals. Semolina, durum, graham, oat, and a variety of whole wheats and rye. We've had wonderful results using Giusto's bread flour and count it one of our favorites.

Gray's Grist Mill (508) 636-6075
P.O. Box 422, Adamsville, RI 02801

Polenta, yellow cornmeal, rye flour, high-protein bread flour, jonny-cake meal, and bread machine mixes. These flours and meals are stone-ground between huge stones powered by a 1946 Dodge Truck they just parked under the floorboards of the mill. You get fresh, fresh stone-ground products. Highly recommended.

Great Grains Milling Co. (406) 783-5588
P.O. Box 427, Scobey, MT 59263

Golden Wheat Flour is their trademark organic bread flour and has made them famous among sourdough enthusiasts. Call for your closest retailer.

Great Valley Mills (800) 688-6455
RD 3, County Line Road
Box 1111, Barto, PA 19504

Stone-ground flours and meals.

Hoppin John's (803) 577-6404
30 Pinckney Street, Charleston, SC 29401

John Taylor sells great grits and corn flour. Use in any polenta bread recipe for terrific results. It can take up to six weeks to get these products, but it's worth the wait.

Kenyon's Corn Meal (800) 753-6966
Box 221 Usquepaugh, West Kingston, RI 02892

Stone-ground cornmeal from a gristmill first built in 1711. They also stone-grind rye flour, whole wheat, and graham flours.

King Arthur Flour (800) 827-6836
P.O. Box 876, Norwich, VT 05055

Here's the source for fine bread flour, white whole wheat, and just about every other kind of flour you ever imagined. Ask for a catalog. We've had great results using their King Arthur's Special and we've ordered diastatic malt powder here, Parrish pans, and a whole slew of baker's cookbooks.

Maison Glass (800) 822-5564
111 East 58th Street, New York, NY 10022

Everything European from figs to foie gras. Their motto is "The Best or Nothing." Believe it. French sugars, fine chocolates, fine European preserves to accompany the breads you make.

Manganaro Foods (212) 563-5331
488 Ninth Avenue, New York, NY 10018

All things Italian including olive oils, polenta, six-foot hero sandwiches. You should stop by when you're visiting New York just so you'll have some standards. Every kind of Italian imported cheese, sun-dried tomatoes, truffles, sausages for pizza, and a comprehensive selection of Italian staples and breads along with a few Italian kitchen gadgets.

Northwest Specialty Bakers (800) 666-1727
15425 SW Koll Parkway, A-1, Beaverton, OR 97006

You want to cheat and keep a stash of bread machine mixes on hand that will make quite acceptable breads! Call up Mark Bonebrake. He sells Classic, whole wheat, and a Garlic Provençal bread machine mix that are quite wonderful.

G.B. Ratto (800) 228-3515
821 Washington Street, Oakland, CA 94607

Oakland's fine grocer, they sell a wide variety of flours and meal including buckwheat, pizza flour, polenta, cassava meal, a sourdough starter packet, spices, and good bulk chocolates.

Sagebrush Mills (806) 983-2527
Route 3, Box 11, Floydada, TX 79235

Good source for organic wheat flour and yellow cornmeal. Very fresh.

Todaro Brothers (212) 679-7766
555 Second Avenue, New York, NY 10016

They'll ship anything they carry, and they carry everything Italian: olive oils, polenta, tomato products, sausages, you name it. If you can eat it and it comes from Italy, Todaro's probably stocks it. Stop in the store and you won't believe how many good things they've crammed into such a narrow New York store.

Vivande (415) 346-4430
2125 Fillmore Street, San Francisco, CA 94115

Ditto Vivande. A terrific inventory in a small space, this is Carol Field's neighborhood store. Such luck. They carry fine durum flour, semolina, polenta, chestnut flour, lots of olive oils, balsamic vinegar, et al. Ask for a catalog.

Walnut Acres (800) 433-3998
Penns Creek, PA 17862

Stone-ground flours, home grain mills, seeds, grains, you name it. They've got it for the home baker.

War Eagle Mill (501) 789-5343
Route 5, Box 411, Rogers, AR 72756

Stone-ground flours and grains certified organic.

Weisenberger Flour Mills (606) 254-5282
Box 215, Midway, KY 40347

Stone-ground but not organic flours. Unbleached all-purpose is excellent.

White Lily Foods Co.
P.O. Box 871, Knoxville, TN 37901

Pure white soft wheat flour so precious we've been known to carry along an empty suitcase on trips to the South just so we could replenish our stash before returning to the Northwest. They also make a fine bread flour that is white as snow and makes a bread with a soft crumb. No bromation is used. Highly recommended.

The Hardware

Bakers' Catalog (800) 827-6836
RR 2, Box 56, Norwich, VT 05055

This is the mail order store for King Arthur flour. Not only can you order divine flours and meals, but every single baker's supply you ever thought about: bowls, scrapers, scales, thermometers, peels, baker's stones. They've got little loaf pans, miniature towers for round crowns of bread, electric bread slicers, four-mold baguette pans, steamed bread molds.

The Baker's Find (800) 966-BAKE
139 Woodworth Avenue, Yonkers, NY 10701

Just a quick subway ride up from Manhattan, this is bakers' nirvana. They sell spices, seasonings, extracts, flours, nuts, seeds, chocolate chips, bakers supplies and lots of professional chef's-quality stuff at wholesale prices. If you love to bake, call for a catalog this instant. They've got gluten flour and filbert flour and California almond flour just for fun. Extra-large sizes of Fleischmann's yeast, and Ambrosia chocolate and cocoa.

Chef's Catalogue (800) 338-3232
3915 Commercial Avenue, Northbrook, IL 60062

Good source for bakers pans, stones, peels, and other supplies. Bread machines.

French Baking Machinery (609) 860-0577
RD 3, Box 799, Cranbury, MD 08512

Bannetons in various sizes for raising dough to authentic French shapes.

Maid of Scandinavia (800) 328-6722
3244 Raleigh Avenue, Minneapolis, MN 55416-2299

Everything you ever thought of and plenty that never crossed your mind in the way of bakers and confectioners supplies. Like those hard-to-find round cooling racks that bakers use to get that concentric round pattern on the tops of rustic breads. And at only $5.65 each. Bulk chocolates, marble molds, commercial rolling pins, dough scrapers, good thermometers—both oven and instant.

H. Roth & Son (212) 734-1111
1577 First Avenue (82nd Street), New York, NY 10028

Quality ingredients and fine cookware. They sell a variety of wooden wares including a good assortment of rolling pins; graters; grinders; knives; a special croissant baking sheet; gugelhupf pans; Turk's head molds; Breton molds; French bread pans; good bread loaf pans from Italy; unglazed baking tiles; as well as specialty flours including buckwheat, chestnut, pumpernickel and rye.

Sassafras Enterprises Inc. (800) 537-4941
1622 West Carroll Avenue, Chicago, IL 60612

Order your baking stone, cloche, and baker's peel here. They have a terrific-looking catalog of cook's stuff. Ask for it.

Williams-Sonoma (800) 541-2233
P.O. Box 7456, San Francisco, CA 94120-7456

Bakers stones, baking ware, high-quality baker's additives, bread machines. The best catalog for cooks that we know of.

BIBLIOGRAPHY

Beard, James. *Beard on Bread.* New York: Ballantine Books, 1973.

Bilheux, Roland, and Alain Escoffier, Daniel Herve, Jean-Marie Pouradier. *Special and Decorative Breads.* New York: Van Nostrand Reinhold, 1990.

Brody, Lora, and Millie Apter. *Bread Machine Baking, Perfect Every Time.* New York: Morrow, 1993.

Brown, Edward Espe. *The Tassajara Bread Book.* Boulder, Colorado: Shambhala, 1986.

Child, Julia. *The Way to Cook.* New York: Alfred A. Knopf, 1989.

Child, Julia, and Simone Beck. *Mastering the Art of French Cooking, Volume Two.* New York: Alfred A. Knopf, 1978.

Clayton, Jr., Bernard. *Bernard Clayton's New Complete Book of Breads.* New York: Simon & Schuster, 1987.

Clayton, Jr., Bernard. *The Breads of France.* New York: Macmillan, 1978.

Couet, Alain, and Eric Kayser. *Special and Decorative Breads.* New York: Van Nostrand Reinhold, 1990.

Costner, Susan. *Great Sandwiches.* New York: Crown Publishers, 1990.

Cunningham, Marion. *The Fannie Farmer Baking Book.* New York: Alfred A. Knopf, 1990.

Duff, Gail. *Bread, 150 Traditional Recipes from Around the World.* New York: Macmillan, 1993.

Eckhardt, Linda West, and Diana Collingwood Butts. *Bread in Half the Time.* New York: Crown Publishers, 1991.

Field, Carol. *The Italian Baker.* New York: Harper & Row, 1985.

Field, Carol. *Italy in Small Bites.* New York: Morrow, 1993.

Glassman and Susan Postal. *The Greyston Bakery Cookbook.* Boston: Shambhala, 1986.

Goldstein, Darra. *The Georgian Feast.* New York: Harper Collins, 1993.

Greene, Bert. *The Grains Cookbook.* New York: Workman Publishing, 1988.

Hensperger, Beth. *Bread.* San Francisco: Chronicle Books, 1988.

Hensperger, Beth. *Baking Bread, Old and New Traditions.* San Francisco: Chronicle Books, 1992.

Jordan, Michele Anna. *The Good Cook's Book of Oil and Vinegar.* New York and Menlo Park, California: Addison-Wesley Publishing, 1992.

Kasper, Lynne Rossetto. *The Splendid Table.* New York: Morrow, 1992.

Leader, Daniel, and Judith Blahnik. *Bread Alone, Bold Fresh Loaves from Your Own Hands.* New York: Morrow, 1993.

McGee, Harold. *On Food and Cooking: The Science and Lore of the Kitchen.* New York: Collier Books, 1984.

Ortiz, Joe. *The Village Baker, Classic Regional Breads from Europe and America.* Berkeley, California: Ten Speed Press, 1993.

Rehberg, Linda, and Lois Conway. *Bread Machine Magic Book of Helpful Hints.* New York: St. Martin's Press, 1993.

Reinhart, Br. Peter. *Brother Juniper's Bread Book.* Menlo Park, California: Addison-Wesley, 1991.

Rutherford, Lyn. *The Book of Antipasti.* Los Angeles: HP Books, 1992.

Scheer, Cynthia. *Breads,* California Culinary Academy. San Francisco: Ortho Books, 1985.

Thorne, John, with Matt Lewis Thorne. *Outlaw Cook.* New York: Farrar, Straus Giroux, 1992.

Wells, Patricia. *The Food Lover's Guide to Paris.* New York: Workman Publishing, 1993.

Wolfert, Paula. *The Cooking of South-West France.* New York: Dial Press, 1983.

INDEX